David Parkinson
is a film critic and the author
of *The Bloomsbury Good Movie Guide*. He has
edited *Mornings in the Dark: The Graham Greene
Film Reader* and written *The Young Oxford Book
of Cinema* and *The Oxford
Dictionary of Film*.

WORLD OF ART

This famous series
provides the widest available
range of illustrated books on art in all its aspects.
If you would like to receive a complete list
of titles in print please write to:
THAMES AND HUDSON
30 Bloomsbury Street, London WC1B 3QP
In the United States please write to:
THAMES AND HUDSON INC.
500 Fifth Avenue, New York, New York 10110

Printed in Italy

David Parkinson

HISTORY OF FILM

156 illustrations, 15 in colour

Thames and Hudson

For my family

Space is at a premium in a concise volume of this kind and, much as I would have liked to have included the original titles of films not in the English language with their translations or trade names, I have elected to refer to productions solely by the title by which they are best known in English. The date given in each case is that of a film's release in its country of origin. Where sources conflict, I have opted for the majority decision.

I am extremely grateful to all at Thames and Hudson for their assistance and unfailing encouragement, and would like particularly to thank Jason Freeman for his invaluable advice on the style and content of this book and all who tolerated me while I completed it.

British Library Cataloguing-in-Publication Data
A catalogue record for this book is available from the British Library

ISBN 0-500-20277-X

Printed and bound in Italy by Conti Tipocolor

Contents

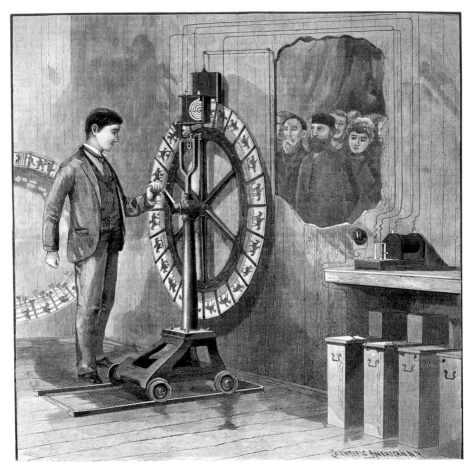

1 Ottomar Anschütz's Electro-Tachyscope (1887) exploited persistence of vision to give the impression of moving pictures as transparencies of sequence photographs passed before brief flashes of light. Anschütz later produced a dual-lens disc projector, premiered in Berlin in November 1894.

CHAPTER ONE

From Science to Cinema

The most modern of all the arts, cinema is fittingly the most dependent on science and technology. The twentieth century's dominant art form was born out of the nineteenth-century predilection for machinery, movement, optical illusion and public entertainment. Film's prehistory is a labyrinth of discoveries, inventions, part-solutions and failures. Some were accidental, others coincidental, but few were devised with the end product of projected moving photographic images in mind. It was an evolutionary process in which each new device or discovery inspired a fresh wave of emulation and experimentation, sometimes for the purpose of entertainment, but often in the cause of science alone. The majority of its pioneers always envisaged the moving picture as primarily a scientific aid, indeed even Louis Lumière claimed that 'my work has been directed towards scientific research. I have never engaged in what is termed "production"'.

However, the key scientific principle on which many of these inventions was based was a false assumption. Persistence of vision had been known to the ancient Egyptians, but in spite of the work of Isaac Newton and the Chevalier d'Arcy, it was not until 1824 that it was satisfactorily defined, by Peter Mark Roget, as the ability of the retina to retain an image of an object for $\frac{1}{20}$ to $\frac{1}{5}$ of a second after its removal from the field of vision. However, it has since been shown that film seems to move because the brain, and not the eye, is accepting stimuli which it is incapable of perceiving as separate. The brain has a perception threshold, below which images exposed to it will appear as continuous and film's speed of 24 frames per second is below that threshold. Persistence of vision or flicker fusion prevents us from seeing the lines between each frame, while the phi phenomenon or stroboscopic effect, analysed between 1912 and 1916 by the psychologists Max Wertheimer and Hugo Münsterberg, provides a mental bridge between the frames to permit us to see a series of static images as a single continuous movement. Cinema is, therefore, the first art form to rely solely on psycho–perceptual illusions generated by machine.

1

7

Roget's conclusions may have been inaccurate, but they still fostered the invention of a number of animating devices critical to the development of the motion picture. Despite its name, the first of these 'optical toys', the Thaumatrope (from the Greek for 'wonder turning') was also the simplest. Based on Sir John Herschel's spinning-coin principle, it was a cardboard disc which merged the pictures on each face into a single image when spun on a piece of thread. Another Roget observation, that a rolling wheel appeared stationary when viewed intermittently through vertical railings, gave rise to three similar toys produced independently in the early 1830s: Michael Faraday's Wheel of Life (1831), the Belgian Joseph Plateau's Phenakistoscope and the Austrian Simon Ritter von Stampfer's Stroboscope (both 1832).

I

The Phenakistoscope was a serrated disc with series drawings about its outer edge which gave the impression of movement when rotated and viewed through its teeth in a mirror. Von Stampfer's device comprised two discs, one slotted and the other bearing the drawings. When viewed through the slots the rotating drawings appeared to portray a continuous action, thus establishing the principle on which the modern shutter is based. George Horner's Daedalum, invented in 1834, replaced the discs with a strip which gave an identical impression when placed around the wall of a spinning slotted drum. By the time the device was marketed as the Zoetrope in the 1860s, an Austrian, Baron Franz von Uchatius, had projected Phenakistoscope images onto a screen using a magic lantern.

Some historians trace the origins of light-projected images back to the Cave of Shadows described in Book VII of Plato's *Republic* or the shadow puppets of China, India and Java. However, shadow shows did not enjoy widespread popularity in Europe until the Enlightenment when, amongst others, Ambroise (or Ambrogio) delighted 1770s London and Goethe founded a shadow theatre at Trefurt in Germany a few years later. Such exhibitions appealed to the rational temper of the age, although they continued to attract audiences throughout the nineteenth century. The most notable shadow show of all, established by Dominique Séraphin in Paris in 1784, prospered until 1870, and Henri Rivière's shadow melodramas at the Chât Noir, which began as late as 1887, remained popular even after the first cinema shows. They were soon surpassed by a more impressive spectacle.

2

This was the Eidophusikon, a theatre of effects devised by the Alsatian painter and theatrical designer Philippe-Jacques de Loutherbourg in the 1780s, in which dozens of miniature scenes were

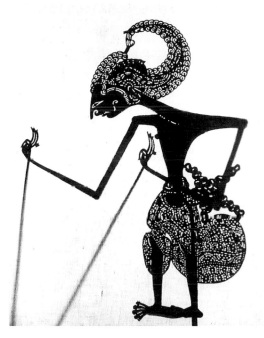

2 A Javanese shadow knight. The *wayang kulit* ('shadow plays') have been performed for over 1000 years and are still enormously popular, with the *dalang* ('puppeteers') as celebrated as film stars.

animated by ingenious variations of light and shade. Robert Barker of Edinburgh harnessed this technique in 1787 and applied it to the paintings of epic content and proportion typical of such realist artists as Benjamin West and Robert Ker Porter. Barker's Panorama was sited in a giant cylinder which surrounded the audience. Its successor, the Diorama, pioneered by the Frenchmen Claude-Marie Bouton and Louis Jacques Mandé Daguerre in 1822, was even more elaborate. Here the audience sat on a dais which revolved as the canvas was illuminated by a battery of lanterns and shutters. John Constable recorded his impressions of the Regent's Park Diorama in 1823: 'It is in part a transparency. The spectator is in a dark chamber, and it is very pleasing and has great illusion. [Yet] it is without the pale of art, because the object is deception. Art pleases by reminding, not deceiving.'

Even more popular was the magic lantern. Its basic elements were   II

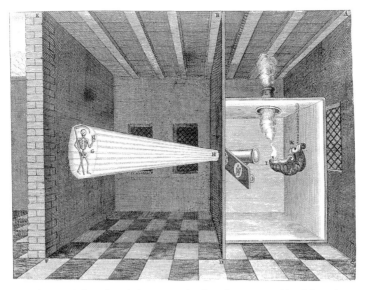

3 The principles of magic lantern projection, demonstrated by Athanasius Kircher in the 1671 edition of his *Ars Magna Lucis et Umbrae*. The diagram shows that the role of lenses was not yet fully understood.

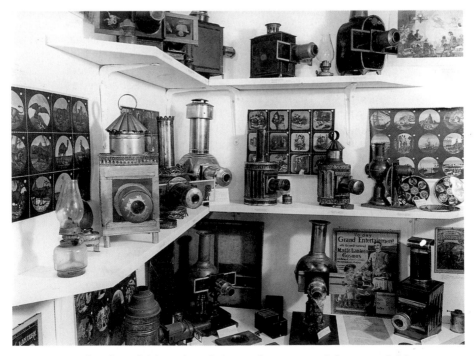

4 A variety of eighteenth- and nineteenth-century magic lanterns and slides.

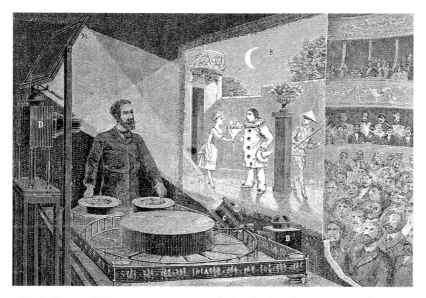

5 Emile Reynaud's 'Pantomimes Lumineuses' played at his Théâtre Optique from 1892 to 1900. Each animated narrative lasted approximately 15 minutes, required some 700 full-colour drawings and was accompanied by specially composed music.

described by the German Jesuit Athanasius Kircher in *Ars Magna Lucis et Umbrae* in 1646 (revised 1671), and probably integrated into a single device by the Dutch scientist Christiaan Huygens a decade later. The 'lanthorn' display Samuel Pepys witnessed in 1666 was probably quite primitive, as candle-light only dimly illuminated the opaque colours of the coarse glass slides. W. J. Gravesande (1721) and Ami Argand (1780) developed oil lamps, which were, in turn, superseded by lime light jet-lamps, whose sharper images could be given depth and sequence by the use of multiple lanterns or lenses. This technique was employed to supernatural effect in the 1790s by the Belgian showman Etienne Gaspard Robert (known as 'Robertson'), whose Fantasmagorie derived additional atmosphere from the smoke swirling around its Gothic setting. Niemiec Philipstahl brought the show to London, where one of his disciples, Henry Langdon Childe, demonstrated the first 'Dissolving Views' at the turn of the century. Movement within an image was made possible by mechanical slides, envisaged by Pieter van Musschenbroeck as early as 1739. The Chromatrope, Eidotrope and Cycloidotrope all relied on gears, rotary

3

4

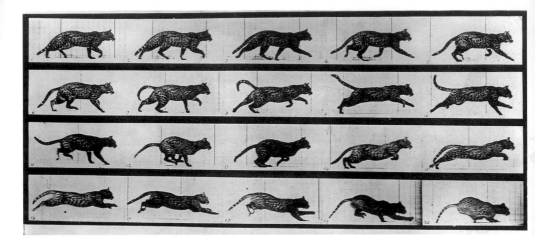

discs and slipping glass for their effects, while the Choreutoscope, patented by the London optician L. S. Beale, was the first projection device to use intermittent movement.

Towering above all other lanternists was the Frenchman Emile Reynaud (1844–1918). His Praxinoscope (1876) replaced the slots of the Zoetrope with a polygonal drum of mirrors placed at its centre, which reflected the rotating drawings to give bright, sharp moving images. By using longer transparent strips and a projecting lens, Reynaud produced the 'Praxinoscope à Projections' with which, from 1892, he presented 'Pantomimes Lumineuses' at his Théâtre Optique. These charming animations played to packed houses and brought the cinema to the verge of existence. It was Reynaud's great tragedy that the successful projection of moving photographs was just three years away.

The history of photography embraces the writings of Aristotle, the Arab mathematician Al Hazen and Leonardo da Vinci, whose theory of a *camera obscura* was put into practice in the mid-sixteenth century by another Italian, Giambattista della Porta. For some two centuries artists used the *camera obscura* and its derivatives as a sketching aid, while scientists including Thomas Wedgwood, J. H. Schultz, Sir John Herschel and Blanquet Evrard conducted the search for the chemical or mechanical means of fixing its image. Still photography became a reality thanks to Joseph Nicéphore Niepce and Louis Daguerre, who displayed the daguerreotype in Paris in 1839, six years after his partner's death. In the 1840s the Englishman William Fox Talbot discovered how to produce photographic images on paper and a

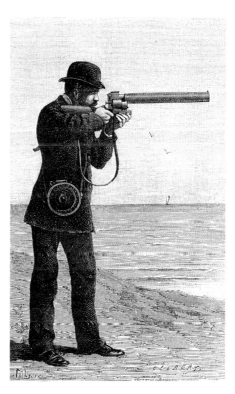

6 Sequence photographs of a running cat taken by Eadweard Muybridge. In 1879 he began projecting moving images from similar pictures with his Zoogyroscope, renamed the Zoöpraxiscope in 1881.

7 Etienne-Jules Marey demonstrating his *fusil photographique* (1882). Nicknamed 'the Birdman of Beaune', Marey developed his sequence technique to record birds in flight. He adapted the gun to paper strips in 1888 and perforated celluloid in 1889.

negative–positive process that enabled the development of his Calotypes (later Talbotypes). His patent for transparencies was purchased by the Langenheim brothers of Philadelphia, who introduced positive images on glass plates in 1849, thus paving the way for the projection of photographs.

Plateau had suggested the union of the photograph and the Phenakistoscope in 1849, but while Henry du Mont's Omniscope (1859) and Henry R. Heyl's Phasmatrope (1870) simulated movement, their stiffly posed photographs only highlighted the need for a method of recording action spontaneously and simultaneously as it occurred. Series photography was to be advanced by the work of two very different characters, the English eccentric Eadweard Muybridge and the French scientist Etienne-Jules Marey, who both lived between 1830 and 1904.   7

An itinerant photographer, Muybridge was hired in 1872 by   6 Governor Leland Stanford of California to determine whether at some stage a galloping horse had all four hooves off the ground at once. The

$25,000 bet that prompted the commission may well have been apocryphal, but Muybridge was successful in proving the point in 1878 when faster exposure times enabled him to perfect his apparatus, a battery of twelve cameras triggered by connecting trip wires along the straight of the Palo Alto racetrack. In 1879 he unveiled the Zoöpraxiscope, a derivative of Uchatius's Projecting Phenakistoscope, which cast onto a screen the drawings made of his photographs by Meissonier. Muybridge later utilized as many as twenty-four cameras to film various species and published his results in 1888 in the eleven-volume *Studies in Animal Locomotion*.

7 Marey was also primarily concerned with the mechanics of movement. In 1882, he adapted the photographic revolver with which his colleague Pierre-Jules-César Janssen had attempted to record the passage of Venus across the face of the sun in 1874. The *fusil photographique* used a revolving plate to record a dozen instantaneous pictures in the course of one second. After experimenting with multiple superimpositions on a single plate, Marey turned first to the paper and then the celluloid roll film marketed by the Eastman Kodak company to produce continuous strips of images called *chronophotographes*. The film's regular, intermittent passage was made possible by the Maltese

8 Peter Bacigalupi's Kinetoscope parlour (San Francisco, 1904). In the first parlour, opened on 14 April 1894, customers paid one nickel to view the films in each row of 5 machines.

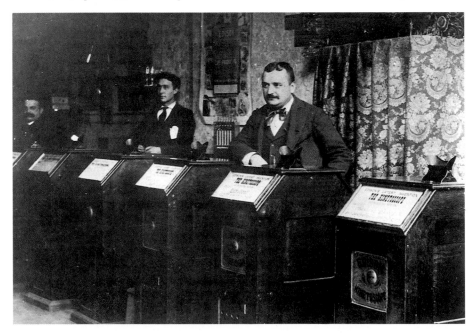

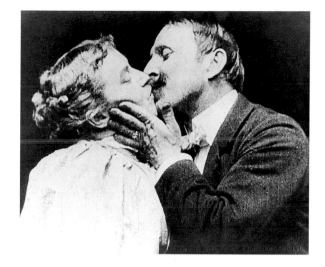

9 *The Rice/Irwin Kiss* (1896). Shot for the Kinetoscope, this kiss between the Broadway stars John Rice and May Irwin provoked outrage when it was projected onto a large screen.

cross mechanism devised by the German Oskar Messter, which is still a key component of much modern movie equipment. Although Marey did not intend to exploit his findings commercially, in 1893 he and his assistant Georges Demenÿ did join, without success, in the race to produce a machine capable of projecting moving photographs.

The first 'movies' were not intended to be projected or silent. They were sponsored by Thomas Alva Edison (1847–1931), who instructed the head of his West Orange laboratory, William Kennedy Laurie Dickson (1860–1935), to copy the design of the Phonograph. However, photographs etched onto metal cylinders proved unworkable and so Dickson, whose genius is too often overlooked, adapted elements from every stage of the evolution of the moving image to produce in 1890 a camera called the Kinetograph and, the following year, a viewer named the Kinetoscope.

Exhibiting action shot in the world's first film studio, the Black Maria, Raff and Gammon's Kinetoscope parlours opened in 1894 and were soon popular throughout America. Items such as *Fred Ott's Sneeze*, the *Rice-Irwin Kiss* and the host of vaudeville acts and boxing bouts were, in effect, little more than unedited lengths of footage, no longer than the action itself or the particular strip of celluloid. Carelessly neglecting to take out overseas patents, Edison completely dismissed the potential of projection and concentrated on exploiting the peepshow, which he believed would be just another fad in a novelty-hungry age. His avaricious misjudgment would ultimately cost him dear.

8
9

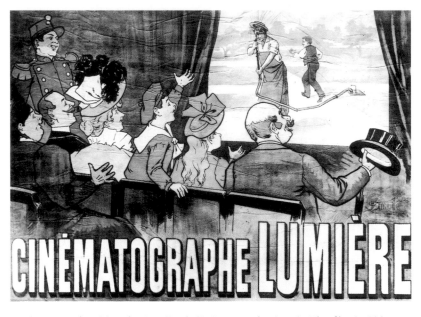

10 A poster advertising the Lumières' Cinématographe (1896). The film is *L'Arroseur arrosé*, in which a mischievous boy steps off a hosepipe when the gardener examines the nozzle to see why the water has stopped.

The age of inventions culminated in the event that traditionally signals the birth of the cinema – the first demonstration to a paying audience of the Lumières' Cinématographe in the Salon Indien, a basement room of the Grand Café in Paris, on 28 December 1895. In essence, Auguste (1862–1954) and Louis (1864–1948) simply won the race to find a workable method of combining the Kinetoscope with the magic lantern. Many contemporaries had competed: the French-born Louis Aimé Augustin Le Prince, who shot and projected street scenes of Leeds in 1888, but who mysteriously vanished before he could complete his work; William Friese-Greene, freely adapting from his fellow Englishmen John Rudge and Frederick Varley, whose apparatus probably worked efficiently only in the 1951 British 'biopic' *The Magic Box*; the London barrister Wordsworth Donisthorpe, whose Kinesigraph experiments were confounded by lack of funds; the German brothers Max and Emil Skladanowsky, inventors of the Bioscope, and the Frenchman Henry Joly, who produced the Photozoötrope. Across the Atlantic, the pioneers included Major

Woodville Latham and his sons Gray and Otway, whose Panoptikon (or Eidoloscope) introduced the 'Latham loop', which prevented the perforated celluloid strip from snapping as it passed before the lens (thus later permitting the production of feature films), and Thomas Armat and C. Francis Jenkins, whose Phantoscope would be accumulated by Edison, renamed the Vitascope, and exhibited at Koster & Bial's Music Hall, New York, in 1896.

The Lumières, the Lathams, the Skladanowskys, Armat and Jenkins, Jean-Aimé LeRoy, Eugene Lauste and Herman Casler had all given public demonstrations of their projectors before 28 December 1895, but it is this date that historians hold sacred. The Lumières merit elevation above their peers. Their portable, hand-cranked cameras (invented by Louis in a single night when unable to sleep), capable of shooting, printing and projecting moving pictures, were soon filming around the world to produce a catalogue of general, military, comic and scenic views, as well as living portraits. The limitations of Dickson's studio-bound shorts were soon exposed alongside the Lumières' more spontaneous 15–20 second slices of life. Reflecting the composed look of contemporary photography rather than the theatrical tableau, their 'pictures in motion' had a depth of scene that contributed to the realism of the train pulling into the Gare de la Ciotat and a basic narrative pattern of beginning, middle and end that informed even the *Workers Leaving the Lumière Factory*. The naturalism and bustle of many of their *actualities* (actuality films) foreshadowed the style of the Soviet Kino-Eye and the Italian Neo-Realists, while *Feeding Baby* has a distinct home-movie feel.

Also on the Lumières' opening bill was *L'Arroseur arrosé*, the first screen gag and the earliest narrative film. Considering the length of its

10

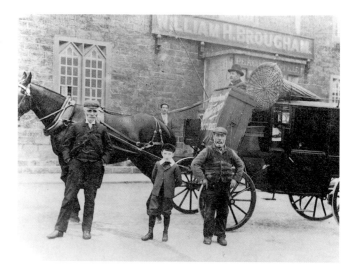

11 The Mottershaws (c. 1902), a Sheffield travelling family who showed their films like *Daring Daylight Burglary* (1903) at fairs and carnivals. Other itinerants included James Bamforth (*A Kiss in the Tunnel*, 1900) and William Haggar (*The Life of Charles Peace*, 1905).

prehistory and the comparative spans required by the novel and the other arts, the speed with which the cinema developed its complex code of instantly recognizable narrative symbols and its own grammar and poetics is all the more remarkable. Yet few were willing to concede that film, with its roots in pulp fiction, comic strips, popular photography and melodrama, was an art, dismissing it as a fairground attraction or a magician's prop. Ironically, it was a French illusionist, George Méliès (1861–1938), considered by many 'the father of the narrative film', who was to become the screen's first true artist.

Between 1896 and 1906, his Star Film company made in excess of 500 films, of which less than 140 survive. Producer, director, writer, designer, cameraman and actor, Méliès is attributed with the first use of dissolves, superimposition, time-lapse photography, art direction and artificial lighting effects. His range of subject was equally impressive: trick shorts (or *féeries*), such as *L'Homme à la tête de caoutchouc* (1901), fantasies (*Cinderella*, 1899), historical reconstructions (*Benvenuto Cellini*, 1904), docudramas (*The Dreyfus Affair*, 1899), and science fiction adventures, the most famous being the thirty-scene *A Trip to the Moon* (1902). Méliès broke from the photographic impulses of the primitives to show that the movie camera could lie. He recognized the difference between screen and real time and conceived a bewildering array of optical effects to expand the parameters of the fictional film story. Chaplin called him 'the alchemist of light' and D. W. Griffith claimed 'I owe him everything', yet his camera was always a spectator with a front-row view of a *tableau vivant*, complete with stage entrances and scenery that prevented action in depth. Some accused him of producing kitsch, others of 'genteel pornography', but Méliès's chief failing was a paucity of imagination which prevented him from exploiting fully the cinematic techniques he had devised.

By the time Pathé Frères bought out Méliès in 1911, they were the major force in production, distribution and exhibition worldwide. In France, only Gaumont could compete, largely owing to the talents of Alice Guy-Blaché (the first woman director and responsible for more than three hundred shorts between 1897 and 1906), Victorin Jasset (the creator of the crime serial) and the prolific Louis Feuillade, who in the twenty years from 1906 directed more than 800 films, scripted some 100 more and collaborated on countless others. However, Charles Pathé, dubbed 'the Napoleon of the screen', could count on the services of the dapper Max Linder, star of more than 400 comedies, and the production chief Ferdinand Zecca (1864–1947), who skilfully plagiarized every new theme and style.

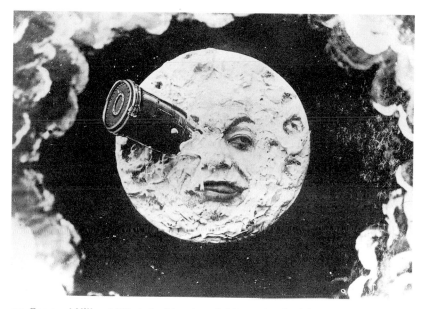

12 Georges Méliès, *A Trip to the Moon* (1902). The rocket fired from a cannon on earth lands in the moon's eye. This action was repeated in the next shot taken from the lunar surface on which the Astronomic Club disembarks.

Yet not even Zecca could reproduce the excitement generated by the films of Edwin S. Porter (1870–1941). During his time as an Edison projectionist, Porter had begun to appreciate that the syntactic unit of the narrative film was not the scene but the shot. The version of *The Life of an American Fireman* owned by the New York Museum of Modern Art suggests that he had acted on his theory as early as 1902. However, the copyright print, held at the Library of Congress, reveals that the film's dramatic rescue was originally shown first from the point of view of the trapped woman and then from that of the fireman and not as parallel actions. Nevertheless, the film remains significant for a number of genuine innovations, including the depiction of on-screen thought and the use of documentary footage for a fictional purpose, while the techniques of 'cross-cutting' and 'creative geography' taught audiences how to make mental associations between events without the benefit of a rigid chronology.

Porter did incorporate parallel cutting into his next film, an embryonic Western, *The Great Train Robbery*, in 1903. The action began by following traditional editing conventions, but Porter soon started cross-cutting for rhythm and pace, overlapping shots to increase tension. The diagonal movement of the characters across the screen, in-camera 'matting' to give the impression of the passing scene, the depth of framing to convey privileged information to the audience, and the use of 'pans' and 'tilts' to follow the action all added to the fluidity and intensity of the narrative. Regrettably, there was no inter-cutting within scenes, the interiors (in stark contrast to the realism of the exteriors) were woefully synthetic and the acting highly theatri-cal; still, *The Great Train Robbery* established the basic principles of continuity editing and did much to widen the vocabulary of film's universal language. Porter's revolution gave cinema a new spatial and temporal freedom, but like Méliès he was unable to keep pace with public demand and retired in 1915.

Although he had included an extreme close-up of the ringing alarm in *The Life of an American Fireman*, Porter had filmed *The Great Train Robbery* exclusively in long or medium shot, apart from its shock

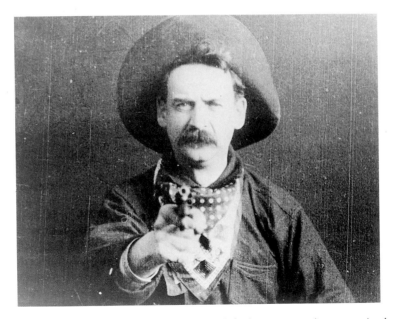

13 Edwin S. Porter, *The Great Train Robbery* (1903), lasting some 12 minutes, consisted of 14 individual shots. The last was completely non-diegetic and depicted the sheriff shoot-ing directly at the audience.

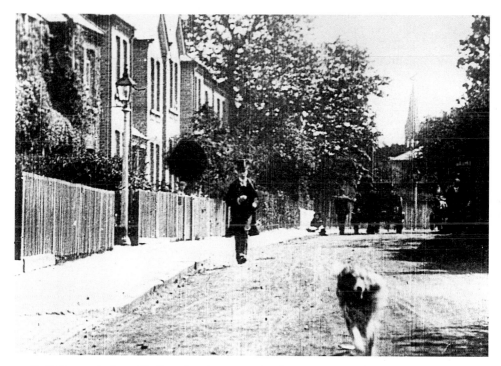

14 Cecil Hepworth, *Rescued by Rover* (1905): an example of consistent direction of movement within the frame, as Rover leads his master to the gypsy shack where his baby is held captive.

finale, a close-up of a bandit firing directly at the viewer. The close-up had first been used to personalize and objectify events by George Albert Smith in *Grandma's Reading Glass* (1900). Smith was a member of the Brighton School that also included Esme Collings and James Williamson. The producer Cecil Hepworth was based near London. His 1905 film, *Rescued by Rover*, expanded on Porter's advances in continuity and ellipsis to demonstrate the contextual value to a film's pace and meaning of cutting on action, 'travelling' shots, '*plan-séquence*', 'screen geography' and implied information. For a brief and isolated moment in film history, Britain led the world. Simple but suspenseful, *Rescued by Rover* was unrivalled in narrative construction and rhythm. Alfred Collins and Zecca harnessed its energy to develop the comic chase, but the chief beneficiary of the advances of Porter and Hepworth was D. W. Griffith.

14

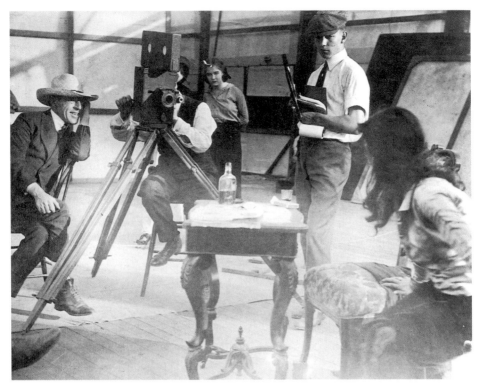

15 D. W. Griffith on the set of *Intolerance* (1916) with Lillian Gish. Behind the camera is Billy Bitzer, whose technical ingenuity enabled Griffith to put many of his ideas into practice during their association (1908–24).

CHAPTER TWO

The Foundations of Classical Hollywood

'D. W. Griffith, Producer of all great Biograph successes, revolution-
izing Motion Picture drama and founding the modern technique of
the art. Included in the innovations which he introduced and which
are now generally followed by the most advanced producers are: the
large or close-up figure, distant views as represented first in *Ramona*,
the "switchback", sustained suspense, the "fade out", and restraint in
expression, raising motion picture acting to the higher plane which
has won for it recognition as a geuine art.'

Thus ran the full-page advertisement Griffith (1875–1948) placed in 15
the *New York Dramatic Mirror* to mark his departure from the famous
Biograph company for the newly founded Mutual in 1913. Few then
would have recognized the earnest theatrical who, on seeing a movie
for the first time in 1905 declared, 'any man enjoying such a thing
should be shot', and who, having had his adaptation of *Tosca* rejected,
acted in Porter's 1907 *Rescued from an Eagle's Nest* (as 'Lawrence'
Griffith) solely out of penury.

Such beginnings make Griffith's achievement all the more remarkable; indeed, it is unparalleled in the emergence of any art form. In the
450-odd films he directed or supervised between 1908 and 1913, he
shaped the basic elements of film-making into the language and syntax
that would serve cinema for over half a century. In the words of Erich
von Stroheim, who graduated from extra to assistant director under
Griffith, he 'put beauty and poetry into a cheap and tawdry sort of
entertainment'. Yet for much of this period Griffith was largely
unaware that he was transforming filmic expression. Contrary to the
above declaration, the 'father of film technique' was not an innova-
tor. Instead, he was an intuitive refiner and extender of existing cinematic methods, which he combined with the conventions of Victorian
art, literature and drama in order to tell his stories in the most effective way.

Within five years of his directorial debut, Griffith had completely
mastered the film form. Although *The Adventures of Dollie* (1908) was
an incongruous mix of realism and clichéd melodrama, it had an

instinctive narrative fluidity and symmetry. Griffith composed carefully to utilize the whole frame and often used deep focus and long shots to heighten the drama. He cut on action throughout, allowing the narrative content to determine the placement of the camera and the timing of the cut, and the last-minute rescue (which was to become something of a trademark) was particularly notable for its rhythm and consistency of screen geography.

Griffith's heavy workload gave him ample opportunity to experiment with film grammar and rhetoric. In addition to exploring the potential of flashbacks, 'eyeline matches' and camera distances, his earliest pictures also showed that individual shots were cinematic phrases that could be edited together into meaningful sequences without a concrete dramatic logic to link them. *The Lonely Villa* (1909), for example, contained 52 separate shots in just 12 minutes, injecting pace and tension into Mack Sennett's scenario. When Biograph bosses questioned whether audiences would be conversant with such a narrative technique, Griffith replied, 'Doesn't Dickens write that way?' His depiction of parallel events and emotions in purely cinematic terms prefigured Eisenstein's 'montage of attractions' and Murnau's 'subjective' camera (*see* pp. 76 and 60). Similarly, his visual metaphors anticipated Soviet theories of associative or intellectual montage.

Each film brought a new sophistication. *A Corner in the Wheat* (1909) heralded an increasing concern with the content of the individual frame, its *mise-en-scène*. To complement his naturalistic exteriors, Griffith disposed of painted backdrops and used domestic props to create angles and shape and deepen the frame. Working closely with the cameraman G. W. 'Billy' Bitzer (1872–1944), he developed Porter's tilts, pans and 'tracks' into decipherable forms of expression, even cross-cutting between tracking shots in *The Lonedale Operator* (1911). Artificial lighting was used to suggest firelight in *The Drunkard's Reformation* (1909), but by *Pippa Passes* (also 1909, but 68 pictures later) he was employing what came to be called 'Rembrandt lighting' as a narrative and characterization device. Graphic techniques, such as the dissolve, 'fade', 'iris' and 'mask', were designated narrative purposes, while split screens and soft focus were sparingly used for additional impact.

Griffith also transformed the art of screen acting, right down to instituting rehearsals. Aware that the camera could magnify even the slightest gesture or expression, he insisted on restraint and an adherence to a range of movements and mannerisms which clearly denoted certain emotions, personality traits and psychological states. He invariably cast to suit particular physical types, and assembled a company that comprised some of the leading names of the silent era, including Lillian and Dorothy Gish, Mary Pickford, Blanche Sweet, Lionel Barrymore, Donald Crisp, Henry B. Walthall and Wallace Reid.

It is often overlooked how versatile Griffith was in his one-reel days. In addition to melodramas, thrillers and literary adaptations, he directed religious allegories (*The Devil*, 1908), histories (*1776*, 1909), morality tales (*The Way of the World*, 1910), rural romances (*A Country Cupid*, 1911), social commentaries (*The Musketeers of Pig Alley*, 1912), satires (*The New York Hat*, 1912) and Westerns (*The Battle of Elderbush Gulch*, 1913). In the process he gave cinema a new social and intellectual respectability, but despite his achievements Griffith remained largely unknown.

By 1913, Griffith was convinced that his revelation of the truth could be satisfactorily expounded only in the 'feature' film. Here again he was to build on the foundations laid by others. The world's first feature, *The Story of the Kelly Gang*, had been made by Charles Tait in Australia in 1906, but Griffith's ambition had been fuelled by the French *film d'art*, *Queen Elizabeth* (1912) and the Italian epic *Quo Vadis?* (1913). Furious that his 1911 two-reeler, *Enoch Arden*, had been released in separate parts, Griffith secretly began work on a four-reel biblical spectacle, *Judith of Bethulia*, in 1913.

Costing an unprecedented $18,000, the film underlines all Griffith's strengths and weaknesses as a director. Sets and costumes were painstakingly authentic, the narrative development taut, and the acting exceptional. The editing, particularly of the battle scenes, in which mass action was never permitted to swamp the drama of the individual, powerfully achieved what Eisenstein was to call 'the shock value of colliding images'. Yet in striving for scale and significance, Griffith discarded experimentation and exposed his intellectual shallowness. His vision overbalanced the rather contrived melodramas which he considered to be 'High Art'. Consequently, sentimentality, pretentiousness and political naivety permeate much of his later work, including his best-known films, *The Birth of a Nation* (1915) and *Intolerance* (1916).

All Griffith had learned during his apprenticeship went into *The Birth of a Nation*, his adaptation of Thomas Dixon's Civil War novels, *The Leopard's Spots* and *The Clansman*, and cinematically, there is much to admire: the reconstruction of period, the historical tableaux, the night photography, the use of tint and the unparalleled power and

16

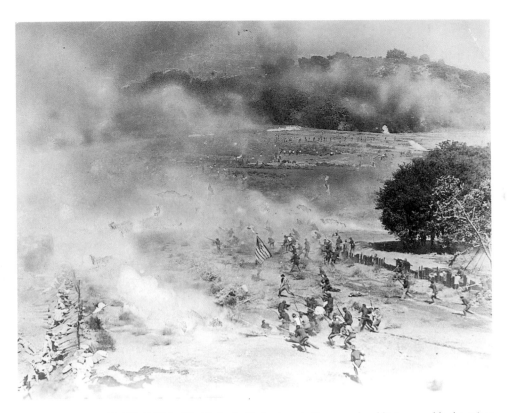

16 D. W. Griffith, *The Birth of a Nation* (1915). Composed and lit to resemble the prints of the Civil War photographer Mathew Brady, the battle scenes were originally tinted red to convey the fury of combat.

control of the editing, which linked 1544 separate shots into a cogent narrative. Overriding all, however, is the film's racial bigotry, which did much to revive the moribund Ku Klux Klan and caused a storm of protest. Still, *The Birth of a Nation* was a huge commercial success, recouping its costs in just two months. Griffith invested much of the profit into his wounded response to the adverse reaction, *Intolerance*.

17

Interweaving four narratives spanning 2500 years, Griffith aimed to show how truth has always been threatened by hypocrisy and injustice, but he was ultimately frustrated by thematic inconsistency and the idealism of his solutions. However, once again there were many cinematic highlights: the tracking shot of the vast Babylon set, the battle scenes, the moments of intimate detail amidst the broad sweep

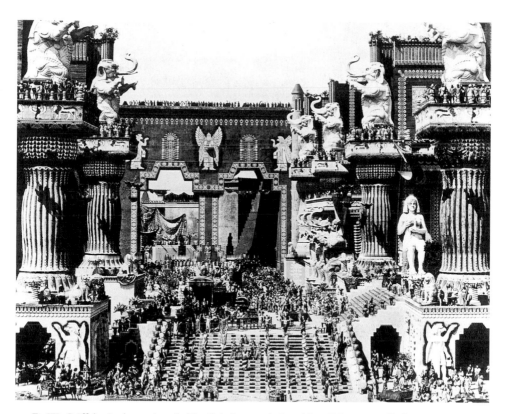

17 D. W. Griffith, *Intolerance* (1916). The Babylon set designed by Walter W. Hall after matte shots taken by Bitzer of the Tower of Jewels at the San Francisco Exposition (1914).

and the abstract, or expressive, montage which unified the individual segments. But audiences were confused by the style and alienated by the sermonizing and Griffith spent the rest of his career paying for its failure. Suffocated by the studio system, his work became increasingly conventional, old-fashioned and, despite fine films from *Broken Blossoms* (1919) to *Orphans of the Storm* (1922), increasingly prone to repetition and sentimentality. Griffith's final film, *The Struggle* (1931), was a failure which forced him to endure a seventeen-year exile from Hollywood, snubbed by the medium he had done so much to fashion.

Suffocation by the strictures of the studio system was a fate shared by many creative film-makers in the 1920s. Yet, as the Jazz Age drew to a close, it was hard to recall that many of the moguls who maintained such a tight grip on every aspect of American cinema had first entered the industry as small-time exhibitors hoping to cash in on what was still considered a disreputable novelty. However, men like Carl Laemmle (1867–1939), Adolph Zukor (1873–1976), William Fox (1879–1952), Jesse Lasky (1880–1958), Samuel Goldfish (later Goldwyn, 1882–1974), Marcus Loew (1870–1927) and Louis B. Mayer (1885–1957), mostly first-generation Jewish immigrants from Eastern Europe, had the acumen and courage to emerge victorious from the business wars of the 1910s.

Following the premiere of the Vitascope in New York in April 1896, there was an instant and insatiable clamour nationwide for projected moving pictures. To satisfy demand, producers and exhibitors flagrantly ignored machine patents and exploited the absence of film-strip copyright. In 1897, armed with the patent on the Latham Loop, Edison began to fight back, systematically suing every company that used the loop in its cameras or projectors. Then, furious at the way Edison had taken the credit for the Vitascope and appropriated its mechanism for his own Projecting Kinetoscope, Thomas Armat also began issuing writs on the strength of the loop patent, including one against Edison himself. As the smaller companies folded, Biograph entered the fray, having secured the Armat and Latham patents. Eventually, in excess of two hundred legal actions came before the U.S. courts.

In the meantime, an exhibition revolution was taking place. Movies had been part of vaudeville bills or fairground attractions before the opening of the first permanent venue, Thomas L. Tally's Electric Palace in Los Angeles in 1902. The first 'store-front' theatre opened in 1905 and by 1910 there were some 10,000 of these 'nickelodeons' across the U.S., drawing up to 80 million patrons each week. Previously, exhibitors had bought strips outright at so much per foot depending on the production costs and the film's box-office potential. However, audiences were now demanding regular changes of programme and to facilitate such rapid turnover, a new player entered the industry. The distributor bought or leased films from the producer and then rented them to the exhibitor, thus guaranteeing a market for the producer and cost-effective availability for the exhibitor. This three-tier system is largely still in effect today.

Edison hoped to exploit the new commercial structure to exclude the mavericks once and for all. In 1908 he invited Armat, the distributor George Kleine and the seven leading companies – Biograph, Vitagraph, Essanay, Selig, Pathé, Lubin and Kalem – to form the

Motion Picture Patents Company (MPPC), to which Méliès was added the following year. Pooling their patents, the members agreed not to lease or sell to any distributor who dealt with any independent company. To strengthen their hand, they signed a deal with Eastman giving them exclusive access to perforated celluloid stock. Effectively, American production lay in the hands of just nine companies, while distribution was limited to the members of the General Film Company, who charged exhibitors a weekly $2 licence fee for the privilege of renting MPPC pictures. To protect their assets further from the moral backlash that accompanied the movie boom, the MPPC also founded the National Board of Censorship in 1908 (renamed the National Board of Review in 1915) to establish a consistent code of standards and principles. But no sooner had the Patents War ended than the Trust War broke out.

Unwilling to brook the MPPC monopoly, the distributors William Swanson and Carl Laemmle went 'independent' and began to produce their own films. Others, including Fox and Zukor, followed suit and by 1910 they, and companies such as Reliance, Eclair, Majestic, Powers, Rex, Champion, Nestor, Lux and Comet, had united to form the Motion Picture Distributing and Sales Company, which sued the MPPC under government anti-trust laws. The MPPC responded violently, employing gangs to destroy equipment and intimidate casts and crews, but despite such strongarm tactics, the independents prospered and by the time the courts outlawed the MPPC in 1917 most of its constituents had already folded. The last, Vitagraph, was taken over by Warners in 1925.

Entrenched in Hollywood folklore is the tradition that the film industry settled there because its distance from the MPPC's New York offices and its proximity to the Mexican border made it an ideal Trust-War haven. In fact, units had been shooting in such suntraps as Jacksonville, San Antonio, Santa Fe and Cuba since 1907 to maintain production levels during the East Coast winter. But in addition to long daylight hours, southern California also offered a diversity of scenery – mountains, valleys, islands, lakes, coastlines, deserts and forests – that could plausibly evoke locations anywhere in the world. Moreover, Los Angeles was a thriving theatrical centre, with a plentiful supply of casual labour, low taxes and an abundance of cheap land, which the companies bought for their studios, standing sets and 'back lots'.

By 1915, 60 per cent of American production was based in Hollywood, but it was the First World War that ensured it also became the cinema capital of the world. Hostilities not only halted most

European production (thus removing Hollywood's serious competition), but also precipitated an economic boom in the U.S., which caused costs and profits alike to soar. The independents, enriched by their successful investment in features, seized the opportunity to strengthen their position through a series of foundations and mergers. Laemmle bought out a number of minors to form Universal Pictures in 1912. William Fox founded the Fox Film Corporation in 1915 (becoming Twentieth Century-Fox in 1935). Paramount Pictures eventually emerged from the union of Zukor's Famous Players, Jesse Lasky's Feature Play Company and the Paramount distribution exchange. Metro-Goldwyn-Mayer (MGM) evolved in 1924 from companies originally started by Mayer, Goldwyn, Loew and Nicholas Schenck. Harry, Albert, Jack and Sam formed Warner Bros. Pictures in 1923 and Harry and Jack Cohn set up Columbia the following year. Together with United Artists and the 'poverty row' studios Monogram and Republic, these were the companies at the core of the studio system that was to sustain Hollywood for some forty years. (RKO was not founded until the sound era.)

The blueprint for successful studio management was devised by Thomas Ince (1882–1924). Actor-turned-director, he made some two hundred shorts for Laemmle's Independent Motion Picture Company (IMP) before graduating to features in 1913. A pragmatic rather than an aesthetic director, Ince was noted for his pace and pictorialism. Despite a keen eye for detail, he was primarily concerned with convincing narrative flow and edited simply to keep the action fast and clear. The French film theorist Jean Mitry wrote: 'If Griffith was the first poet of an art whose basic syntax he created, one can say that Ince was its first dramaturgist.' Apart from the pacifist tract *Civilization* (1916), his best-known films were Westerns, particularly those starring William S. Hart. A major influence on John Ford, they established many of the genre's dramatic conventions and introduced its characteristically sharp, deep-focus photography.

In 1915, Ince, now a partner in the Triangle Film Corporation along with Griffith and Sennett, vacated his 'Inceville' studio for a vast new complex at Culver City, abandoning directing for a purely supervisory role two years later. Hollywood's first executive producer, Ince divided the studio's artistic and administrative functions and introduced detailed shooting scripts, tight schedules and production notes to ensure that films came in on time and budget. He oversaw every stage of production, from story conference to final print, and his 'front office' method resulted in a number of expertly constructed features,

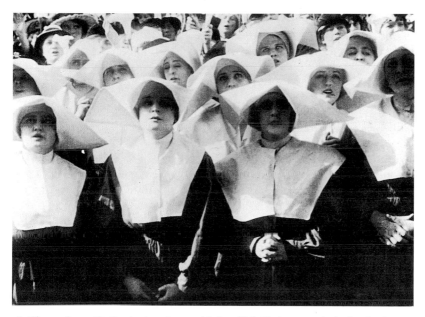

18 Thomas Ince, *Civilization* (1916), a parable in which Christ enters the body of an inventor to reveal the evils of war to a Teutonic king. Ince's death (allegedly, catching a bullet meant for Charlie Chaplin) was one of the many Hollywood scandals in the early 1920s.

including *The Patriot* (1916) and *Anna Christie* (1923), as well as imparting film craft to directors of the calibre of Henry King, Frank Borzage and Fred Niblo. Ironically, Ince's fortunes declined under the system he had helped to create.

A similar fate awaited another studio pioneer and one of Griffith's most fervent disciples, Mack Sennett (1880–1960), whose frantic comedies owed as much to his mentor's editing techniques as they did to burlesque, pantomime, the *commedia dell'arte*, circus and the chase films of Zecca and Max Linder. Sennett was the progenitor of the most beloved and durable of all silent screen techniques – slapstick. Whether parodying popular styles (*The Iron Nag* and *The Uncovered Wagon*, both 1923) or treating caricatured humans as unbreakable props in a hostile world (*The Rounders*, 1914 and *The Surf Girl*, 1916), Sennett had just two rules: that movies *moved* and that no gag should be longer than 100 seconds. A master of location and improvisation, he made the camera the servant of the action, enhancing the comedy with trick photography, 'undercranking' and the inspirational timing of his editing. He also had an instinctive nose for talent: Harry Langdon, Ben Turpin, Charley Chase, Chester Conklin, Billy Bevan and Fred Mace all made their names at his Keystone studio, as did Frank Capra, as a gag-writer. By the mid-1910s, Sennett could style himself the 'King of Comedy', with his Keystone Kops and troupe of Bathing Beauties renowned throughout the world. However, his pace, *non sequiturs* and zaniness did not suit the style of perhaps his most important discovery, Charlie Chaplin (1889–1977).

Joining Keystone from Fred Karno's music-hall troupe in 1913, Chaplin was originally hired, at $150 a week, as a foil for more established performers, such as Mabel Normand and Roscoe 'Fatty' Arbuckle. After just twelve shorts he was directing himself, as well as writing and editing much of his material. He devised the tramp character that would make him the screen's first international star for his second film, *Kid Auto Races at Venice* (1914), although his personality was to be continuously developed and refined throughout Chaplin's career. Arbuckle's trousers, Mack Swain's moustache and Ford Sterling's shoes, together with the derby, cane and ill-fitting jacket, were allegedly selected at random, but their 'messy elegance' irresistibly recalls Linder's dapper dandy. Crude but romantic, fallible but resilient, the 'little fellow' was a cynic with a poetic eye, a rascal with a prudish morality. Audiences everywhere identified with this outsider who yearned for comfort though despising its shallowness.

Consistently rooted in the poverty of his London childhood, Chaplin's comedy was always very personal, combining nostalgia with a horror of social injustice. Deriving much of his humour from character and locale, he used films like *Easy Street* and *The Immigrant* (both 1917) to tackle such controversial topics as drug abuse, street crime and prostitution, while balletic comedies, including *The Rink*, *The Floorwalker* (both 1916) and *The Cure* (1917), which Debussy admired for their rhythm and energy, allowed him simply to demonstrate his genius as a clown. Chaplin slowed Sennett's pace and reduced the gag count to exploit fully the comic potential of each situation, so that scenes depended on the impact of the jokes and not on their mere existence. His use of props showed the range of his comic ingenuity. Although they were always unpredictable and likely to turn against him, as in *One A.M.* and *The Pawnshop* (both 1916), Chaplin's props were employed to define character and express inner feelings, giving depth to the surface comedy. But central to the success of all Chaplin's films were the intelligence and grace of his own performance.

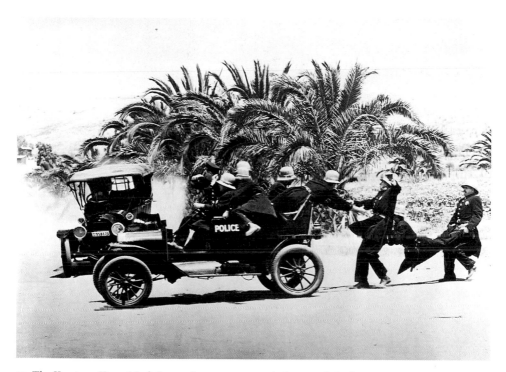

19 The Keystone Kops. Mack Sennett's seven-man comic force made its first appearance in December 1912. Led by Ford Sterling's Chief Teheezel, the Kops became a proving ground for aspiring comics.

There is an irony in the title of Chaplin's debut film, *Making a Living* (1914), for, as a founder of the star system, his value rose and his artistic independence grew enormously with each new contract. Leaving Keystone in 1915, he joined Essanay to make fourteen films a year at $1250 per week, where he began his association with Rollie Totheroh, Edna Purviance and Eric Campbell, respectively his regular cameraman, leading lady and adversary. He switched to Mutual in 1916, where he made twelve films for a weekly $10,000, before securing in 1918 a $1-million deal to make just eight pictures for First National, one of which, *The Kid* (1921), was his first feature. In 1919, he co-founded United Artists with Griffith, Mary Pickford and Douglas Fairbanks, through which he released all subsequent work from *A Woman of Paris* in 1923.

20

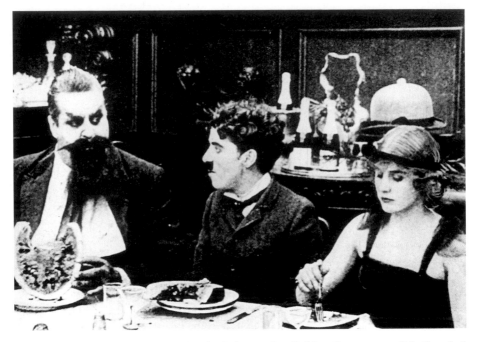

20 Charles Chaplin, *The Count* (1916). Chaplin's comedy relied heavily on typage. Eric Campbell played Charlie's adversary in 11 shorts, while Edna Purviance personified the ideal woman in the majority of his films from 1915 to 1923.

21   Periods of inactivity began to lengthen and although *The Gold Rush* (1925), *City Lights* (1931) and *Modern Times* (1936) are among his most famous films, Chaplin was increasingly seduced by highbrow acclaim from the mid-1920s. As the Tramp lost his common touch, Chaplin became more and more self-conscious and fluency and spontaneity gave way to pretension and sentimentality. His directorial style had intimacy and a natural instinct for establishing the dynamic between camera and performer, but his methods were highly conventional. While his seamless editing never detracted from the action, his preference for bright, flat lighting, carefully composed sets, long shots and 'sequence takes' betrayed a technique still firmly rooted in the stage tradition. His limitations as both director and intellectual were ultimately exposed in his 'talkies', *The Great Dictator* (1940), *Monsieur Verdoux* (1947), *Limelight* (1952), *A King in New York* (1957) and *The Countess from Hong Kong* (1966).

34

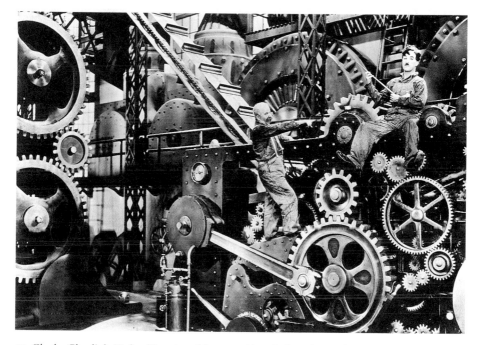

21 Charles Chaplin's *Modern Times* (1936) borrowed heavily from René Clair's *A Nous la liberté* (1931) but its greater debt was to Soviet revolutionary cinema, causing it to be banned as Communist propaganda by Hitler and Mussolini. Chaplin took his revenge with *The Great Dictator* (1940).

If Chaplin's style remained largely theatrical, Buster Keaton's was wholly cinematic, despite his own vaudeville background. In 1917, Keaton (1895–1966) began working with Fatty Arbuckle and over the next two years produced fifteen two-reelers of increasing sophistication. In 1919 he formed his own production company and between 1920 and 1923 made nineteen supremely visual shorts, including *One Week* (1920), *The Playhouse*, *The Boat* (both 1921), *Cops* (1922) and *The Balloonatic* (1923), whose elaborate structure and fluid editing rank them among the finest of the period. Beautifully photographed, with meticulous attention to location and *mise-en-scène*, Keaton's features showed an even greater awareness of the camera's ability to register comedy, *Sherlock Jr* (1924) and *The Cameraman* (Edward Sedgwick, 1928) actually exploring the cinematic process itself.

Unlike other silent comics, Keaton required complex and credible dramatic situations from which his humour could naturally emerge,

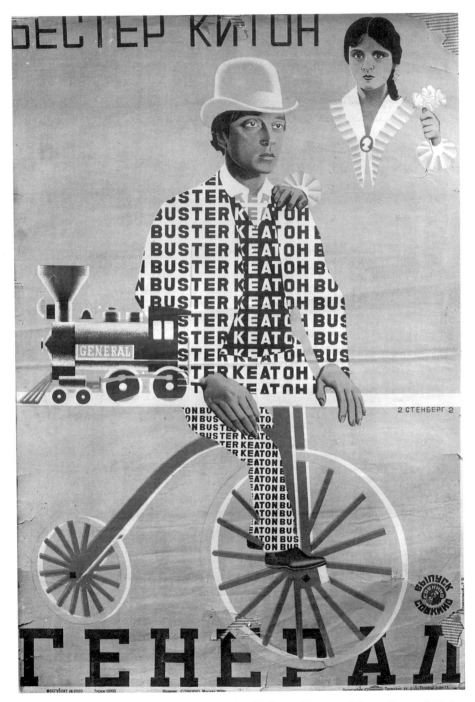

22 A 1929 Soviet poster for *The General* (1927), with Buster Keaton as Johnny Gray and Marion Mack as Annabelle Lee.

such as the family feuds in *Our Hospitality* (1923) and *Steamboat Bill Jr* (1928). Once the plot was established, he unleashed a series of 'trajectory' gags, which impelled him through numerous dramatically connected incidents that culminated in hilarious pay-offs. Superbly constructed and timed, these energetic, yet precise and often dangerous, gags pitted the stone-faced Keaton against such giant props as a train, a boat, a waterfall, cascading boulders and falling house-fronts, as well as battalions of pursuers in chases whose pace belied their intricacy. Although Keaton often shared the directorial credit with Eddie Cline, there is only one creative force behind such pictures as *The Three Ages* (1923), *The Navigator* (1924), *Seven Chances* (1925), *Battling Butler* (1926) and *College* (1927).

Chronicling the daring resue of a locomotive at the height of the Civil War, *The General* (1927) is Keaton's undoubted masterpiece. A 22 dexterous blend of period authenticity, glorious location photography, dramatic action and thrilling comedy, the film was nevertheless a commercial failure and Keaton was to make only two more features for his own production company before it was bought out by MGM in 1928. Despite the adherence of such European avant-gardists as Ionesco, Lorca, Buñuel, Dalí and Beckett (who is said to have written *Waiting for Godot* with Keaton in mind), he enjoyed relatively little success with American critics and audiences. Personal and professional problems blighted the remainder of Keaton's career, although it was studio discipline, rather than the coming of sound, that seemed to take the power and poetry out of his comedy.

Sound certainly accounted for the decline of both Harry Langdon (1884–1944) and Harold Lloyd (1893–1971). Joining Sennett in 1924, Langdon, a baby-faced innocent trapped in a cruel world, enjoyed brief fame thanks to his collaboration with Frank Capra (1897–1992), which yielded *Tramp, Tramp, Tramp, The Strong Man* (both 1926) and *Long Pants* (1927). His whimsical, pantomimic style required great subtlety, but such self-directed features as *The Chaser* (1928) disclosed Langdon's limited range, and his later appearances were confined to minor character roles.

Lacking the depth of Langdon's comedy of emotions and responses, Lloyd's pictures had a compensatory pace and *joie de vivre*. He started as a Universal extra and spent two years playing the Chaplinesque hobos Lonesome Luke and Willie Work, before creating the familiar, bespectacled boy-next-door in *Over the Fence* (1917). Earnest, decent, yet ruthlessly ambitious, Lloyd's character typified the 'can do' mentality of 1920s America, although there was little social commentary or satire in such films as *Grandma's Boy* (1922), *Girl Shy* (1924) and *The Freshman* (1925). But Lloyd will be best remembered for his 'comedy of thrills', expertly constructed gags entirely dependent on his agility and the illusion of highrise peril, typified by his hanging from the hands of a wallclock in *Safety Last* (1923).

23

Sound may not have suited Lloyd's kinetic humour, but it greatly enhanced the appeal of two more Hal Roach (1892–1992) comedians, Stan Laurel (1890–1965) and Oliver Hardy (1892–1957). First appearing together in *Slipping Wives* in 1926, they became, over the next ninety-nine films and twenty-five years, the finest comedy team in cinema history. Perfect physical foils, they quickly developed the characteristics that parodied American bourgeois pettiness and ambition: Hardy – pompous, boastful and bullying, Laurel – naive, incompetent and vengeful. Perpetually bowler-hatted and down on their luck, they were the classical exponents of Henri Bergson's 'snowball' theory of comedy, as seemingly harmless situations descended into

24

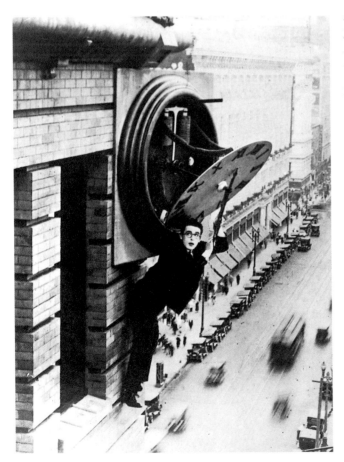

23 Harold Lloyd in *Safety Last* (Fred Newmeyer and Sam Taylor, 1923). Despite losing a thumb and part of a forefinger during the making of *Haunted Spooks* (1920), Lloyd invariably performed his own stunts.

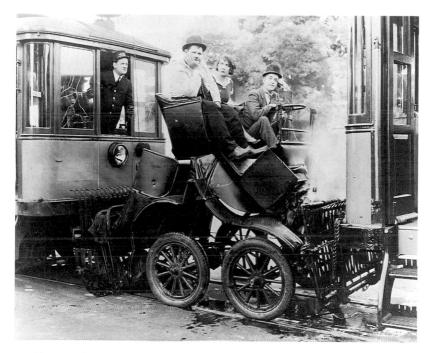

24 Oliver Hardy, Fay Holderness and Stan Laurel in *Hog Wild* (James Parrott, 1930). Only Laurel and Hardy could meet such an end in attempting to erect a radio aerial.

chaos and destruction in such two-reelers as *Two Tars* (1929), *Laughing Gravy* (1931), *The Music Box* (1932) and *Busy Bodies* (1933). Laurel devised much of their business, in which props played a key part, whether to throw, fall over, smash or simply hit each other with. Features such as *Pardon Us* (1931), *Sons of the Desert* (1933), *Our Relations* (1936), *Way Out West* (1937) and *Blockheads* (1938) increased their popularity worldwide, but their careers dipped after 1940, when executives at Fox and MGM curtailed the freedom they had enjoyed under Roach; their later films were essentially contrived vehicles for recycled routines.

More than a quarter of a century after Laurel and Hardy's last feature in 1950, Adolph Zukor, another of the leading architects of the studio system, was still an important Hollywood figure. Zukor had continued to thrive after the failure of the all-or-nothing block-booking system he had introduced in 1916 to guarantee nationwide screen-time for his products. Undaunted by the formation of the First National Exhibitors Circuit, which began making its own films in 1917, Zukor sought Wall Street backing and began buying theatres, transforming them into opulent movie palaces along the lines of Samuel L. Rothafel's Roxy and Radio City Music Hall in New York and Sid Grauman's Chinese Theatre in Hollywood itself. Seducing working and middle class alike, the tawdry splendour of the 'dream palaces' mirrored that of the majority of the silent movies they exhibited, many of which have been lost for ever and many more long forgotten.

Whatever their quality, motion pictures represented a huge investment that had to be protected: as the studios transmuted into film factories, art became increasingly subservient to industrial and business practices. Nothing was left to chance. Anticipating and pandering to public taste, the moguls devised a diet of prestige pictures and potboilers, all made according to proven formulae and backed by mass publicity and advertising. Vital to the success of these marketing campaigns was the cornerstone of the entire studio set-up, the star system.

The snobbery of theatricals and the miserliness of producers had kept screen performers in anonymity until 1910, when Laemmle lured the 'Biograph Girl' to his IMP studio and, by circulating fictitious reports of her death, turned Florence Lawrence into a star. As with the films themselves, the stars were manufactured according to type. Among actresses there were vamps such as Theda Bara, Pola Negri and Vilma Banky, flappers like Louise Brooks and Colleen Moore, 'It' girls in the mould of Clara Bow, worldly women such as Gloria Swanson and Norma Talmadge and serial heroines like Ruth Roland and Pearl White, while among actors there were Latin lovers like Rudolph Valentino, Ramon Novarro and Rod La Rocque, soulful juveniles such as Richard Barthelmess and Charles Ray, 'It' boys along the lines of John Gilbert, jaded playboys like Adolph Menjou and Owen Moore and cowboys like William S. Hart. In addition there were child and animal stars like Jackie Coogan and Rin Tin Tin, and such indefinable stars as Greta Garbo (1905–91), 'the cinema's first truly Existentialist figure', and Lon Chaney, 'the man of a thousand faces'. The biggest stars of the period were Mary Pickford (1893–1979) and Douglas Fairbanks (1883–1939). Pickford, 'America's Sweetheart', was a better actress than her films suggest, her instinct for character, grace and comic timing wasted in the wholesome (and

25

25 Pola Negri as Catherine the Great in *Forbidden Paradise* (1924). Best known as a vamp, Negri here gave a memorable comic performance in her last collaboration with Ernst Lubitsch, with whom she made 7 films.

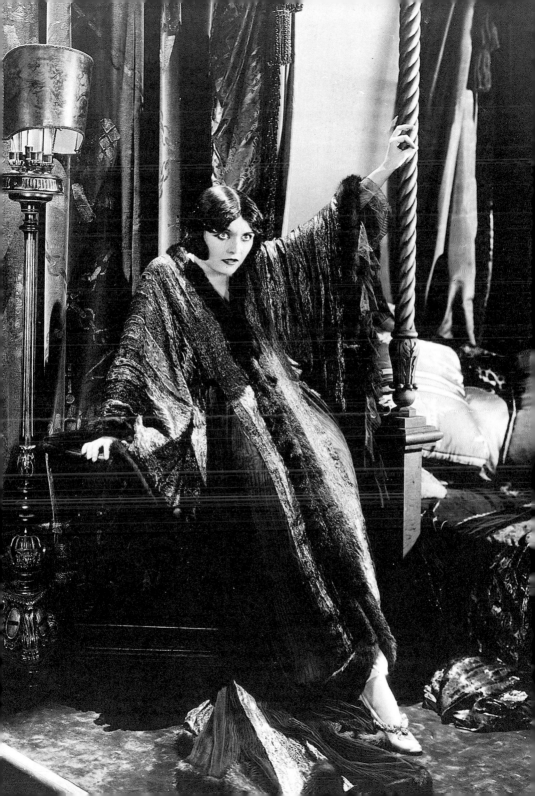

largely forgotten) roles like *Rebecca of Sunnybrook Farm* (1917) and *Pollyanna* (1920) in which the public typecast her. Fairbanks made his name in smart social satires and genre parodies before finding his *métier* in swashbuckling adventures like *The Mark of Zorro* (1920), *The Three Musketeers* (1921), *Robin Hood* (1922) and *The Thief of Bagdad* (1924).

The entire process was punctiliously managed, with the stars' private lives promoted in terms of their screen personae; by 1915 such fictionalized truths had turned movie performers into powerful cultural icons. Many believed their own publicity and the pressures and rewards of fame led to the excesses which earned Hollywood its Babylonian reputation and the series of scandals which jeopardized its privileged position in American life in the early 1920s. If Mary Pickford's divorce from Owen Moore and marriage to Douglas Fairbanks offended, it paled alongside the furore sparked by the involvement (and subsequent acquittal) of Fatty Arbuckle in a manslaughter case, the murder of the director William Desmond Taylor and the drug-induced death of leading man Wallace Reid. Faced with a box-office slump (partly caused by the spread of such new pastimes as motoring and the radio) and fearing intervention by Congress, Hollywood opted for self-regulation and in 1922 appointed Will H. Hays as President of the Motion Picture Producers and Distributors of America (MPPDA). The Hays Office was charged with restoring the industry's positive image (by keeping deleterious stories from the press) and encouraging producers voluntarily to submit films for pre-release scrutiny.

The MPPDA's loose invigilation was turned to his advantage by one of the screen's great showmen, Cecil B. De Mille (1881–1959). The director of the first feature Western, *The Squaw Man* (1914), De Mille had subsisted on adaptations (*Carmen*, 1915) and patriotic melodramas (*Joan the Woman*, 1917) before latching onto the twin Jazz Age preoccupations of wealth and sex, which he exploited in such comedies of manners as *Old Wives for New* (1918), *Don't Change Your Husband*, *Male and Female* (both 1919) and *Forbidden Fruit* (1921). Straining for easy sophistication but overwhelmed by 'Belasco staging', Rembrandt lighting and stylized *mise-en-scène*, these vulgar comedies, located more often in the bathroom than the drawing-room, could only offer tantalizing glimpses of sin and decadence. But with the coming of Hays and his discovery of the biblical epic, De Mille was able to show violence and debauchery in more graphic detail than ever before, providing it was punished in the final reel. *The Ten Commandments* (1924), *King of Kings* (1927), *The Sign of the Cross*

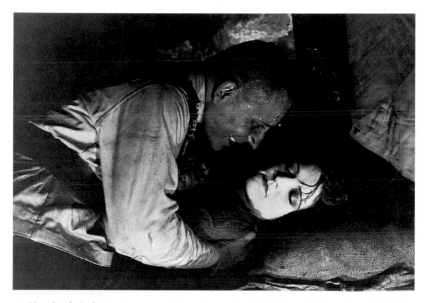

26 Von Stroheim's Russian count attempts to seduce Miss Dupont's American wife in his *Foolish Wives* (1921). The extended shoot and his insistence on hand-colouring and sets that replicated Monte Carlo drove the film's cost up to $1,124,500.

(1932) and *Samson and Delilah* (1949) rendered him in the eyes of the British critic and producer Paul Rotha, 'a pseudo-artist with a flair for the spectacular and the tremendous', possessing 'a shrewd sense of the bad taste of the lower type of the general public, to which he panders and a fondness for the daring, vulgar and pretentious'. His later career was founded on equally extravagant epics, including *Cleopatra* (1934), *The Crusades* (1935), *Union Pacific* (1939) and *The Greatest Show on Earth* (1952).

Theorists such as Vachel Lindsay and Hugo Munsterberg had been paying cinema serious critical attention since 1915, but Hollywood in the 1920s was content to act as a barometer of American social and political wellbeing rather than immerse itself in the Modernist rebellion that was sweeping all other art forms (and, indeed, cinema elsewhere). As a consequence, while Paramount was happy to encourage De Mille's facile brand of spicy morality, Universal reined in the understated naturalism and intelligence of Erich von Stroheim 26 (1885–1957).

Griffith's former assistant and military adviser, von Stroheim portrayed caddish Prussians that made him familiar to millions as 'the man you love to hate'. He reprised the role in his directorial debut, *Blind Husbands* (1918), a comedy of uncommon maturity, wit and sophistication with a precision of lighting, costume and decor that offered psychological insights into the motives and emotions of characters trapped in a sexual triangle. Von Stroheim's obsession with symbolic naturalism chillingly exposed the cruelty and ugliness of the worlds he satirized, but the intricacy of his detailed realism was dismissed as extravagance by the studio heads. The rhythmic montage (with alternating tints and tones) of *The Devil's Passkey* (1919) and the vast sets constructed for *Foolish Wives* (1921) hoisted costs and prolonged schedules. The most expensive film ever, *Foolish Wives* brought von Stroheim into conflict with Universal's head of production, Irving J. Thalberg, who, considering him an inefficient and insubordinate egomaniac, slashed 14 of the film's proposed 24 reels.

Dismissed by Thalberg during the shooting of *Merry-Go-Round* (1922), von Stroheim joined Goldwyn Pictures, where his first project was an adaptation of Frank Norris's novel *McTeague*. Attempting to reproduce its Zolaesque naturalism in purely cinematic terms, he opted for a documentary realism composed of long takes, deep-focus photography and an almost static camera. Completed in 1924 at a cost of $500,000, the finished print of *Greed* ran to 42 reels with a screen-time of nine hours. Von Stroheim himself cut it to 24 reels and his friend, Rex Ingram, shaved another 6, but its reduction to 10 reels at the instigation of Thalberg, now production chief at the newly formed MGM, was an act of vandalism that corrupted von Stroheim's vision and destroyed much of the story's logic. The three-hour prologue became a five-minute treatise on gold, while fragments of the many extirpated sub-plots and Expressionist sequences were erroneously reinstated as 'symbolic' asides. However, such was the power of von Stroheim's *mise-en-scène* that the film was not utterly devalued and it remains one of cinema's finest achievements.

Unable to withstand the strict supervision under which he made *The Merry Widow* (1925), von Stroheim left MGM for Paramount only to be replaced on *The Wedding March* (1927), *Queen Kelly* (1928) and his sole talkie, *Walking Down Broadway* (1932) – released the following year as *Hello Sister!* after much reshooting by several hands. Debarred from directing, he resumed his acting career and appeared in fifty-two films between 1934 and 1955, most notably in Renoir's *La Grande Illusion* (1937) and Wilder's *Sunset Boulevard* (1950).

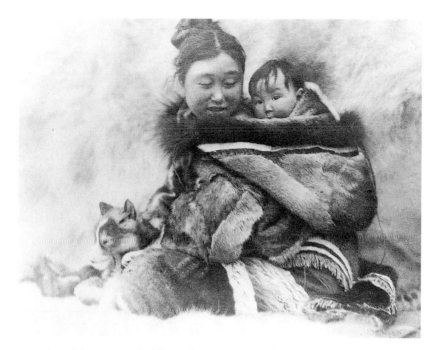

27 Robert Flaherty, *Nanook of the North* (1922). Shot on the eastern shore of Hudson Bay's Ungava Peninsula, *Nanook* made pioneering use of the gyroscope camera to achieve its pans and tilts.

While von Stroheim strove for narrative power through documentary realism, Robert Flaherty (1884–1951) used the techniques of narrative editing to heighten the realism of his documentaries. Shot with a 'participatory camera', the scenic footage and dramatic reconstructions of *Nanook of the North* (1922) captured the spirit of the Eskimo lifestyle through an inspired montage of close-ups, 'reverse angles', pans and tilts. Utilizing 'panchromatic' stock and telephoto lenses, Flaherty's second feature, *Moana* (1926), was criticized for being a poetic fantasy on Samoan life rather than an anthropological study, but as John Grierson, the British film-maker, pointed out, the very purpose of the documentary film was to make 'creative use of actuality'. However, Paramount saw Flaherty primarily as a talented photographer of exotic backgrounds against which it assigned W. S. Van Dyke and F. W. Murnau to fashion the melodramas *White Shadows in the South Seas* (1928) and *Tabu* (1931). Disillusioned with

27

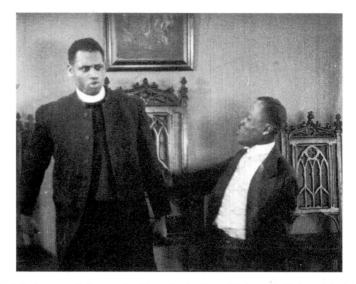

28 Paul Robeson and Chester A. Alexander in Oscar Micheaux's *Body and Soul* (1925). From 1918 to 1948, Micheaux (1884–1951) made some 30 films, all with exclusively black casts. Achieving some glamour despite budgetary constraint, features such as *Birthright* (1924), *The Exile* (1931), *God's Step Children* (1938) and *The Notorious Elinor Lee* (1940) were hugely popular in black neighbourhoods and Latin America. Few, however, have survived.

Hollywood, Flaherty emigrated to Britain where, after *Man of Aran* (1934), he again found himself confined to location work on Zoltan Korda's *The Elephant Boy* (1937). Returning to the U.S., he made two powerful films, *The Land* (1942) and *Louisiana Story* (1948), for restricted release.

The sanitized conditions of the studio system may have militated against experiment and overtly personal expression, but they did not preclude the fostering of genuine talent and the production of some fine films. Clarence Brown, Frank Borzage, Sidney Olcott and Henry King all lent dignity to the sentimental melodrama, the Soviet director Vsevolod Pudovkin hailing King's 1921 *Tol'able David* as a model of construction that instructed and entertained through its 'plastic material' and authenticity. Allan Dwan, Herbert Brenon, Rupert Julian and Fred Niblo were among the most versatile directors of the period, Niblo's 1925 *Ben-Hur* being one of its most spectacular and best-remembered epics.

28

29

Amidst the plethora of matinee pulp, the Western came of age courtesy of *The Covered Wagon* (James Cruze, 1923), *The Iron Horse* (John Ford, 1924) and *Tumbleweeds* (King Baggott, 1925), while Josef von Sternberg's atmospheric *Underworld* (1927), *The Dragnet* and *The Docks of the Underworld* (both 1928) performed a similar service for the gangster movie. Apart from a series of pernicious 'Red Scare' pictures, Hollywood largely steered clear of politics, although Rex Ingram's *The Four Horsemen of the Apocalypse* (1921) and King Vidor's *The Big Parade* (1925) and *The Crowd* (1928) were persuasive pacifist statements and Lois Weber's 'problem pictures' powerful social commentaries. She was just one of thirty women directors active in the 1920s, but Dorothy Arzner, Margaret Winkler Mintz and even established stars like Lillian Gish and Mary Pickford were afforded only limited

30 Ramon Novarro in Fred Niblo's *Ben-Hur* (1925). Completed after 3 years, at a cost of $4 million, Hollywood's most spectacular silent epic was rightly famed for its sea battle and chariot race, here supervised by the second unit director, B. Reeves Eason.

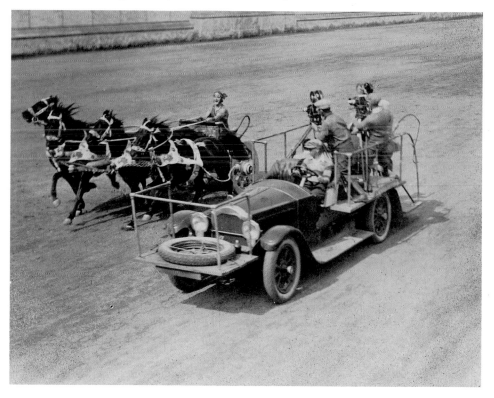

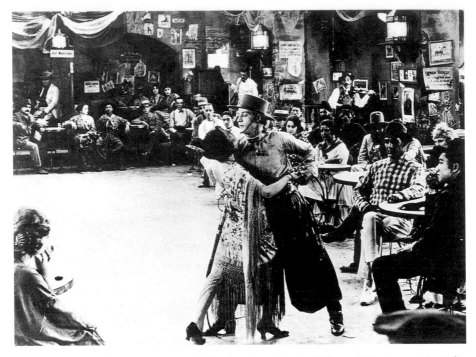

30 Rex Ingram, *The Four Horsemen of the Apocalypse* (1921). Telling of the Argentinian Julio Desnoyer's exploits in the Great War, this 150-minute epic made an international star of Rudolph Valentino.

opportunities behind the camera. These were further diminished by the influx of European personnel following the Parufamet Agreement of 1926 (*see below*).

In pursuit of Continental refinement, Hollywood had been importing directors like Ernst Lubitsch (1892–1947) since the early 1920s. He responded with a series of elegant and ironic comedies, including *The Marriage Circle*, *Forbidden Paradise* (both 1924), *Lady Windermere's Fan* (1925) and *So This Is Paris* (1926), which demonstrated a consummate skill for symbolic detail and innuendo. Mary Pickford called him a 'director of doors, not people' and the 'Lubitsch Touch' stood in stark contrast to the vulgarity of De Mille.

Yet where he and the Hungarian director Michael Curtiz succeeded, many others failed. The Germans Murnau, Paul Leni, Lothar Mendes and Ludwig Berger all arrived in Hollywood in 1926 as part of the Parufamet Agreement, by which Paramount and MGM eased the Germany company Ufa's (*see* p. 57) financial worries in return for

48

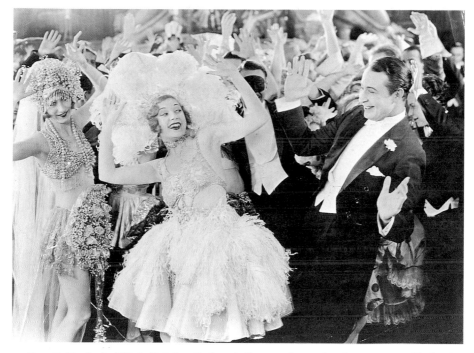

31 Ernst Lubitsch, *So This Is Paris* (1926). A typically assured comedy of manners, notable for the precise nuances of gesture and expression that characterized the 'Lubitsch Touch' and its superbly choreographed camera movements.

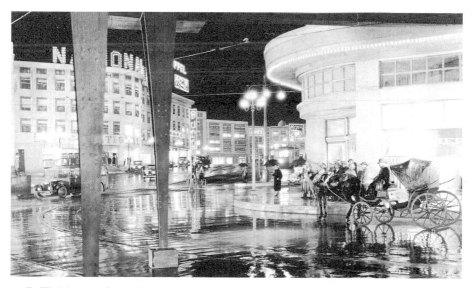

32 F. W. Murnau, *Sunrise* (1927). Murnau's preoccupations in his Hollywood debut were with camera movement and the play of light. In order to realize his designs, the cinematographers Charles Rosher and Karl Struss made pioneering use of panchromatic stock, nondirectional lighting and 'day-for-night' photography.

collaborative rights to facilities and personnel. However, together with the Swedes Mauritz Stiller and Victor Sjöström, they were prevented from imposing their personalities on the formulaic product they had been hired to transform and departed bitterly disenchanted, although their legacy was apparent in the lighting, decor and cinematography of the classical Hollywood style. Of the performers, Garbo was virtually alone in surmounting the problems presented for foreigners by the coming of sound. The rise of Fascism would beget a second exodus, but in the meantime the disillusioned returned to mixed fortunes within their native industries.

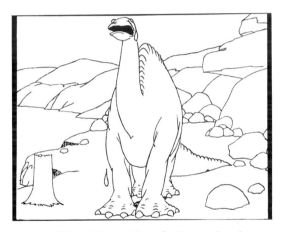

33 Winsor McCay, *Gertie the Dinosaur* (1909).
Along with J. Stuart Blackton and Emile Cohl, McCay
was a pioneer of the animated film and the mischievious
Gertie was its first star. This 7-minute film required
10,000 drawings by McCay, inked onto rice paper.

CHAPTER THREE

Film Art 1908–30

In his 1916 manifesto on film, the Italian F. T. Marinetti, the founder of Futurism, called the cinema 'a new art, much more agile and vast than any other', yet, he continued, 'except for certain films on travel, hunting, wars, film-makers have done no more than inflict on us the most backward-looking dramas, great and small. The cinema is an autonomous art. The cinema must therefore never copy the stage.' However, too many producers worldwide misguidedly believed that by duplicating the theatre's method on film, they could import its cultural respectability.

In France, apart from the intricate *courses comiques* of Zecca, Linder and Jean Durand, which combined parallel editing with Mélièsian trick photography, the majority of films betrayed theatrical influence. Even *Fantômas* (1913–16), *Judex* (1916) and the other crime serials of   34

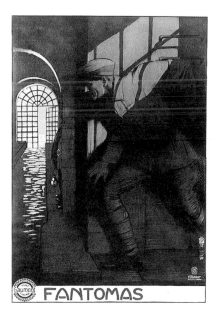

34 A poster for Louis Feuillade's serial *Fantômas* (1913–14). Following the formula of Victor Jasset's *Nick Carter* series (1908), the serial (5 episodes of 4 to 6 parts each) was composed in depth and atmospherically photographed on location in Paris.

FANTOMAS

Louis Feuillade, in spite of their use of real Paris locations, were essentially tableaux shot from the front with a static camera. However, his films had a compositional depth and density that exploited the artificiality of their interiors to intensify mystery and excitement. Managing to convey both naturalism and fantasy, the atmospheric beauty of each episode derived from Feuillade's poetic imagination and his emphasis on the creative use of movement and space within shots, rather than on their juxtaposition – what the theorist André Bazin was later to call *mise-en-scène*. Neglected for some forty years, this great *metteur-en-scène* was lionized in the 1950s by the critics of the French film journal *Cahiers du cinéma*, and in many ways his singularly personal style qualifies him for their highest accolade, *auteur*.

Feuillade's serial style, popular with public and intelligentsia alike, was a conscious revolt against the conventions established in the 'high-art' productions known as *films d'art*. Founded in 1908, the Société Film d'Art aimed to seduce the middle classes into cinemas by elevating the aesthetic and intellectual content of the moving picture through the staging of prestigious plays on the screen. Unfortunately, despite the participation of some of France's leading literary and dramatic luminaries, *films d'art* remained exactly that – screened plays. Notwithstanding a script by the Academician Henri Lavédan, a score by Camille Saint-Saëns and a cast from the Comédie Française, the first *film d'art*, *The Assassination of the Duke of Guise* (1908), stylistically predated Méliès. Imported from the theatre, the directors Charles Le Bargy and André Calmettes had no filmic sense whatsoever, spurning the dramatic potential of intercutting in favour of capturing the action from a single angle in long or medium shots.

Initially acclaimed as a cultural landmark and emulated worldwide, *film d'art* was to enjoy only a fleeting vogue, its technical limitations increasingly exposed as grandiose producers added ballets and operas to the repertoire of literary classics. However, it still had a number of significant ramifications. *Film d'art* brought cinema an unprecedented social and artistic respectability. It taught film-makers that the bombastic acting methods of the stage were wholly unsuitable for the screen and, thanks to pictures such as Louis Mercanton's fifty-minute *Queen Elizabeth* (1912), starring Sarah Bernhardt, it convinced producers of the viability of feature films.

35

Nowhere was increased running time more eagerly seized upon than in Italy. Although Filotea Alberini, founder of the Cines studio, had produced *The Capture of Rome* in 1905, he had failed to see the potential of the historical melodrama and concentrated on saucy short

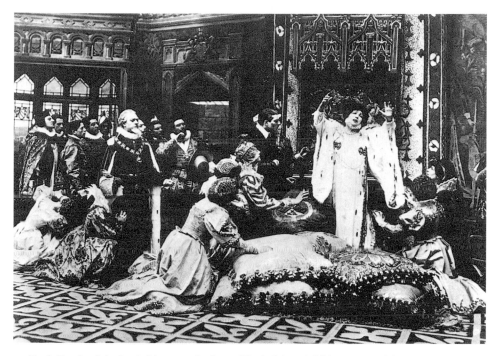

35 Sarah Bernhardt in Louis Mercanton's *Queen Elizabeth* (1912). This most prestigious and influential *film d'art* was imported into the U.S. by Adolph Zukor and persuaded Griffith, among others, of the viability of features.

comedies starring the *femme fatale* Lyda Borelli. However, following the success of Luigi Maggi's *The Last Days of Pompeii* for Ambrosio Films in 1908, he returned to ancient history and the boom in costume epics began.

Leading the pack were Mario Caserini (*Lucrezia Borgia*), Enrico Guazzoni *(Brutus)*, and Giovanni Pastrone (*The Fall of Troy*, all 1910), and each was to supersede the other in the production of the multi-reel superspectacles that were to inspire Griffith. Caserini's nine-reel 1913 remake of *The Last Days of Pompeii* was immediately outshone by Guazzoni's *Quo Vadis?* (1913). Featuring vast three-dimensional sets and more than five thousand extras, *Quo Vadis?* was little more than a series of impressive, if loosely bound, set-pieces, yet it made a twentyfold return on its budget. Based on over a year's research, Pastrone's *Cabiria* (1914) was even more grandiose, its twelve reels 36 boasting some of the most sophisticated special effects of the silent era. Pastrone made pioneering use of artificial light and 'process photog-

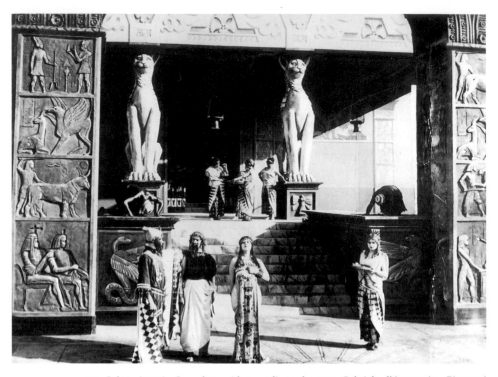

36 *Cabiria* (1914). Complete with a credit to the poet Gabriele d'Annunzio, Giovanni Pastrone's Second Punic War epic profoundly influenced the Babylonian scenes in Griffith's *Intolerance*.

36 raphy', and invented a dolly and a primitive crane to achieve a series of slow, extended tracking shots initially known as '*cabiria* movements'. War prevented *Cabiria* from eclipsing *Quo Vadis?* at the box office and, indeed, ended Italy's brief hegemony of world cinema.

In fact, the First World War was virtually to decimate European film production for five years. With governments slow to appreciate the value of propaganda and morale-boosting escapism, many studios were closed down, their materials and finances diverted to the war effort, and their personnel conscripted to record newsreels or to fight. Only the film industries of neutral Scandinavia continued to prosper, enjoying short-lived 'golden ages' that ended in decades of doldrums.

Renowned for its artistry and controversial films such as Holger Madsen's *The Morphine Takers* (1911), Danish cinema reached its peak in 1916 in order to meet the demands of German theatres suffering from wartime isolation. Yet, as normality began to return in 1917, the industry spiralled into decline. Nordisk, founded in 1906 and still operating today, saw output drop from 124 features in 1916 to just one in 1928. The directors Stellan Rye (1880–1914) and Urban Gad (1879–1947) and the silent superstar Asta Nielsen (1883–1972, creator of the vamp) had already departed for Germany in 1912 because of the limited resources generated by the small domestic market, and this new crisis prompted a similar exodus. Benjamin Christensen (1879–1959) went to Sweden, where he shot his best-known film, *Witchcraft through the Ages* (1922), while Carl Theodor Dreyer (1889–1968), already known for his abstract composition and use of intimate close-up, sought opportunities in Germany and France.

Swedish cinema also eventually fell prey to foreign competition, with the leading directors Victor Sjöström (1879–1960) and Mauritz Stiller (1883–1928) and the latter's protégée Greta Garbo all in Hollywood by 1925. They had left a legacy of remarkable features that explored the expressive possibilities of film art.

Sjöström specialized in slow, serious studies of moods and emotions, many of them, like *The Girl from the Marsh Croft* (1917) and *The Phantom Carriage* (1921), adapted from the novels of Selma Lagerlöf. 37

37 Victor Sjöström, *The Phantom Carriage* (1921). Sjöström's use of natural landscape and stylized sets gave his films a unique texture and almost mystical atmosphere. Chaplin considered him 'the greatest director in the world'.

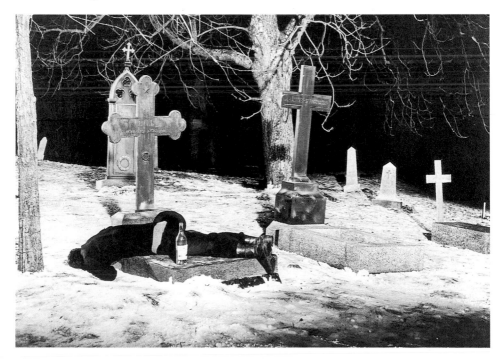

A sensitive director of performers, Sjöström also had great feeling for the natural landscape, which he used, along with spare, stylized sets, to convey atmosphere and psychological states. His earliest work, including *Ingeborg Holm* (1913), was noted for its mosaic narrative, poetic imagery, deep-focus photography and heightened perspectives, achieved by placing objects at 90° to the camera. As his technique became more assured, Sjöström began holding shots to reinforce the significant interaction of character and setting, and experimenting with structure. In *Kiss of Death* (1916), for example, he examined the central incident from several viewpoints by means of flashback. Despite completing nine films for MGM, including acclaimed adaptations of *The Scarlet Letter* (1926) and *The Wind* (1927), both with Lillian Gish, Sjöström (known as Seastrom in Hollywood) was unable to settle and returned to Sweden to resume his acting career, his most notable role being the tormented academic in Ingmar Bergman's *Wild Strawberries* (1957).

Mauritz Stiller was as capable of producing sombre, powerful dramas as Sjöström, although he too often sacrificed thematic range and emotional depth for technical ingenuity and epic scale. In films such as *Sir Arne's Treasure* (1919), *Gunnar Hede's Saga* (1922) and *The Atonement of Gösta Berling* (1924), he depicted the darker side of the soul by means of a symbolic fusion of mood and landscape. His detached style allowed him to judge images in purely filmic terms, and his juxtaposition of key elements within the *mise-en-scène* in many ways anticipated Soviet associative montage. As *Thomas Graal's Best Film* (1917) and the witty comedy of sexual manners *Erotikon* (1920) testify, Stiller was equally adept at comedy, but his career, following disastrous spells at MGM and Paramount, was to be cut short by illness. He was 45 when he died in 1928, the same year the Swedish film industry, broken by the coming of sound and an unfavourable co-production deal with the German company Ufa, went into long-term decline.

The thematic and stylistic concerns of the Scandinavians had a considerable impact on German cinema, which had been rendered still more stagebound by the advent in 1912 of *Autorenfilme*, the German equivalent of *film d'art*. Intended by their producer, Paul Davidson, to raise standards and status, they were chiefly noteworthy for the introduction to film of the legendary stage director Max Reinhardt. Famed for his use of functional sets and *chiaroscuro* lighting, and his skilled choreography of performers, Reinhardt not only fashioned the look of German silent cinema, but also discovered many of its leading personalities, including Ernst Lubitsch, Emil Jannings, Conrad Veidt, Fritz Kortner, and Albert Basserman.

The first German film to break with the theatrical tradition was Stellan Rye's variation on the Faust theme, *The Student of Prague* (1913), which combined location shooting with an impressive array of photographic illusions. Stylistically and thematically prefiguring the Expressionism of the Weimar period, the film spawned numerous imitations, including *The Golem* (1915), directed by Rye's leading man, Paul Wegener, and the 1916 serial *Homunculus*, but it failed to break the proscenium mould.

Production increased rapidly during the war, particularly after the merger in December 1917 of all branches of the German industry into Universum Film Aktiengesellschaft (Ufa), a single, state-subsidized conglomerate, detailed by General Ludendorf to upgrade output and counter anti-German propaganda. The government sold its shares in 1918 and for the next decade under Erich Pommer, Ufa's vast Neubabelsberg studio operated almost as a collective of directors, performers, cinematographers and designers, primarily engaged in the pursuit of artistic excellence. Athough concentrating more on distribution and exhibition than production, the films that Ufa did sponsor were, almost without exception, classics.

The same could not be said for the *Aufklärungsfilme* ('facts of life films'), which followed the relaxation of censorship in 1919. With titles such as *Prostitution*, *Hyenas of Lust* and *A Man's Girlhood*, they were essentially pornographic and could not have been much more divorced from the *Aufbruch* ('departure'), the vibrant spirit of intellectual radicalism that pervaded much early Weimar art. Avant-garde in style and Marxist in overtone, it swept aside both outmoded filmmaking practices and highbrow prejudices against the medium.

Ufa also capitalized on this new-found freedom, consciously courting overseas success with its first peacetime productions, a series of Italianate *Kostümfilme*, beginning with Joe May's *Veritas vincit* in 1918. However, the master of the genre was 'the great humanizer of history', Ernst Lubitsch. Invariably starring Pola Negri and employing lavish, period sets, Reinhardt-style lighting, bold camera angles and rapid cutting, films such as *The Eyes of the Mummy Ma* and *Carmen* (both 1918), *Madame Dubarry* (1919) and *Anna Boleyn* (1920) explored the sexual intrigues that simmered beneath the pageantry of the past. While he made dynamic use of crowds, Lubitsch was never totally comfortable with the epic scale, preferring the intimate detail or innuendo that illuminated a scene, a predilection that served him well in

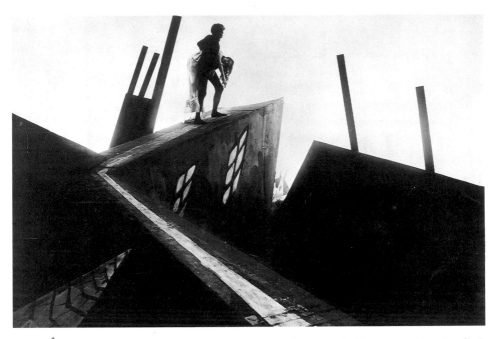

38 Robert Wiene, *The Cabinet of Dr Caligari* (1919). To some critics the film's Expressionist designs were a conscious departure from the classical Hollywood style or a reflection of post-war national angst; to others they are early examples of self-reflexivity and cinematic deconstruction.

his cynical social satires *The Oyster Princess* and *The Doll* (both 1919). Studiously avoiding local subjects, films such as Dmitri Buchowetski's *Danton* (1921) and Richard Oswald's *Lady Hamilton* (1922) covertly mocked the heritage of Germany's vanquishers and insinuated that history was shaped more by passionate whim than socio-economic or military force.

Their popularity waned, however, with the return of prosperity in 1924, unlike that of *Schauerfilme*, horror fantasies that were the direct descendants of the one truly Expressionist film of the era, *The Cabinet of Dr Caligari* (1919). Written by Carl Mayer and Hans Janowitz, the film, telling of an evil asylum director who forces a patient (the narrator) to commit murder on his behalf, was intended to be an allegory on the misuse of power. However, through the addition of a framing story, devised by Fritz Lang (1890–1976) as a means of increasing the Expressionist significance of the *mise-en-scène*, it was revealed that the narrator was an inmate of the director's institution, thus inverting the meaning or, at best, leaving it ambiguous.

58

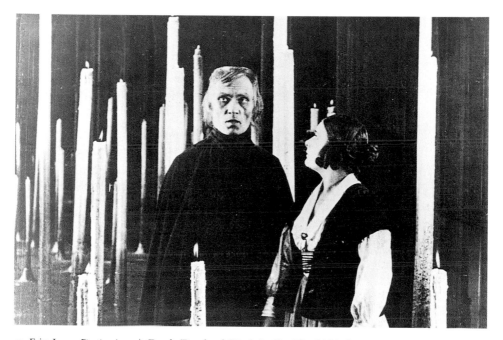

39 Fritz Lang, *Destiny* (1921). Death (Bernhard Götzke) offers The Girl (Lil Dagover) the chance to save her lover by proving love can conquer death. The thin white candles symbolize the fragility of human life.

In order to convey in objective terms the subjective realities of the narrator's disturbed mental state, the director Robert Wiene (1881–1938) hired the Expressionist artists Hermann Warm, Walter Röhrig and Walter Reimann to design sets with exaggerated dimensions, altered spatial relationships and distorted perpendiculars. The sinister unnaturalness of Caligari's world was further compounded by the thick, frozen make-up of the performers and the stylized representations of light and shade painted onto the backdrops which, for all their impact and significance, were rather forced on the production by electricity rationing. What lighting was available was low-key to accentuate the artwork.

Notwithstanding the conservatism of its structure (arranged scenes with little camera movement or intercutting) or the restriction of its Expressionism to décor and staging, *Dr Caligari* brought a non-narrative and poetic dimension to film art. Unforgettable but unrepeatable, it had little tangible influence on world cinema, yet its implications and its deployment of *Stimmung* (the means of conveying mood with light and setting) dominated the *Kino-debatte* on the role of film in German art in the 1920s. To some it was 'painting in motion', but the German theorist Siegfried Kracauer, in his book *From Caligari to Hitler* (1947), controversially arraigned it for preconditioning the national subconscious in favour of Nazism. He levelled a similar charge against the glorified heroism of Dr Arnold Fanck's 'mountain films', disregarding the fact that 50 per cent of the films which contemporary German audiences saw were imported. *Warning Shadows* (Arthur Robison, 1920), *Waxworks* (Paul Leni, 1924) and remakes of *The Golem* (Paul Wegener, 1920) and *The Student of Prague* (Henrik Galeen, 1926) were among the many *Schauerfilme* that continued to explore what Kracauer called Germany's 'deep and fearful concern with the foundation of the self'.

The struggle between love and death, however, was the theme of Lang's *Destiny* (1921). Set in ninth-century Baghdad, Renaissance Venice and a mythical China, it was less cerebral than *Caligari*, but undeniably more handsome, using light to achieve striking geometrical stylizations of architecture and space. In stark contrast was Murnau's *Nosferatu* (1922), which the contemporary critic Béla Balázs claimed had 'a chilling draught from doomsday' whistling through every frame. Subtitled 'A Symphony of Horror', its menace was derived as much from Murnau's use of real locations, negative footage, and dislocated editing and from the cinematographer Fritz Arno Wagner's angular, low-contrast compositions as from the grotesqueness of Max Schreck's vampire.

Lang was at his best with such commercial subjects as crime (*Dr Mabuse, the Gambler*, 1922, and *M*, 1931), fantasy (the *Nibelungen*, 1922–4) and science fiction (*The Woman in the Moon*, 1929). His middlebrow outlook and political naivety were exposed, however, when he attempted the deeper themes of totalitarianism and the dehumanization of labour in *Metropolis* (1926). Even so, that film remains memorable for its brilliant depiction of futuristic architecture and technology courtesy of the Schüfftan Process, which combined miniature sets with live action. Refusing Hitler's offer to head Nazi film production, Lang left Germany in 1933, although his wife and regular screenwriter, Thea von Harbou, remained.

Murnau (1888–1931), on the other hand, was capable of tackling more complex topics. In 1924, Carl Mayer, the creator of *Caligari*, conceived his theory of 'unchained' or 'subjective camera'. 'The camera should not remain immobile,' he wrote, 'it must be everywhere. It must come close to things and it must above all come close

39

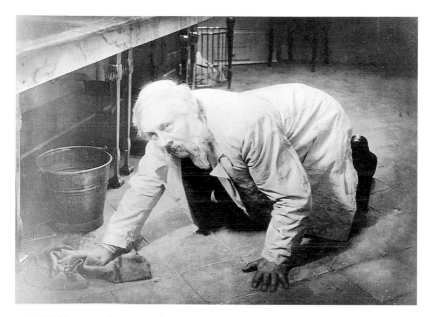

40 F. W. Murnau, *The Last Laugh* (1924). Emil Jannings as the pompous doorman stripped of his uniform and demoted to lavatory attendant.

to human beings. It must spy on their sorrows and joys, the sweat on their brows, their sighs of relief.' He built such camera movements into his script for Murnau's *The Last Laugh* (1924), a complex parable 40 on the failure of militarism and Germany's salvation by American investment. In order to assume the physical perspective of Emil Jannings's humiliated hotel doorman, Murnau and the cinematographer Karl Freund variously mounted the camera on a bicycle, a fire-engine ladder, overhead cables, and even Freund's chest. To represent Jannings's sensory perceptions they resorted to superimpositions, unfocused lenses and distorting mirrors, thus using the subjective camera in an Expressionist way. So clear was Murnau's symbolism that the film's only caption was to explain the doorman's unexpected inheritance towards its end.

Recognizing that 'objectivity' was actually the sum of a number of conscious decisions about camera placement and lighting, Murnau chose to employ the camera as a performer, whose movements were always logical and whose stillness always significant. The roving camera also permitted him to experiment with long takes, which he

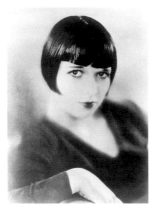

41 Louise Brooks (1906–85), who transformed the art of screen acting as Lulu in *Pandora's Box* (1928) and Thymiane in *The Diary of a Lost Girl* (1929). Henri Langlois later declared: 'There is no Garbo! There is no Dietrich! There is only Louise Brooks!'

enlivened with deft editing. Following *Tartuffe* (1925) and *Faust* (1926), Murnau went to Hollywood in 1927 to make *Sunrise* for Fox. His discovery of the first- and third-person camera was critical to the development of the classical Hollywood narrative style, although the less restrained subjectivity of E. A. Dupont's *Variety* (1925) was better received at the American box-office.

The Last Laugh ended the series of intimate studies of lower bourgeois life, or *Kammerspielfilme*, that Mayer had started in 1921 with the scripts for Leopold Jessner's *Backstairs* and Lupu Pick's *Shattered*. Dealing with morbid themes in realistic settings, they were both an extension of Expressionism and a reaction against it. As the Depression lifted they were supplanted by *Strassenfilme* like Karl Grune's *The Street* (1923), exercises in studio-controlled realism that reflected the *neue Sachlichkeit*, or 'New Objectivity', the art movement that portrayed everyday conditions under Weimar with cynical resignation.

The key work of German social realism was *The Joyless Street* (1925), a slice of Viennese life during the inflation period, directed by G. W. Pabst (1886–1967). Gritty and graphic, with little sentimentality or symbolism, the film succeeds because of the astute performances of Asta Nielsen and Greta Garbo and the dynamism generated by Pabst's almost seamless editing. Influenced by Eisenstein's montage (*see* p. 76), Pabst's 'invisible' or 'continuity editing' disguised fragmentation by cutting during a movement which was then completed, from a new perspective, in the next shot. The technique, later essential for smooth transitions in sound films, was even more evident in *The Love of Jeanne Ney* (1927), which includes a two-minute sequence containing forty barely perceptible cuts across both subjective and objective action.

Using angle and composition, rather than camera movement and symbolism, to establish character and psychological truth, Pabst's perceptive social analyses were diluted by his reluctance to delve too far beneath the surface and by a fondness for such melodramatic material as *Pandora's Box* (1928) and *Diary of a Lost Girl* (1929), both starring Louise Brooks. He was to achieve verbal and visual realism in the pacifist dramas *Westfront 1918* (1930) and *Kameradschaft* (1931), but his later work became increasingly conservative in form and content.

Since he was responsible for so much innovation during this Expressionist period, it is hardly surprising that Carl Mayer was a prime mover in the break with sanitized studio production. However, although he conceived the idea for *Berlin, Symphony of a Great City* (1927), it was Walter Ruttmann who, exulting in the shapes and rhythms of daily life, edited Karl Freund's candid-camera footage into a dazzling 'city symphony'. Unlike educational documentaries (or *Kulturfilme*), this was an abstract celebration of the city, as was *People on Sunday* (1929), a collaboration between Robert Siodmak, Fred Zinnemann, Edgar G. Ulmer and Billy Wilder. All four would later prosper in Hollywood, along with the many others who had left Germany following the Parufamet Agreement. Their exile and Ufa's

42 *Berlin, Symphony of a Great City* (Walter Ruttmann, 1927): a 'montage documentary', one of many fine 'city symphonies' of the period, including Cavalcanti's *Rien que les heures* (1926), Vertov's *The Man with the Movie Camera* (1929), Joris Ivens's *The Bridge* (1928) and *Rain* (1929) and Vigo's *A Propos de Nice* (1929).

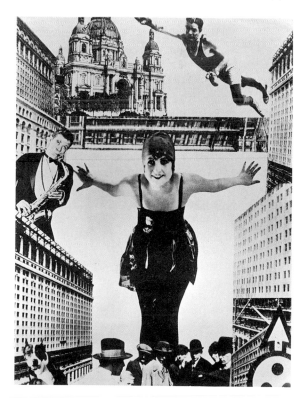

continued financial plight were to be more culpable of the decline of German cinema than either the coming of sound or the industry's appropriation by the Nazis.

In another part of his film manifesto, Marinetti wrote: 'The cinema, being essentially visual, must above all fulfil the evolution of painting, detach itself from reality, from photography, from the peaceful and solemn. It must become anti-graceful, deforming, impressionistic, synthetic, dynamic, free-wording'. His ideas found expression in *Vita futuristica* (1916), in which he and the director Arnaldo Ginna used mirrors, superimposition, split screens and dots handpainted onto the celluloid to distort their images, and in the *fotodinamismo* films of the Bragaglia brothers, which made recordings of movement similar to those of Marey's *chronophotographe*.

These themes were also echoed in the writings of film's first aesthetic theorist and the 'father of French cinematic art', Louis Delluc (1890–1924). Initially hostile to cinema, since he believed it could never reproduce the impressionistic imagery of Baudelaire's poetry, Delluc finally succumbed to the work of Ince, Chaplin, the Swedes and the Expressionists. Working within the commercial industry ('the masters of the screen are those who speak to the masses'), he resolved in 1921 to fashion a truly national cinema: 'The French cinema must be *cinema*; the French cinema must be French.' Delluc dismissed the Italian theorist Ricciotto Canudo's term *écraniste* for those artistically involved in film-making in favour of his own coinage, *cinéaste*, and insisted film was the fifth, rather than the seventh, art. None the less, in collaboration with Léon Moussinac, he based the Cinés film clubs on Canudo's CASA (Club des Amis du Septième Art) model and through their journals, lectures and viewings popularized his concept of the photogenic, cinematography's unique ability to transform objects into symbols for thought and emotion.

Rejecting detailed scripts in favour of lyric impulse, Delluc manipulated the temporal and spatial unity of his fatalistic urban dramas in order to convey place and atmosphere and depict inner passion. Intimate in form and literary in flavour, films such as *Fever* (1921), *The Woman from Nowhere* (1922) and *L'Inondation* (1924) challenged the viewer to decipher the true nature of events suggested by the ambiguous arrangement of selective realism, subtle imagery and cinematic trickery. Labelled Impressionist or 'narrative avant-garde', Delluc's work harked back to the experiments of Méliès, yet it established the distinctive visual style that still characterizes French cinema. It also inspired his closest associates – Germaine Dulac (1882–1942), Marcel

L'Herbier (1890–1979) and Jean Epstein (1897–1953) – who employed such devices as irises, masks, superimpositions, filters, distorting lenses, vertiginous camera movements, and rhythmic and point-of-view editing to reinforce the disturbing ambiguity of their images.

Already known for her wartime proto-feminist films, Dulac used soft-focus photography and variegated speeds in her intense psychological study of a stale bourgeois marriage, *The Smiling Madame Beudet* (1923). In order to achieve an Impressionist interpretation of Antonin Artaud's Surrealist analysis of sexual repression, she filled *The Seashell and the Clergyman* (1927) with a series of chaotic incidents and grotesque images. Unable to raise funds to continue her experiments in the sound era, Dulac moved into newsreel production.

L'Herbier, the most faithful and cerebral of Delluc's disciples, was preoccupied with abstract form and the visual representation of the psyche. Incorporating Impressionist and Cubist influences, films such as *El Dorado* (1921) and *L'Inhumaine* (1924) were criticized for sacrificing depth for pictorialism. He atoned with *L'Argent* (1929), a bold updating of Zola's novel, notable for its imaginative camera movements and dislocated editing. Originally a film theorist, Epstein exploited his own and Delluc's ideas in *The Faithful Heart* (1923), a virtuoso fusion of documentary realism, lyrical imagery and rhythmic cutting. Gradually disregarding narrative structure altogether, he utilized a range of technical effects to adapt Poe's *The Fall of the House of Usher* (1928), which the archivist Henri Langlois considered to be 'the cinematic equivalent of a Debussy creation'.

On the edge of Delluc's coterie was the maverick film-maker Abel Gance (1889–1981). Beginning with Impressionist experiments like *Dr Tube's Mania* (1915) and such melodramas as *The Tenth Symphony* (1918), Gance chose to concentrate on technically innovative epics after seeing *Intolerance*. Having earned the epithet 'the Griffith of France' with his metaphorical antiwar tract *J'accuse* (1919), he moved cinema ever closer to Dulac's 'the symphonic poem based on images' with *La Roue* (1922), which prompted Jean Cocteau to write: 'There is the cinema before and after *La Roue* as there is painting before and after Picasso.' Shot on location over three years, the nine-hour film was cut on Pathé's orders to just two and a half, yet its sophisticated construction, based on accelerated and associative montage, allowed its evocative realism and vulgar romanticism to transcend the truncation. Four years in the making, his next film, however, was to surpass even that achievement.

Originally comprising twenty-eight reels and intended as the first

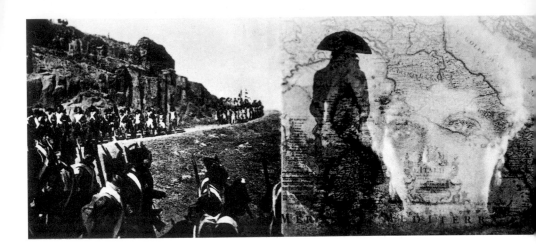

43 of a six-part biography, *Napoléon* (1927) starred Albert Dieudonné and traced Bonaparte's career from his youth to the Italian campaign. According to Kevin Brownlow, who reconstructed a six-hour version in 1979, 'the visual resources of the cinema have never been stretched further than in *Napoléon vu par Abel Gance*. The picture is an encyclopedia of cinematic effects – a pyrotechnical display of what the silent film was capable of in the hands of a genius'. In order to attain fluid, subjective camera movements, Gance variously strapped the newly invented portable Debrie Photociné Sept camera onto a galloping horse's back, a pendulum, a flying football and into a plunging waterproof box, while to achieve the vast panoramas that he would project onto triptych screens he mounted three synchronized cameras in an arc. This Polyvision process also enabled him to effect powerful lateral montages of contrasting or complementary images. Flamboyant and energetic, his metaphorical editing was also ingenious, at one point filling the screen with sixteen superimposed images. In 1934 Gance reassembled the cast for dubbing and two years later issued a single-screen version, complete with the world's first stereophonic soundtrack. With the possible exception of *The Life and Loves of Beethoven* (1936), he was never again to reach such heights.

Although Delluc died in 1924, his Cinés clubs continued to explore the film's abstract potential, and it was their increasing demand for a *cinéma pur* ('pure cinema'), providing intellectual challenge through an absence of figurative meaning, that ushered in the avant-garde's second wave. The American photographer Man Ray adopted just such an illogical materialist approach to his *Return to Reason* (1923), a

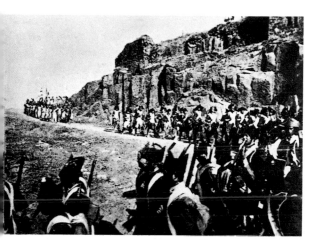

43 Bonaparte's entry into Italy, in Abel Gance's *Napoléon* (1927). The sequence was also filmed in 3-D and colour, but the footage was never used. Gance regarded the central screen as the prose story and the side screens as poetry.

non-camera film derivative of his Rayograph technique, in which objects were placed directly onto the celluloid and then exposed to light. His later films, *Emak Bakia* (1927) and *L'Etoile de mer* (1928), were more akin to abstract collages of randomly edited photographic images. Made in collaboration with the American Cubist Dudley Murphy, the painter Fernand Léger's *Le Ballet mécanique* (1924) was an exercise in 'art in motion', which choreographed household utensils and other plastic forms in non-associative rhythms, much in the same way that Alberto Cavalcanti arranged his images of Paris in the poetic documentary *Rien que les heures* (1926).

René Clair (1898–1981) allied *cinéma pur* with comic creativity in *The Crazy Ray* (1923) and *Entr'acte* (1924). The latter, originally shown during the intermission of Francis Picabia's ballet *Relâche*, featured such leading avant-garde figures as Man Ray, Marcel Duchamp and Erik Satie and borrowed comic business from Méliès, Zecca and Sennett. Clair's 1927 adaptation of Labiche and Michel's stage farce *An Italian Straw Hat* so successfully blended a moving camera with precise comic editing that Henri Bergson used it to demonstrate his theory of comedy. While Clair used Surrealism to amuse, the Spaniard Luis Buñuel (1900–83) seized upon it as a means to satirize and shock. Financed by his mother and the Vicomte de Noailles, *Un Chien* 44

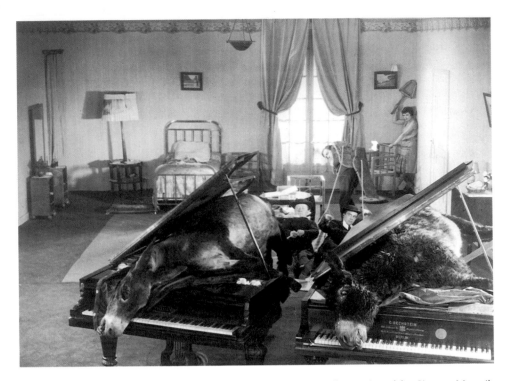

44 Luis Buñuel, *Un Chien andalou* (1928). Having been rejected by Simone Mareuil, Pierre Batcheff drags the symbolic burdens of modern society, including the priests Jaime Miravilles and Salvador Dalí.

andalou (1928) was intended by Buñuel and his co-scenarist Salvador Dalí as a violent and outrageous attack on Surrealist cinema's over-dependence on Freudian psychology. 'Nothing in this film symbolizes anything', Buñuel insisted, in spite of the apparent significance of such nightmarish images as the slicing of an eyeball, ants scurrying from a hole in a man's hand and his dragging a pair of grand pianos each bearing a dead donkey and towing a priest. *L'Age d'or* (1930), however, did possess a theme to which Buñuel was to return through-out his career – the conflict between sexual desire and religious and political repression. He considered the film, which provoked riots in Paris on its release, 'a desperate and passionate call to murder', although André Breton, the founder of Surrealism, called it 'the only authentically Surrealist film ever made'.

Among many others, Dmitri Kirsanov (*Ménilmontant*, 1924), Jean Cocteau (*The Blood of a Poet*, 1930), the microcinematography pioneer

Jean Painlevé (*The Seahorse*, 1934) and Jean Vigo (*A Propos de Nice*, 1930) all made significant contributions to the avant-garde. In addition, the period also saw the emergence of Jacques Feyder (1885–1948) as a key commercial director with *L'Atlantide* (1921), *Crainquebille* (1922) and *Thérèse Raquin* (1928); and Jean Renoir (1894–1979), who, despite a rather erratic silent career, still gave witness in *Nana* (1926) and *The Little Match Girl* (1928) to the skill with performers, careful composition of *mise-en-scène* and tone of melancholic irony that would characterize his mature work. However, the most important French film of the late 1920s was *The Passion of Joan of Arc* (1927), directed by the Dane Carl Theodor Dreyer.   45

Based on authentic trial records and drawing on artistic styles from Renaissance iconography to abstraction, the film traces the last six hours of St Joan's life, focusing on her torment as opposed to the evidence itself. Shot in sequence on panchromatic stock to enhance psychological realism, the action consists of a series of uncompromising close-ups from symbolic angles of faces devoid of make-up, which contrast the Maid's serenity and sincerity with the duplicity of her accusers. Emotion is often conveyed in extreme close-ups of eyes and mouths, and similarly the courtroom is only defined by props, fragments of the set and the stark white background. Joan (Renée Falconetti) is shown in full only three times. The cameraman Rudolph Maté made abrupt use of zooms, tilts and pans to shift dramatic emphasis, yet for all the intellectual and emotional sophistication of its visual expression, the rhythm and pictorial unity are perhaps too often disrupted by intrusive intertitles.

The film was banned in Britain for its portrayal of the English soldiers. British cinema itself was securely in a Hollywood stranglehold, which the Cinematograph Films Act (1927) only served to intensify. Stipulating that British films had to occupy 30 per cent of domestic screen time, the 'Quota Act' relegated such reliable craftsmen as Maurice Elvey, Graham Cutts, Herbert Wilcox and Victor Saville to the production of 'Quota Quickies', target-oriented, low-budget features that diverted the minimum investment away from imports. However, the foundation of Gainsborough Pictures by Michael Balcon (1896–1977) in 1924 and the emergence of the directors Alfred Hitchcock (1899–1980) and Anthony Asquith (1902–68) raised hopes for a brighter future.

Indeed, Hollywood influence was almost universal. Brazil's *Bela época*, with its *fitas cantatas* (silent operettas lip-synched by singers behind the screen), fell victim to it in 1911, while Mexican,

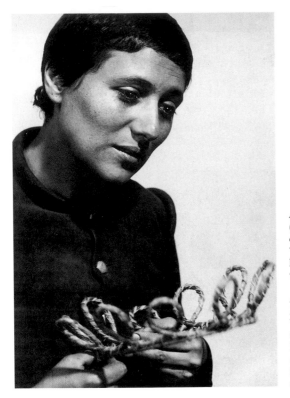

45 Carl Dreyer, *The Passion of Joan of Arc* (1927). Renée Falconetti as Joan, her only screen role. Jean Cocteau wrote: '*The Passion of Joan of Arc* seems like an historical document from an era in which the cinema didn't exist.'

46 Teinosuke Kinugasa, *A Page of Madness* (or *A Page Out of Order*, 1926). Yoshie Nakagawa as a mother confined to an asylum after attempting to drown her son. Shunning intertitles and logical continuity, Kinugasa was profoundly influenced by *Caligari's* Expressionist stylization and psychological intensity.

Argentinian and Australian production was virtually reduced to local variations on the Western. Egypt's film community was known as 'Hollywood on the Nile' and even China's Asia Company, under the directors Zhang Shichuan and Zheng Zhengqui, was backed by American money. India endured a British monopoly, apart from the work of Dadasaheb Phalke, who made over 100 features between 1913 and 1931. Only Japan and the Soviet Union managed to resist the wholesale usurpation of their national cinemas.

The popular appeal and intellectual respectability enjoyed by early Japanese cinema derived from its close links with Noh and Kabuki theatre. Although the *gendai-geki* (contemporary dramas made in Tokyo) and the *jidai-geki* (period pieces shot in Kyoto) had a measure of success, audience conservatism frustrated the attempts of Norimasa Kaeriyama to heighten realism by doing away with female impersonators (*oyoma*), narrators (*benshi*) and live-action sequences (*rensa-geki*).

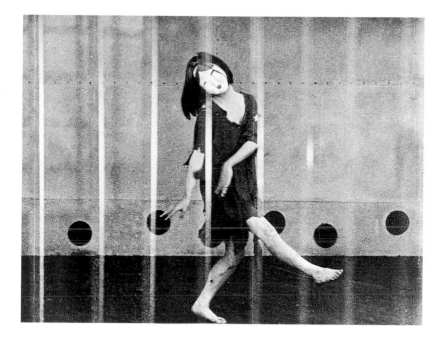

However, the impact on Japanese social and cultural susceptibilities of the earthquake of 1923 and the influx of foreign films that followed the subsequent suspension of production led to an upsurge in thematic and stylistic experimentation. While Daisuke Ito and Hiroshi Inagaki specialized in *jidai-geki*, the majority of Japan's young film-makers chose to work in the newest genre, the *shomin-geki* or petit bourgeois drama. Except for Teinosuke Kinugasa's *A Page of Madness* (1926), 46 which recalled the Expressionism of *Caligari*, the majority of these films bore the influence of the Bluebird series of simple, naturalistic melodramas produced by Universal in Hollywood. The leading exponents were Minoro Murata (*Seisaku's Wife*, 1924), Yasujiro Shimazu (*Father*, 1922), Heinosuke Gosho (*The Village Bride*, 1927), and Yasujiro Ozu (1903–63) and Kenji Mizoguchi (1898–1956), both of whose best work was to come in the sound era.

Russia's first studio had been founded as late as 1908 and strict tsarist censorship had limited production to mediocre escapist entertainment. Although imports occupied 90 per cent of Russian screen time, a number of significant films were made, including Vladimir Mayakovsky's avant-garde *Drama in a Futurist Cabaret No. 13* (1913),

71

Vsevolod Meyerhold's *The Portrait of Dorian Gray* (1915) with its impressively cinematic *mise-en-scène* and Yakov Protazanov's sophisticated adaptation of Tolstoy's *Father Sergius* (1918). Censorship was abolished after the fall of the Romanovs in 1917 and the production of anti-tsarist films ordered, but Lenin, who seized power in October that year, had a greater awareness of the value of silent cinema as a propaganda tool in a country of 160 million people speaking more than 100 different languages: 'The cinema is for us the most important of the arts.'

However, White (that is, anti-Bolshevik) film-makers had reached the same conclusion and absconded to the West with their equipment and experience, while trade embargoes prevented the acquisition of new film stock. Thus, in order to ensure the rapid and effective communication of revolutionary propaganda, all available celluloid was placed at the disposal of such young film-makers as Dziga Vertov (1896–1954), whose Kino-Eye newsreels were shot, edited and exhibited around the country on board a fleet of 'agit-prop' ('agitational propaganda') trains and steamers. Assembled according to Marxist historical dialectic and the principles of the art movement Constructivism, films such as the twenty-three-part *Kino-Pravda* ('cinema truth') series (1922–5) metaphorically intercut candid-camera footage with extracts from pre-revolutionary features, emphasizing points with angular composition, double exposure and accelerated motion. In his later work, including *The Man with the Movie Camera* (1929), Vertov and his co-editor, Elizaveta Svilova, used prismatic lenses, dissolves, multiple superimpositions, split screens, tints, animation, microcinematography and staccato editing, thus disregarding reality and entering the realm of ciné-poetry in order to show both the spirit of the Revolution and the vital role of cinema within it.

Lenin nationalized the cinema within the Commissariat of Education under his wife, Nadezhda Krupskaya, and in 1919 she founded the All-Union State Institute of Cinematography (VGIK) or the Moscow Film School, the first of its kind in the world. On its periphery was Lev Kuleshov (1899–1970), who along with Vertov established the key principles and practices on which much Soviet cinema would be based.

Deprived of equipment, Kuleshov had his students make 'films without celluloid', in which they performed screenplays before an empty camera and edited set-ups sketched on paper. When *Intolerance* arrived in Moscow, he had duplicates made, which he endlessly re-edited to illustrate both the value of a shot as a photographic representation of reality and how its meaning could be altered through montage. He further demonstrated the importance of what became known as the 'Kuleshov effect', with his celebrated experiment in which the impassive face of Ivan Mozhukin, when juxtaposed with a bowl of soup, a corpse in a coffin and a child with a toy bear, appeared to register hunger, grief and joy respectively. Similarly, by linking shots of a man, a woman, a Moscow street and the White House in Washington, D.C. into a logical sequence, he showed how editing could create temporal and spatial unity, what he called 'creative geography'. Whereas Griffith had linked shots for narrative impact, Kuleshov's work evinced that montage could also have a metaphorical or associational function, the power of which lay, not in the images themselves, but in the audience's perception of them. The Kuleshov Workshop was prevented from putting its theories into practice until 1924, but *The Extraordinary Adventures of Mr West in the Land of the Bolsheviks*, a sharp parody of American detective thrillers, proved a sophisticated and effective showcase. However, Kuleshov's main talent was as a tutor and it was to him that Sergei Mikhailovich Eisenstein (1898–1948) came in 1923 during preparations for his debut feature, *Strike*.

47

A Latvian by birth, Eisenstein had trained as an engineer before joining the Red Army in the Civil War (1918–22), during which time he had designed agit-prop posters and helped stage troop plays. After the war, he became a set designer at the Proletkult Theatre, where he encountered Meyerhold, his 'artistic father', from whom he learned how to combine stylization with improvisation. He organized his directorial debut, *The Wise Man* (1923), into a 'montage of attractions', 'units of impression combined into one whole' that were 'mathematically calculated to produce certain emotional shocks'. The play also included his first film, the short *Glumov's Diary*, and when, later in the year, he set his third play, *Gas Masks*, in a factory, it was clearly evident that cinema alone could do justice to his ideas.

Strike was to be the fifth in an eight-part history of the Revolution sponsored by the Proletkult Theatre. Recognizing his inexperience in film technique, Eisenstein watched hundreds of Expressionist and Hollywood pictures, apprenticed himself to the documentarist Esther Shub while she re-edited Lang's *Dr Mabuse, the Gambler* for Soviet consumption and spent three months with Kuleshov. Nevertheless, he still relied heavily on Eduard Tissé, who was to become his regular cinematographer, to capture the realism of the locations.

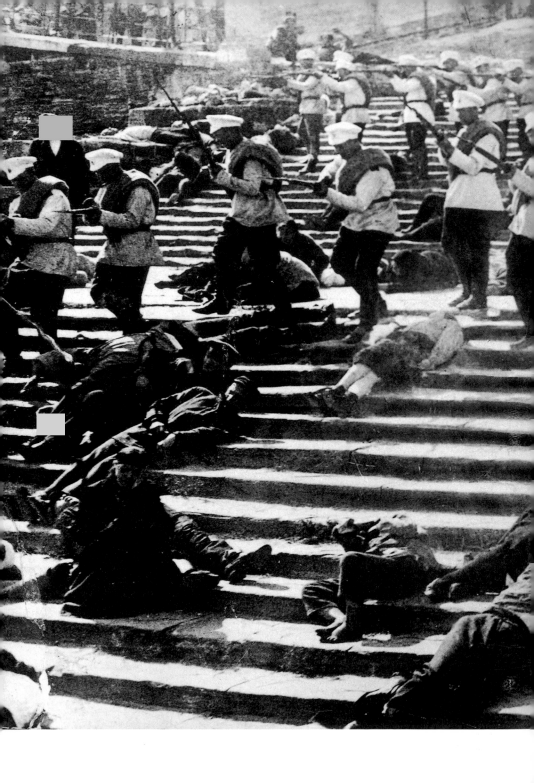

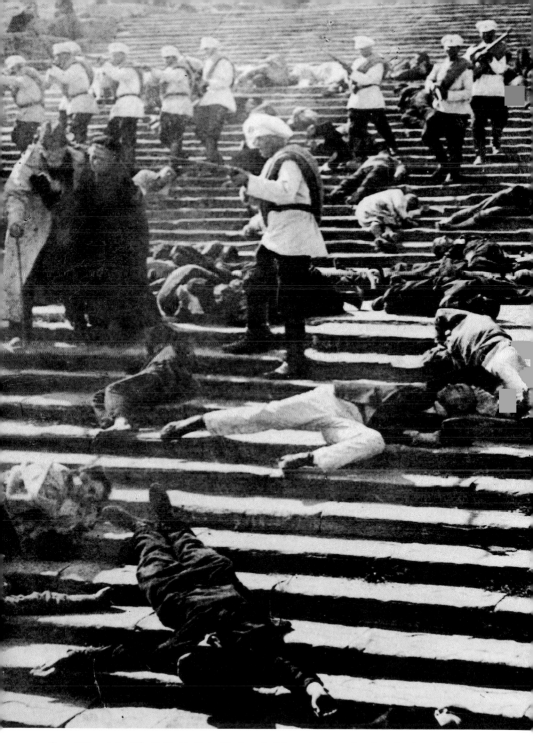

47 Sergei Eisenstein, *The Battleship Potemkin* (1925). A long shot covering the relentless advance of the Tsarist troops against the crowd during the Odessa Steps sequence.

Tissé shot the complex geometrical patterns made by the 'mass hero' of the action, the strikers. What transformed this 'kino-eye' footage into the 'kino-fist' Eisenstein envisaged was the power of his editing.

Eisenstein saw montage as a process that operated according to Marxist theory, which considered history and human experience to be a series of conflicts in which a thesis collides with an opposing force, or antithesis, to produce a new phenomenon, or synthesis, which is greater than its causal parts. However, as Kuleshov had shown, while montage, or the collision of independent shots, might give a film its dynamic, its meaning came only from audience perception, so Eisenstein drew on the example of Japanese pictographs (bird + mouth = sing, and so on) to show how juxtaposed images could convey more complex or abstract concepts.

According to Eisenstein, there were five types of montage, which could be employed independently or simultaneously within a sequence. 'Metric' montage determined the tempo of the editing, and was dictated by the duration, rather than the content, of each shot. 'Rhythmic' montage, on the other hand, did take the shot content into account and gave it a valuable emphatic or contrapuntal function, as in sequences of sustained tension. The texture or emotional feel of the shots was the basis of 'tonal' montage, while 'overtonal' montage was a synthesis of metric, rhythmic and tonal which, while not existing in a single frame or in an edited sequence, became evident, as Eisenstein wrote, the moment the 'dialectical process of the passing of the film through the projection apparatus' commenced.

However, Eisenstein was most preoccupied with the fifth method, 'intellectual' montage, the linkage of contrasting shots to make ideological statements or express abstract ideas, such as the comparison of the massacred workers in *Strike* with slaughtered cattle. His theories, later published in *The Film Sense* (1942) and *The Film Form* (1948), found almost perfect expression in his next film, *Battleship Potemkin* (1925). Originally planned as a 42-shot sequence in a twentieth anniversary account of the 1905 Revolution, *Potemkin* came to stand as a metaphor for the uprising as a whole. Abandoning his completed scenario and plans to shoot in thirty sites around the country, Eisenstein spent 10 weeks on location in Odessa and a further 2 weeks editing his footage into an 86-minute film that contained 1346 shots (compared with 600 in the average 90-minute Hollywood feature).

Eisenstein wrote that '*Potemkin* looks like a chronicle or newsreel of an event', and for this he was once more indebted to Tissé, whose contrasts of light, shade and volume deftly counterpointed the graphic

47

line and movement within the frame to achieve the dialectic inside individual shots. 'But', he continued, 'it also functions as a drama', and this was entirely due to his own editorial skills. The film was divided into five 'acts': 'Men and Maggots', 'Drama on the Quarterdeck', 'An Appeal from the Dead', 'The Odessa Steps' and 'Meeting the Squadron'. Memorable scenes abounded – the smashing of the plate, given additional impact by the use of repetition and extended time; the 'fog montage', which acted as a caesura between the mutiny and the events on land; and the Constructivist glorification of the ship's engines as she steams out to confront the fleet – but it was Act Four, in which the protesting citizens are callously murdered by advancing troops, that was to become the best-known and most influential montage sequence in cinema history.

The sequence took a week to film and has an average shot length of 52 frames, or 2 seconds. Intercutting moments of personal tragedy into the scene's documentary realism, Eisenstein forced the viewer to empathize with, as well as witness, the events through his use of long shots, close-ups, objective and subjective angles, distorted lenses, variegated speeds, jump cuts and static shots. Recalling the 'agit-Guignol' of his second play, *Do You Hear, Moscow?* (1923), the rhythm, texture and tone of such scenes as the relentless advance of the soldiers, the appeal of the mother with an injured child, the descent of the pram and the rising up of the stone lion ensured that the film achieved both its intellectual and emotional aspirations. 47

Widely acclaimed abroad, *Potemkin* enjoyed relatively little popular or critical success inside the Soviet Union, and Eisenstein's next film, *October* (1928), recounting the overthrow of Kerensky in 1917, fared no better. Bitingly satirical and overtly political, it was a conscious experiment in intellectual montage, but the obscurity of some of its imagery and the uncomfortable blend of symbolism and realism rendered it less dramatically unified, thematically consistent or emotionally powerful than its predecessor. *The General Line* (1929), an exercise in overtonal (or, as Eisenstein later called it, 'polyphonic' or 'harmonic') montage, contained some of the most subtle editing of his career, but it was attacked by the authorities for formalism (the subjugation of content to style) and he was prevented from completing a project for another nine years, during which time he endured an unhappy sojourn in Hollywood.

Much has been made of Eisenstein's theoretical debate with Vsevolod I. Pudovkin (1893–1953). Although both agreed that 'the foundation of film art is editing', they diverged on the optimum

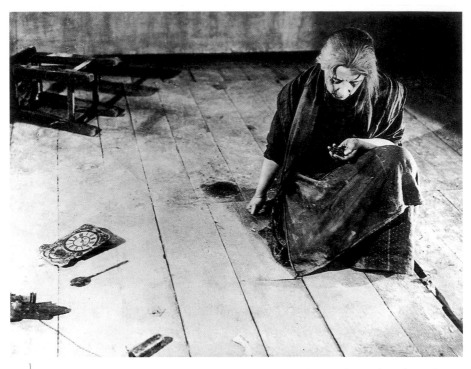

48 Vsevolod Pudovkin, *Mother* (1926). Vera Baranovskaya as the mother who embraces the revolutionary cause after the death of her husband and her unintentional betrayal to the authorities of her son.

method of conveying cinematic meaning. Pudovkin, a Kuleshov graduate, rejected the dialectical technique of collision in favour of a more Constructivist one of linkage: 'the expression that a film is "shot" is entirely false, and should disappear from the language. The film is not *shot*, but *built*, built up from the separate strips of celluloid that are its raw material.' Similarly, although they concurred that a performer's role within a scene was dependent upon how she or he was edited into the film as whole, Pudovkin preferred an identifiable central character to Eisenstein's predilection for mass heroes, and was less reliant on 'typage' or representational casting. These human touches, reminiscent of Griffith, made him considerably more popular with Soviet audiences. However, in 1928, both directors were to agree in a manifesto on the use of non-naturalistic sound.

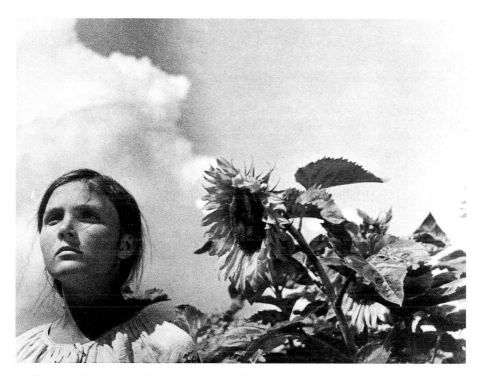

49 Alexander Dovzhenko's *Earth* (1930), a study of the natural cycle in a Ukrainian community, was considered 'a luminous contribution to the realm of lyric cinema' by Western critics and denounced as 'counter-revolutionary' and 'fascistic' by the Soviet authorities.

Pudovkin began his career with *The Mechanics of the Brain* (1926), a study of Pavlovian reflexology, and *Chess Fever* (1925), a Keystonesque comedy wholly dependent for its gags on creative continuity. Moussinac wrote that 'a film of Eisenstein's resembles a scream, one of Pudovkin's a song' and this is borne out in *Mother* (1926). Rarely engaging in intellectual abstraction, the film's sophisticated montage often served simultaneously metaphorical and narrative functions, as in the celebrated thaw sequence. Based on Gorky's novel and starring Vera Baranovskaya, this political parable employed careful composition and selective detail to trace the evolution of an individual's revolutionary fervour, a theme Pudovkin was to revisit in *The End of St Petersburg* (1927) and *Storm over Asia* (1928).

Another great humanizer of momentous events was Alexander

48

Dovzhenko (1894–1956), whose affinity for stylized narrative, lyrical imagery and Impressionist editing was first evident in *Zvenigora* (1928), an allegorical journey through four periods of Ukrainian history. Focusing on the miseries of poverty and war and notable for its use of extended metaphors and oblique, or 'Dutch', angles, *Arsenal* (1929) was a poetic expression of the indefatigable spirit of the Ukrainian people. The juxtaposition within the largely non-narrative structure of talking horses, animated portraits and sequences of graphic realism prompted Eisenstein to praise the film for its 'liberation of the whole action from the definition of time and space'. Even less conventional and more poetic was *Earth* (1930), a slow, richly evoked study of life and death, which paid tribute to the Ukrainian soil and the people who worked it. Sumptuously photographed with a virtually static camera, the natural imagery was given an almost mystical quality by the simplicity of Dovzhenko's editing.

49

Although rather overshadowed by Eisenstein, Pudovkin and Dovzhenko, numerous other film-makers also did much to enhance the Soviet's cinema's international reputation. Paramount among them was the pairing of Grigori Kozintsev and Leonid Trauberg, founders of the Factory of the Eccentric Actor (FEKS), who moved from stage to screen in 1924 with *The Adventures of Oktyabrina*. Their finest achievement, *The New Babylon* (1929), a stylized account of the Paris Commune set in a department store, incorporated a score by Dmitri Shostakovich. Yakov Protazanov, one of the few directors to make notable films either side of the Revolution, produced the science-fiction adventure *Aelita* in 1924, the only Soviet film to have a Constructivist set. Abram Room (*Bed and Sofa*, 1927) and Boris Barnet (*The House on Trubnaya Square*, 1928) made their names with satires and social comedies, while Olga Preobrezhenskaya (*Women of the Riazan*, 1927) specialized in sombre social realism. Fashioned from existing newsreel and feature footage, Esther Shub's 'compilation films', such as *The Fall of the Romanov Dynasty* (1927), were admired as cinematic chronicles of the times, while Viktor Turin's *Turksib* (1929) was to have a profound influence on the British documentary movement of the 1930s.

On becoming head of state in 1927, Stalin announced that as the cinema was 'the greatest medium of mass agitation . . . the task is to take it into our hands.' Mistakenly believing that ideological content alone could make great art, he reorganized the film industry under Boris V. Sumyatsky, an adherent of didactic melodrama, who levelled accusations of formalism against all leading film-makers. Gradually he insisted that every film conform to a code of 'socialist realism', an artistic method 'whose basic principle is the truthful, historically concrete depiction of reality in its revolutionary development, and whose most important task is the Communist education of the masses.' Soviet cinema was thus plunged into an artistic crisis, which was compounded by the growing need to assimilate the new technology of sound.

According to the film historian Arthur Knight, 'the silent film had created a world of persuasive reality despite the absence of voices and the verifying clangour of natural sound.' Indeed, in little over thirty years film-makers from Méliès and Porter to Griffith and Eisenstein had developed the motion picture from a novelty entertainment into 'a subtle, complex and highly expressive art form'. Despite this, by 1927 – the year Eisenstein began work on *October*, Lang released *Metropolis* and Gance completed *Napoléon* – American audiences were demonstrating an increasing dissatisfaction with the visual conventions, melodramatic formulae and intrusive captions of the typical Hollywood product and the moguls were forced to turn to talkies as a means of averting financial disaster. Such was Hollywood hegemony that within three years silent production had virtually ceased throughout the world. It is the great tragedy of the silent screen that its achievements were so rapidly and completely forgotten. Few of its stars have been remembered, most of its films have been destroyed, while those that have survived are rarely shown. Cinema would never again experience a period of such intense theoretical debate or diverse formal experimentation, but as Knight concludes: 'the audience's wholehearted acceptance of the new order, despite all the grave head-shakings of industry leaders, despite the shocked protests of the film aestheticians, suggests a certain, dimly sensed inadequacy in the silent film itself.'

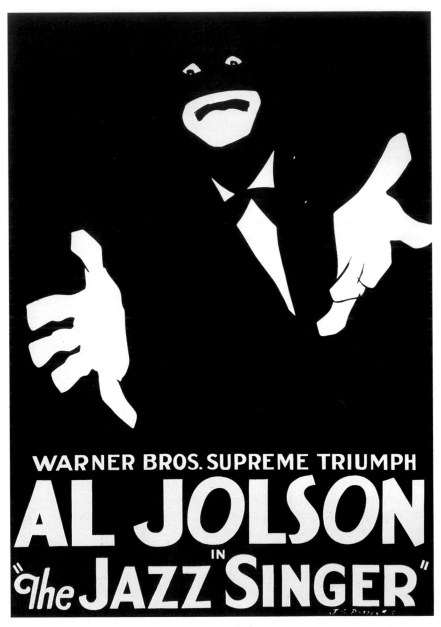

50 A poster for Alan Crosland's *The Jazz Singer* (1927). Sam Warner, the driving force behind Warner Brothers' experiments with Vitaphone, died on 5 October 1927, the day before the film's legendary premiere.

CHAPTER FOUR

The Golden Age of Hollywood 1927–41

Cinema's pioneers had never intended their moving pictures to be silent. Reynaud's 'Pantomimes Lumineuses', for example, had been accompanied by scores specially composed by Gaston Paulin. The Lumières, however, resorted to piano improvisations for their first programme and for the next decade key scenes were to be similarly underscored. With the coming of features, distributors began providing cue sheets of appropriate pieces to be played throughout an entire film, while from 1908 exhibitors started investing in Allefex or Kinematophone sound-effects machines and huge Wurlitzer or Kimball organs capable of a range of orchestral effects. Original scores were commissioned for prestigious productions and Saint-Saëns, Antheil, Satie, Honegger, Sibelius, Shostakovich and Milhaud all composed for the screen.

Pursuing a different technology, Edison had always considered the Kinetoscope to be a corollary of his phonograph and as early as 1889 Dickson had achieved accurate sound and image synchronization in his Kinetophone productions. Henri Joly, Georges Demenÿ, Auguste Baron and William Friese-Greene all experimented with sound on disc (or cylinder) apparatus for use with projected films before the turn of the century, and three similar systems – the Phonorama, the Photo-Cinéma-Théâtre and Gaumont's Chronophone – were demonstrated at the Paris Exposition of 1900. Within three years, Gaumont and Oskar Messter were appending recorded accompaniments to much of their output, while Cecil Hepworth's Vivaphone and Dickson's new Cinephonograph films enjoyed reasonable success in Britain and America respectively.

III

Sound-on-disc was fraught with drawbacks, however. The synchronization of sound and image was, at best, haphazard and the need to change discs in mid-film could irretrievably throw screenings out of sync, as could a damaged record or reel. Moreover, few systems could adequately amplify sound for large auditoriums before 1910, the year that sound-on-film first became feasible.

Attempts to record sound as striations of light on the film strip had begun as early as 1896 with the American Joseph T. Tykociner, but his experiments with a gas flame were soon superseded by those of Eugene Lauste, whose Photocinematophone used a photoconductive selenium cell to convert sound-modulated light into electrical impulses. In 1919, the German inventors Josef Engl, Hans Vogt and Joseph Massole patented the Tri-Ergon system, which used a photo-electric cell to convert sound waves into electrical impulses and thence into light waves, which were then photographed onto the edge of the celluloid. The original sound was reproduced when the strip passed through another photoelectric cell in the head of the projector. Synchronization was maintained by means of a flywheel.

Three years later, the New York-based Lee de Forest, whose Phonofilm system had much in common with Tri-Ergon, perfected the audion tube, a vacuum that intensified electronically received sound and forced it into speakers which provided sufficient amplification for even the largest theatre. By mid-1924, he was producing several films each week, featuring famous opera singers, instrumentalists, vaudeville acts and personalities such as President Coolidge and George Bernard Shaw. De Forest made more than a thousand sound films between 1923 and 1927 and some eighty theatres worldwide were wired for Phonofilm, but Hollywood remained unconvinced.

The studio system owed much of its success to its 'no risk' policy and the conversion to sound involved too many imponderables. There was no guarantee that sound films were anything more than a temporary novelty, whose passing would render obsolete expensively re-equipped sound stages and theatres. If they did prove viable, the studios would be left with a huge backlog of silent films and much of their overseas market would collapse. In addition, Hollywood feared that dialogue would deprive silent stars of their ethereal appeal. However, in 1926, when Sam Warner persuaded his brothers to incorporate sound films into their aggressive expansion plan, he had no intention of producing 'talking' pictures; rather he hoped that synchronized scores would improve business at the company's smaller theatres.

Backed by the bankers Goldman Sachs, Warners leased Western Electric's Vitaphone disc system and invested over $3 million in the promotion of the New York premiere of its first synchronized feature, Alan Crosland's *Don Juan*. The programme began with an hour of 'Preludes', including a short featuring Will Hays, who proclaimed 'the beginning of a new era in music and motion pictures'. Complete with orchestral score, dramatic sound effects and a dashing silent performance from John Barrymore, *Don Juan* was a critical and commercial success. Yet the other studios remained cautious. However, undeniable proof that the sound era had dawned came in the form of *The Jazz Singer* (1927).

Also directed by Crosland, this melodrama about the cantor's son 50 who abandons the temple for the theatre was scheduled to have seven songs by Al Jolson as well as a synchronized score. However, having finished 'Dirty Hands, Dirty Face', Jolson proceeded to *speak* to the audience: 'Wait a minute, wait a minute. You ain't heard nothin' yet! Wait a minute, I tell you. You ain't heard nothin' yet! Do you want to hear "Toot, Toot, Tootsie"?', and later he talked to his mother while singing 'Blue Skies'. *The Jazz Singer* may have been the first feature to contain speech, but audiences were too accustomed to filmed monologues to be thrilled simply by the sound of a voice. What was significant about Jolson's *ad libs* was that they were so unconscious, giving the viewer the feeling of eavesdropping on a real conversation.

Warners' shrewd decision to leave the improvised dialogue in the release print reaped a handsome reward and caused a cinematic revolution. Yet Vitaphone was to play little further part in it, nor were William W. Case and Earl I. Spondable's Fox Movietone system or RCA's Photophone, despite their feasibility. Anxious to avoid another patents war during the Depression, the studios decided to adopt a uniform system in July 1930. Ironically, they opted for a sound-on-film format produced by Western Electric, the manufacturers of Vitaphone.

Although silent and sound-on-disc production continued until 1931, in order to meet small-town and export requirements, the transition to sound was virtually instantaneous, and its success saved the American cinema in the wake of the 1929 Wall Street Crash. Conversion was a tortuous process which cost the industry some $300 million and delivered it into the thrall of big business. However, weekly attendances rose from 60 million in 1927 to 90 million in 1930, and the 50 per cent increase in receipts financed the round of mergers and takeovers that resulted in the formation of the five major, three minor and cluster of 'poverty row' studios that were to dominate the industry until the 1950s.

Sound may have eased financial concerns, but it posed a profusion of artistic and technical problems which engendered the most static films ever made. So limited was the range of the earliest microphones that performers had to deliver their dialogue directly into them, thus restricting intra-frame movement to silent passages. Concealed about the set by sound technicians, who often usurped the director's function, the 'mikes' were also omni-directional and picked up the noises of the arc lamps and the camera, causing the latter to be banished to a soundproofed box which permitted only 30° tripod tilts. A concentration on the foreground meant that décor was neglected and space was robbed of its dramatic and psychological import. In an attempt to recapture the fluidity of the silent screen, film-makers used lenses of differing focal lengths within set-ups or varied angles by shooting with multiple cameras. However, sound signals ran twenty frames in advance of the visual image and while editors assimilated the requisite new skills, cutting was confined to transitions.

Furthermore, the studios insisted that if films had to talk they should have the highest quality dialogue. Consequently, Broadway talent was imported to deliver lines crafted by America's leading writers; heavily accented silent stars (Emil Jannings, Pola Negri and Vilma Banky) or those with voices at odds with their screen image (Colleen Moore, Clara Bow and, to a large extent, John Gilbert) were cast into oblivion. However, films such as *Lights of New York* (1927) – the first '100% all-talkie' – were little more than 'canned theatre' or 'illustrated radio' productions of 'teacup dramas' and, unsurprisingly, the public soon tired of them.

To purists like Paul Rotha, who considered the amalgam of sound and vision to be 'contrary to the aim of the cinema', these movies were a 'degenerate and misguided attempt' to destroy the 'culture of the public' solely for financial gain. Such pronouncements, however, disregarded the fact that much of the art of silent cinema resided in the search for visual compensations for the lack of natural sound and shortsightedly ignored the benefits that sound could bring to film art. Diegetic sound was capable of establishing space outside the frame and creating temporal continuity, while non-diegetic sound could fulfil narrative, atmospheric and psychological functions. Moreover, dialogue removed the need for the captions that had disrupted the rhythm of many a silent film.

Wholly in accord with Clair, Eisenstein and Pudovkin's views on asynchronous or contrapuntal sound and their denouncement of the laboured depiction of all sound sources, certain Hollywood directors began to experiment with post-synchronization or dubbing techniques. These circumvented direct recording and thus, once more, liberated the camera. Lubitsch was one of the first to post-synchronize sound and to use dialogue, effects and silence in expressive ways. Indeed, Alfred Hitchcock would later call such films as *The Love Parade*

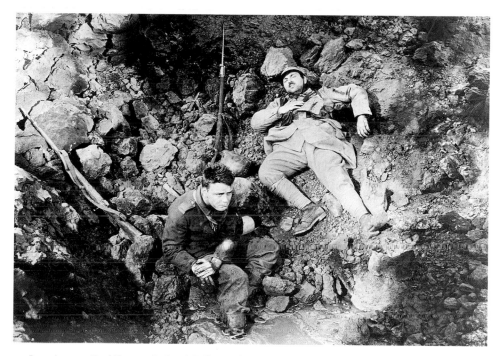

51 Lew Ayres as Paul Baumer in Lewis Milestone's *All Quiet on the Western Front* (1930). Faithfully adapted from Erich Maria Remarque's novel, this was the first sound film to use a giant mobile crane to shoot its realistic battle sequences.

(1929), *Monte Carlo* (1930) and *Trouble in Paradise* (1932) 'silent Talkies'. King Vidor (1894–1982) dubbed the soundtrack of his controversial, all-black musical *Hallelujah* (1929) onto silent location footage, while Lewis Milestone (1895–1980) added battle effects to the sweeping action sequences in his powerful pacifist statement *All Quiet on the Western Front* (1930).

However, the most original uses for sound were discovered by Rouben Mamoulian (1897–1987), who had arrived in Hollywood as part of the Broadway migration. He achieved overlapping dialogue in *Applause* (1929) by mixing recordings made with two separate microphones, while in *City Streets* (1931), he suggested memory by playing extracts of flashback dialogue over a close-up of Sylvia Sidney. His supreme achievement, however, was the experiment in synthetic sound that accompanied Fredric March's adroit on-screen transitions in *Dr Jekyll and Mr Hyde* (1932). 'Mamoulian's stew' included the

87

sound of his own heartbeat and bells ringing in an echo chamber, as well as bytes painted or photographed directly onto the soundtrack.

Solutions to the logistical problems of sound filming emerged throughout the 1930s. The camera was freed from its 'icebox' by the invention of the 'blimp', a lightweight casing that muffled the whirr of the motor, and was given unprecedented mobility by the development of manoeuverable dollies and boom cranes. Boom arms soon bore multidirectional microphones, which, towards the end of the decade, were fitted with suppressors to limit track noise and compressors to eliminate distortion. A new Moviola cutting table appeared in 1930, complete with sound and image heads that could be operated in tandem or isolation. Two years later editing was further facilitated by the introduction of 'rubber' numbers, which were stamped onto the edges of the film strip to ensure precise resynchronization.

Recorded sound added new dimensions to all existing Hollywood genres, inaugurating many sub-genres in the process. It gave rise to only one completely new type, the feature-length musical. The success of *The Jazz Singer* and Jolson's second film, *The Singing Fool* (1928), persuaded producers that 'all-talking, all-singing, all-dancing' pictures were guaranteed box-office successes. Consequently, Broadway hits like *Rio Rita*, *The Desert Song* (both 1929) and *Sunny* (1930) were imported, together with the biggest stars of the musical stage and songwriters of the calibre of Jerome Kern, Irving Berlin, George Gershwin, Rodgers and Hart, and Cole Porter. However, these productions, along with such vaudeville-inspired revues as *Broadway Melody* (Harry Beaumont, 1929) and *On with the Show* (Alan Crosland, 1929), failed to escape their stage origins and stood in stark contrast with the fluidity of Lubitsch's musical comedies. The screen musical was eventually to attain similar levels of sophistication through the work of Busby Berkeley (1895–1975) and Fred Astaire (1899–1987).

Although he later turned director, Berkeley made his name as a choreographer on the 1933 'backstage' musicals *42nd Street* and *Footlight Parade* (both directed by Lloyd Bacon) and *The Gold Diggers of 1933* (Mervyn LeRoy). Transforming production numbers into surreal, stage-defying extravaganzas, Berkeley employed all manner of gimmickry to fashion 'chorines' into series of mobile geometric or abstract patterns and tableaux (which have subsequently been attacked for their dehumanizing and misogynistic regimentation). He also experimented with zoom and kaleidoscopic lenses, mattes and rhythmic montage, but what set Berkeley's work apart was his dynamic use

52 Lloyd Bacon, *Footlight Parade* (1933). An elevated shot from Busby Berkeley's 'By a Waterfall' routine.

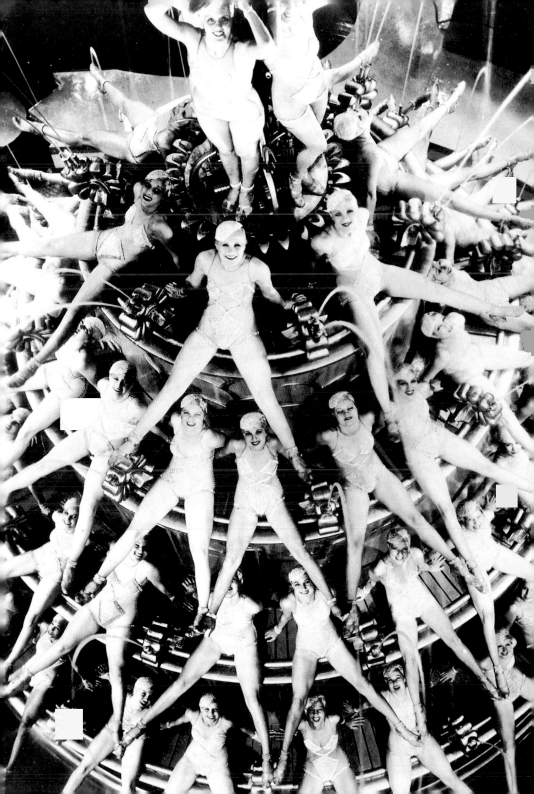

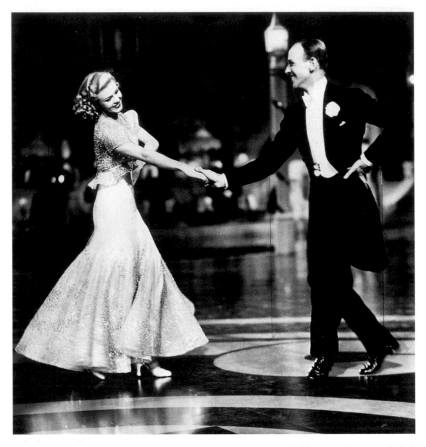

53 Mark Sandrich, *Top Hat* (1935) 'Can't act. Slightly bald. Can dance a little.' Notwithstanding his screen test report, Fred Astaire demonstrated throughout his career a command of cinema craft that matched his dance technique. Katharine Hepburn summed up his working relationship with Ginger Rogers: 'She gave him sex, and he gave her class.'

of the camera. He attached it to swooping cranes, ran it along a mono-rail of his own invention and located it high above the action (the 'top shot') or in trenches below the 'sound stage' in order to achieve his characteristically audacious angles.

Astaire, on the other hand, in collaboration with Hermes Pan, achieved a perfect union of sound and visual rhythm through a prefer-ence for unobtrusive pans (to keep figures in full-length view) and infrequent invisible edits (to redefine space). While Berkeley's routines were essentially self-contained, Astaire used dance as an expression of emotion, integrating it into the action of the nine films in which he co-starred with Ginger Rogers (1911–95), including *Top Hat* (Mark Sandrich, 1935) and *Swing Time* (George Stevens, 1937). 53

The gangster film similarly benefitted from the addition of sound. Gunshots, screeching tyres and rattling, idiomatic dialogue brought a sense of brutal realism to such punchily edited pictures as *Little Caesar* (Mervyn LeRoy, 1930), *Public Enemy* (William Wellman, 1931) and *Scarface* (Howard Hawks, 1932), which respectively made stars of Edward G. Robinson (1893–1973), James Cagney (1899–1986) and Paul Muni (1895–1967). 54

54 James Cagney as Tom Powers in William Wellman's *The Public Enemy* (1931). By 1934, Hollywood had been compelled to soften the violence in its gangster pictures and rethink the hoodlum as 'tragic hero'.

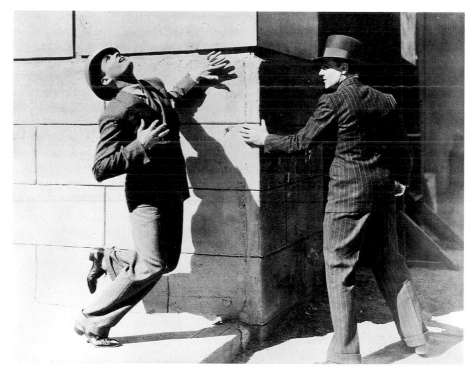

However, much of the power of the gangster genre was to be diluted by the imposition of the Production Code in 1934. The Catholic Legion of Decency had been lobbying the MPPDA to reinforce its control over the content of films since the publication, the previous year, of Henry Forman's study of the influence of cinema on youth, *Our Movie-Made Children*. The coincidence of its aims with those of corporate capitalism prompted the Hays Office to adopt the strict moral charter drafted by the Legion, and place it under the administration of Joseph I. Breen. Upholding the sanctity of marriage and forbidding the depiction of nudity, passion, prostitution, homosexuality and miscegenation, the Code also demanded the demythologization of the hoodlum. Consequently, in films like *G-Men* (William Keighley, 1935), government agents triumphed over the gangsters, whose glamorous image was further tarnished by prison pictures such as *20,000 Years in Sing Sing* (Michael Curtiz) and *I Am a Fugitive from a Chain Gang* (Mervyn LeRoy, both 1932) and 'crime does not pay' pieces like *Dead End* (William Wyler, 1937) and *Angels with Dirty Faces* (Curtiz, 1938).

Ever mindful of its dependence on Wall Street, the Hollywood 'dream factory' hoped, through its skilful espousal of conservatism and isolationism, to show its backers that its highly selective delineation of the contemporary scene could serve as an effective means of social control. However, the studios' bland, optimistic exposition of traditional American values virtually prevented film-makers from tackling topical themes in a mature way. Consequently, apart from the round of cynical newspaper pictures like *The Front Page* (Lewis Milestone) and *Five Star Final* (Mervyn LeRoy, both 1931), ventures into the realms of realism were rare. Yet those sorties that somehow slipped through the net were among the most remarkable films of the period – *Fury* (Fritz Lang, 1936) and *They Won't Forget* (LeRoy, 1937) dealing with lynch law; *Black Fury* (Michael Curtiz, 1935), labour relations; *Black Legion* (Archie Mayo, 1936), racism; *Wild Boys of the Road* (William Wellman, 1933), the Depression; and *Massacre* (Alan Crosland, 1934), the plight of Native Americans.

While series and serials, and inherently escapist genres like horror, the Western, melodrama and the historical biography (or biopic) all thrived at different intervals throughout the 1930s, comedy frequently found itself at odds with the studio system or the Code. Of the silent clowns, only Laurel and Hardy made a comfortable transition to sound. Keaton, Langdon and Lloyd had slipped progressively further into obscurity, while Chaplin elected to remain essentially silent until 1940. Slapstick was replaced by the sharp visual and verbal wit of

XIII

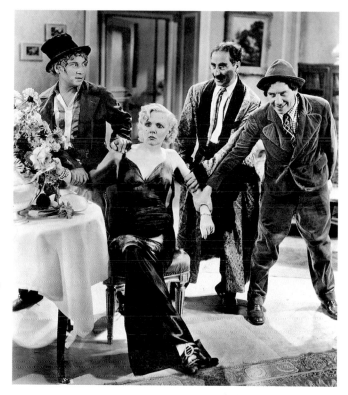

55 Sam Wood, *A Day at the Races* (1937). Harpo, Groucho and Chico torment Esther Muir. Although Irving Thalberg brought the Marx Brothers to MGM, he cluttered their pictures with musical and romantic interludes that hampered their anarchic comic style.

vaudeville and burlesque, whose principal film exponents (the Marx Brothers, W. C. Fields and Mae West) all prospered, initially, at Hollywood's least interventionist studio, Paramount.

Lampooning everything from art and authority to class and language, the Marx Brothers' manic, absurd comedy relied little on plot and heavily on the ingenious interchanges between Groucho and Chico, the silent lunacy of Harpo and the stooging of Margaret Dumont. The films were largely improvised and shot with a predominantly passive camera: *Animal Crackers* (Victor Heerman, 1930), *Horse Feathers* (Norman McLeod, 1932) and *Duck Soup* (Leo McCarey, 1933) were packed with wounding one-liners and inspired prop gags. However, MGM, to whom they transferred in 1935, offered less creative latitude. Although *A Night at the Opera* (Sam Wood, 1935) and *A Day at the Races* (Sam Wood, 1937) still contained many memorable moments, the Brothers' films were increasingly handicapped by formulaic situations and prolonged musical interludes, showcasing Chico and Harpo.

55

Writing much of his own material under pseudonyms including Mahatma Kane Jeeves and Otis Criblecoblis, W. C. Fields (1879–1946) specialized in the comedy of harassment and disillusion. Almost devoid of structure and pace, features such as *It's a Gift* (1934), *The Man on the Flying Trapeze* (1935) and *The Bank Dick* (1940) were wholly dependent on his physical appearance, precise gesturing, bibulous irascibility and throwaway *bon mots*. Like Fields, Mae West (1892–1980) supplied many of her own screenplays, which similarly skirted narrative convention. Hedonistic comedies like *She Done Him Wrong* and *I'm No Angel* (both 1933) relied on acerbic, monotone putdowns, double entendres and West's provocative demeanour. Yet the Code was to expunge her sexual wit and in later films, such as *Klondike Annie* (1936), she was compelled to caricature her previously prurient parody of the screen vamp.

With its breathless combination of wisecracking dialogue and mild slapstick, screwball was another comic style fully to exploit the potential of sound. Ridiculing the Victorian mystique of womanhood, films such as *It Happened One Night* (Frank Capra, 1934), *My Man Godfrey* (Gregory La Cava, 1936), *Nothing Sacred* (William Wellman, 1937) and *Bringing Up Baby* (Howard Hawks, 1938) were invariably battles of the sexes in which repressed males were ultimately liberated by free-spirited women. The screwball format was harnessed by the writer-director Preston Sturges (1898–1959) for his dark social satires, which ran contrary to traditional Hollywood values in exposing a range of American foibles: corruption (*The Great McGinty*, 1940); sexual hypocrisy (*The Lady Eve*, 1941); consumerism (*The Palm Beach Story*, 1942); provincialism (*The Miracle of Morgan's Creek*, 1944); and wartime complacency (*Hail the Conquering Hero*, 1944). In *Sullivan's Travels* (1941), Sturges even held up the mirror to the cinema itself.

Walt Disney (1901–66) had also started as a satirist, with a series of animated shorts called Laugh-O-Grams. On arriving in Hollywood in 1923, with his longtime collaborator Ub Iwerks, he made a number of *Alice in Cartoonland* live-action and animation films before creating the character of Mickey Mouse in 1928. Debuting in the silent *Plane Crazy*, Mickey found his voice in *Steamboat Willie* later that year, by which time Disney had begun a series of experiments to perfect sound and image synchronization. The last of the resultant 'Silly Symphonies' was an immensely popular all-colour version of *The Three Little Pigs* (1933) and, encouraged by its reception, Disney engaged his factory in the production of the first animated feature, *Snow White and the Seven Dwarfs* (1937). *Pinocchio* followed in 1940,

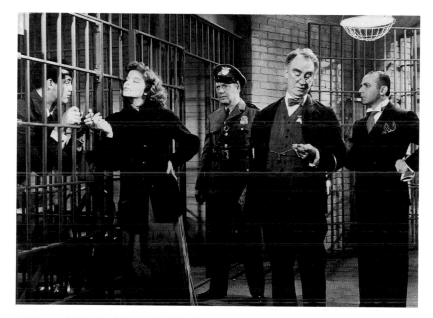

56 Howard Hawks, *Bringing Up Baby* (1938). The paleontologist Cary Grant's ordered world is turned upside down by the heiress Katharine Hepburn, a bone-stealing dog and a leopard named Baby.

along with *Fantasia*, which, at the suggestion of Oskar Fischinger, attempted to fuse the rhythm of classical scores with animated narratives and abstractions. Benefitting from animation's independence of photographic reality, Disney's features exploited to the full the potential of sound and colour, although the rest of the industry remained unconvinced of the value of the latter.

Coloration had been a component of films since their earliest days. Frame-by-frame handtinting had been superseded first by the Pathéchrome (1905) and Handschiegl (1916) stencil systems and then by the processes of tinting or toning the print. By the early 1920s, over 80 per cent of American films contained toned or tinted sequences. Yet the dyes used to stain the celluloid interfered with the sound strip and by the time Eastman Kodak introduced Sonochrome, its tinted raw stock, in 1929, the emphasis had shifted to the search for a viable method of colour cinematography.

The principles of colour photography had been explained first by the Scottish physicist James Maxwell in 1861. He discovered that the

VII

colours of the spectrum were composed of combinations of the colours red, green and blue and that when these were mixed together equally they produced white. Maxwell proceded to demonstrate that colour could be produced either by mixing various measures of the primaries or by removing them from white. The earliest cinematographic colour processes were to employ the 'additive' method.

IV   Devised by G. A. Smith and exploited as early as 1908 by Charles Urban, the Kinemacolor process fused red and green into a range of colours by means of persistence of vision, although its registration of blues was poor and it tended to fringe moving objects. However, Kinemacolor was far in advance of its main competition, Gaumont's Chronochrome (1912) and Cinechrome (1914), a two-colour additive process that used prisms to split the light beam into two pairs of red and green exposures, which were superimposed during projection.

In 1917, frustrated by the complexities and imprecisions of such additive systems, Herbert T. Kalmus, Daniel F. Comstock and W. Burton Wescott began experimenting with a 'subtractive' process, in which separate transparent relief prints were dyed red and green and then joined together to produce a single, colour-registered strip. The first film shot with this Technicolor 'cement positive' process was Loew's Inc.'s *The Toll of the Sea* in 1922. Kalmus improved his colour quality in 1928 by using the relief prints as matrices for the transfer of dyes to a third print through a process called 'imbibition'. Two-colour

VI   Technicolor, as it was known, enhanced sequences in a number of early revue musicals and was used throughout *On with the Show*, but indifferent registration and lurid flesh tones caused its popularity to wane after 1931.

The following year, Kalmus perfected the three-colour Technicolor system, which was to become the industry standard for the next twenty years. Here, a prismatic beam-splitter exposed three

IX   monochrome negatives as they ran through two gates at right angles to each other inside the camera. The right-hand gate contained a single green-sensitive negative, the one on the left a 'bipack' of two negatives, the front one of which absorbed blue light and filtered red through to the one behind. Each colour-separated negative then acted

VIII   as a matrix during imbibition. The first three-colour feature, *Becky Sharp* (Rouben Mamoulian), appeared in 1935 and although a number of films employed colour throughout the period, it was considered an expensive luxury worthy only of prestige films. However, in 1939, Kalmus introduced a faster, fine-grained stock that reduced the need for intensive lighting and in 1941 marketed the Monopack, a multi-

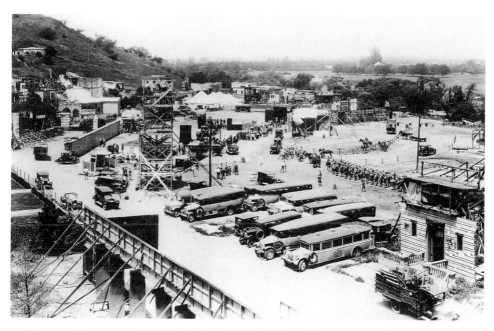

57 Diverse activity on a studio backlot in the early days of the Hollywood Golden Age.

layered film that was capable of producing direct colour positives from exposure in a conventional camera.

The majority of pictures made in Golden Age Hollywood were shot on Eastman panchromatic stock. The classical 'soft' look of the 1930s was achieved mainly through the use of Super X film, diffused lighting and shallow focus, while the sharper, deep-focus style of the 1940s was made possible by the introduction of sensitive Super XX stock and the high-intensity arc lamps that had been developed originally for Technicolor cinematography. Although each studio had its own distinctive personality, many stylistic traits were held in common, not least the insistence on the highest quality production values (that is costumes and *mise-en-scène*). Sets were invariably lit for scene, stars and atmosphere in that order. Editing was largely functional and limited to transitions, 'shot-reverse-shot' and rapid-time passages, achieved by a combination of cuts and superimpositions known as 'Hollywood montage'. The stars, no longer paid the astronomical salaries of the silent era, were now bound by rigid contracts and compelled to accept roles on pain of suspension or loan to another studio. Directors, too, were left little scope for individualism. Excellence,

57
8

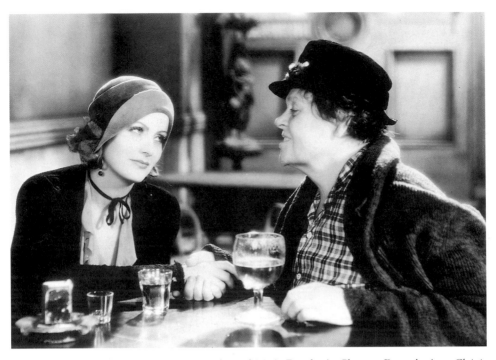

58 'Garbo Talks!': Greta Garbo and Marie Dressler in Clarence Brown's *Anna Christie* (1930), best remembered for Garbo's heavily accented first line: 'Gimme a whisky, with ginger ale on the side, and don't be stingy, baby.'

efficiency and eclecticism were the watchwords of an industry that between 1930 and 1945 was to produce more than 7500 features.

Financed by the Chase National Bank and run by the dictatorial production chief Louis B. Mayer, MGM was Hollywood's biggest and most prolific studio, specializing in literary adaptations, musicals, melodramas and series such as Andy Hardy, Dr Kildare and Tarzan. Characterized by high-key lighting and lavish production values, its films were glamorous, optimistic and escapist family entertainment. Boasting 'More Stars Than There Are In Heaven', the MGM galaxy included Garbo, Jean Harlow, Norma Shearer, Judy Garland, Joan Crawford, Jeanette MacDonald, Nelson Eddy, Spencer Tracy, William Powell, James Stewart and Mickey Rooney, as well as the King and Queen of Hollywood, Clark Gable and Myrna Loy. In addition, gifted producers like Irving Thalberg, David O. Selznick

58

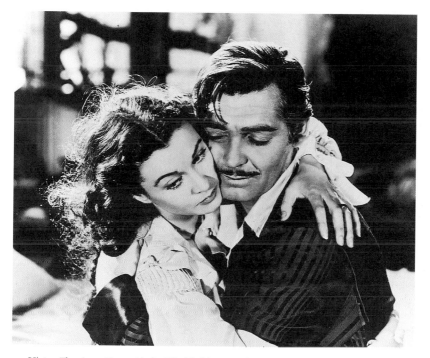

59 Victor Fleming, *Gone with the Wind* (with uncredited sequences by George Cukor and Sam Wood, 1939). While Clark Gable was everyone's choice for Rhett Butler, Vivien Leigh was only cast as Scarlett O'Hara after a 2-year search, during which some 1400 women were auditioned for the part.

(1902–65) and Albert Lewin could draw on the services of designers like Cedric Gibbons (who had created the Oscar statuette in 1927) and cinematographers such as Karl Freund and Harold Rosson.

Also on the payroll were a number of intelligent journeyman directors who found the studio system conducive to their partcular styles: Clarence Brown (*Anna Christie*, 1930, and *Anna Karenina*, 1935); Sam   58 Wood (*A Night at the Opera*, 1935, and *Goodbye Mr Chips*, 1939); W. S. Van Dyke (*The Thin Man*, 1934, and *San Francisco*, 1936); George Cukor (*David Copperfield*, 1935, and *Camille*, 1936); King Vidor (*The Citadel*, 1938, and *Northwest Passage*, 1940) and Victor Fleming (*The Wizard of Oz*, 1939). Fleming also completed *Gone with*   59 *the Wind* (1939) after Cukor and Wood had been dismissed. One of the glories of the studio era, it was distributed by MGM on behalf of Selznick International in return for the loan of Clark Gable.

While MGM proclaimed the virtues of American life, Paramount, thanks to the opulent sets of Hans Dreier and the soft, diffused lighting of Theodore Sparkuhl, alluded to the supposed decadence of Europe. Advocating such themes as wealth, status and desire, the studio bosses Adolph Zukor and Barney Balaban maintained a relaxed regime that allowed directors like Lubitsch, Mamoulian and De Mille to retain their individuality and gave unparalleled licence to its iconoclastic comedians the Marx Brothers, W. C. Fields and Mae West. In spite of having at its disposal such proficient directors as Mitchell Leisen (*Easy Living*, 1937, and *Midnight*, 1939), Henry Hathaway (*Lives of a Bengal Lancer*, 1935), Dorothy Arzner (*Christopher Strong*, 1933), Leo McCarey (*Ruggles of Red Gap*, 1935, and *Going My Way*, 1944) and Preston Sturges, and durable performers like Cary Grant, Fredric March, Gary Cooper, George Raft and Claudette Colbert, Paramount spent much of the 1930s in receivership. Solvency was regained thanks to a number of successes during the Second World War, most notably the 'Road' movies staring Bob Hope, Bing Crosby and Dorothy Lamour.

The most remarkable talent on the Paramount lot, however, was Josef von Sternberg (1894–1969). A disciple of Murnau and von Stroheim, contemptuous of narrative, von Sternberg placed so much emphasis on the texture of his films that, for all their surface beauty, these 'poems in fur and smoke' eventually bore out John Grierson's contention that 'when a director dies, he becomes a photographer'. Allied to a penchant for chiaroscuro lighting, baroque production values and exotic studio sets was an insatiable desire to fill the 'dead space' between the camera and its subject. Von Sternberg went some way to solving the problem with nets, veils and streamers in *The Blue Angel* (1930), but by the time he made *The Devil Is a Woman* in 1935, he had discovered that he could deepen the image by flooding the screen with light passed through a variety of gauzes, filters and diffusers. Produced by Ufa and starring Emil Jannings, *The Blue Angel* was notable for its expressive use of simultaneously recorded sound; moreover, it marked the beginning of a seven-film collaboration with Marlene Dietrich (1901–92). While *Morocco* (1930), *Shanghai Express* (1932) and *The Scarlet Empress* (1934) made Dietrich one of Hollywood's most glamorous stars, their profligacy resulted in von Sternberg's dismissal and he rarely rediscovered his unique cinema of mood and atmosphere.

In stark contrast were the brisk, tightly structured narratives of Warner Brothers. With flat, low-key lighting, austere sets and a ten-

60

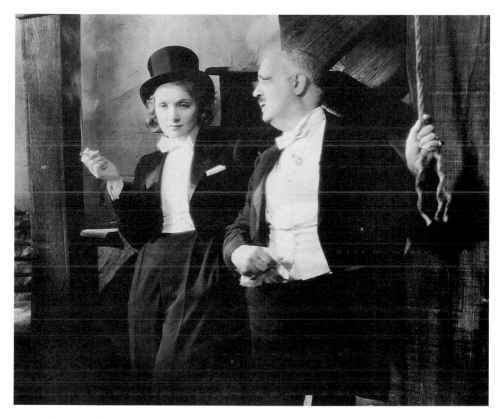

60 Josef von Sternberg, *Morocco* (1930). Marlene Dietrich's androgynous allure made her one of Hollywood's top stars. Eisenstein told the director: 'Of all your great works, *Morocco* is the most beautiful.'

dency to cut single frames from each shot to inject extra momentum, Warners possessed the tough, realistic style that was perfectly suited to gangster, prison and social problem pictures, as well as Berkeley's backstage musicals. Even the literate biopics of William Dieterle – *The Story of Louis Pasteur* (1936), *The Life of Emile Zola* (1937), *Juarez* (1939) and *Dr Ehrlich's Magic Bullet* (1940) – were made to embrace contemporary issues, although he was also capable of flights of fancy such as *A Midsummer Night's Dream* (co-directed by Max Reinhardt, 1936). Despite the affluence bestowed by sound, Warners remained parsimonious, with strict production methods and such low salary scales that its staff were among the prime movers in the strikes that hit Hollywood in 1941.

Warners' indefatigable stars included Bette Davis, Barbara Stanwyck, James Cagney, Paul Muni, Edward G. Robinson and Errol Flynn, while among its leading directors were William Wellman, Mervyn LeRoy, Raoul Walsh, Anatole Litvak and Lloyd Bacon. The versatility of these consummate film-makers – essentially studio men permitted little personal input – is exemplified by the oeuvre of Michael Curtiz (1888–1962). Detested by his casts, Curtiz none the less produced memorable entries in each Hollywood genre: horror (*Doctor X*, 1932); the gangster (*Angels with Dirty Faces*, 1938) and prison picture (*20,000 Years in Sing Sing*, 1932); swashbuckling adventure (*The Adventures of Robin Hood*, 1938); historical romance (*The Private Lives of Elizabeth and Essex*, 1939); the Western (*Dodge City*, 1939); the musical (*Yankee Doodle Dandy*, 1942) and melodrama (*Mildred Pierce*, 1945). He also directed the film considered by the U.S. film historian James Monaco to be 'more an icon than a work of art', *Casablanca* (1942), starring Humphrey Bogart and Ingrid Bergman.

61

The eclectic Howard Hawks (1896–1979), who worked for various studios independently of the system, went one better in directing undisputed classics in each of the main studio subject areas. A natural storyteller, his genius was for screwball comedy – *Twentieth Century* (1934), *Bringing Up Baby* (1938) and *His Girl Friday* (1940) – and action adventure – *The Dawn Patrol* (1930), *The Crowd Roars* (1932) and *Only Angels Have Wings* (1939) – but he also made such key genre films as *Scarface* (1932, gangster), *The Criminal Code* (1930, prison), *The Big Sleep* (1946, *film noir*) and the Westerns *Red River* (1948) and *Rio Bravo* (1959). Professionalism, courage and duty were the typical themes of Hawks's tough narratives, which made up in pace and power what they lacked in pyschological and emotional depth. Proclaiming a good director to be 'someone who doesn't annoy you', Hawks favoured a cinema of implication and understatement, which used *mise-en-scène* and eye-level medium shots to achieve what amounted to a studio look.

Hawks dealt with archetypically American issues in an unsentimental manner that made him one of the heroes of the French New Wave. John Ford (1895–1973), on the other hand, produced films of a sentimentality and conservatism that often recalled Griffith, yet they were to influence film-makers as diverse as Eisenstein, Akira Kurosawa, Ingmar Bergman, Hawks himself, and Orson Welles, who, when asked to name his favourite directors replied, 'The old masters . . . by which I mean John Ford, John Ford and John Ford.'

Ford directed 125 films in a career that spanned fifty-three years.

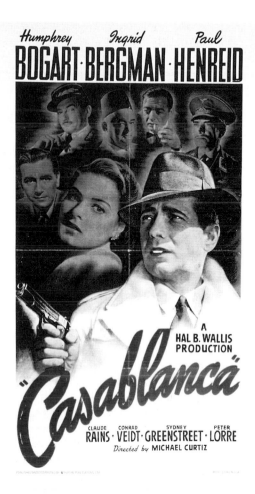

61 A poster for Michael Curtiz's *Casablanca* (1942): Humphrey Bogart and Ingrid Bergman in the roles of Rick and Ilsa Lund that had been rejected by Ronald Reagan and Ann Sheridan.

Starting with low-budget Westerns for his brother Francis at Universal, he was profoundly influenced by Murnau's *Sunrise*, and his first significant sound film, *The Informer*, made for RKO in 1935, had a distinctly Murnauesque feel. In addition to contrapuntal sound, brooding *Kammerspiel* lighting and subjective camera effects, Ford used dissolves, distorting lenses and symbolic mists to convey the psychological torment being suffered by Victor McLaglen's treacherous IRA informant. Winning Ford the first of his six Academy Awards, it was followed by a series of routine studio assignments for the newly formed Twentieth Century-Fox, before he was approached by the independent producer Walter Wanger to make *Stagecoach* (1939), his first Western for thirteen years.

Scripted by Ford's longstanding associate Dudley Nichols, the film employed a *Narrenschiff* ('Ship of Fools') format in order to explore one of the director's key themes, the triumph of community spirit over urban prejudice in the face of frontier crises. Swiftly delineating character through its economical dialogue, the film established many Western conventions and remains a model of structural unity and visual impact. Extreme long shots served to contrast the grandeur of Monument Valley with the intimacy of the interiors, while the chase sequences, with their exceptional stunt work, were intercut with close-ups to retain human interest. The film transformed the career of John Wayne (1907–79), who was to become Ford's favourite man of action in such allegorical Westerns as *Fort Apache* (1948), *She Wore a Yellow Ribbon* (1949), *The Searchers* (1956) and *The Man Who Shot Liberty Valance* (1962), as well as Second World War re-creations like *They Were Expendable* (1945).

The typical Ford man of conscience was to be portrayed by Henry Fonda (1905–82) in *Young Mr Lincoln* (1939), *Drums along the Mohawk* (1939) and *The Grapes of Wrath* (1940), an eloquent yet populist adaptation of John Steinbeck's novel that stylistically resembled Pare Lorentz's Depression documentaries *The Plow that Broke the Plains* (1936) and *The River* (1937). Following *How Green Was My Valley* (1941), Ford joined the Navy and became chief of the Field Photographic Branch during the Second World War. Although it continued to espouse his personal creeds of honour, courage, discipline and duty, his post-war work, ranging from the poetic *My Darling Clementine* (1946) to the whimsical *The Quiet Man* (1952), was noticeably more eclectic and less dictated by form.

Ford was far and away the leading director at Twentieth Century-Fox, which had been formed in 1935 following William Fox's ruinous attempt to retain exclusive American rights to the Tri-Ergon sound system. Controlled by Darryl F. Zanuck (1902–79), the studio was renowned for its production-line manufacture of hard, glassy musicals, sound remakes of silent hits, folksy comedies and exercises in period nostalgia. It also boasted the best special effects department in Hollywood (as in *The Rains Came*, Clarence Brown, 1939), a newsreel service and a chain of theatres and film exchanges. Charles Boyer, Tyrone Power, Don Ameche, Betty Grable, Alice Faye and Loretta Young were among its top stars, but its (and Hollywood's) biggest attraction throughout the 1930s was Shirley Temple (b. 1928).

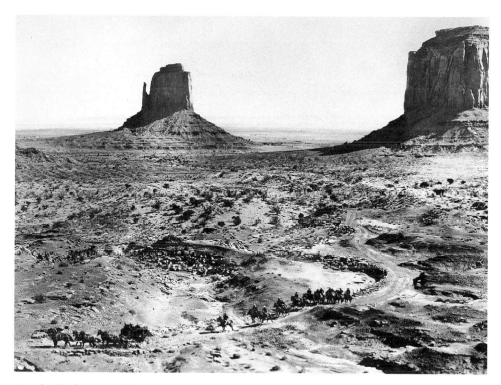

62 John Ford, *Stagecoach* (1939), the first of many Westerns that Ford shot in Monument Valley, Utah. He considered it 'the most complete, beautiful and peaceful place on earth'.

Another musical child star, Deanna Durbin, did much to keep Universal afloat during this period. Remaining under the control of its founder Carl Laemmle until 1936, the studio's financial difficulties stemmed largely from its failure to acquire a major theatre chain. Its early sound successes included John M. Stahl's melodramas *Back Street* (1932), *Imitation of Life* (1934) and *Magnificent Obsession* (1935), but Universal was to become best known for its horror movies, the first of which was Tod Browning's *Dracula* (1931), starring Bela Lugosi. The leading horror specialist on the lot was the Englishman James Whale, whose debt to the German *Schauerfilm* was evident in such pictures as *Frankenstein* (1931), *The Old Dark House* (1932) and *The Bride of Frankenstein* (1935), all of which starred his compatriot Boris Karloff, and in *The Invisible Man* (1935), which featured another stalwart of Hollywood's British community, Claude Rains.

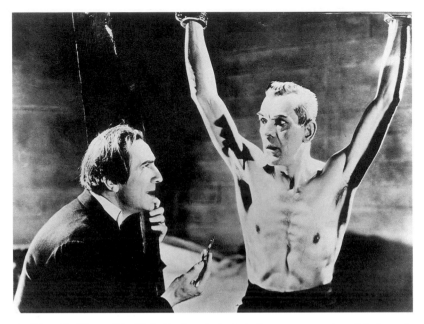

63 Edgar G. Ulmer, *The Black Cat* (1934). In their first screen teaming, Bela Lugosi's Dr Vitus Werdegast exacts his revenge on Boris Karloff's occultist Hjalmar Poelzig for corrupting his wife and daughter.

63   *The Murders in the Rue Morgue* (Robert Florey, 1932), *The Mummy* (Karl Freund, 1932) and *The Black Cat* (Edgar G. Ulmer, 1934) were among Universal's other more interesting contributions to the genre. By the 1940s, however, it was tending (unwittingly at first, but later consciously) towards self-parody, leaving the studio ever more dependent on the production of such low-budget second-features as the Basil Rathbone and Nigel Bruce 'Sherlock Holmes' series and the comedies of Abbott and Costello. Universal was also home to Lewis Milestone at the time he made *All Quiet on the Western Front*. Elsewhere, he made a number of stylish films, such as *The Front Page* (1931) and *The General Died at Dawn* (1936), which managed to combine the kind of characters usually associated with Howard Hawks with the themes beloved of Frank Capra.

Capra was almost single-handedly responsible for keeping Columbia off 'poverty row' until the founder Harry Cohn

(1891–1958) elevated Rita Hayworth to stardom in the early 1940s. 64
Rising above the round of series and programme Westerns, Capra exploited Cohn's genius for single-picture deals to entice Gary Cooper (1901–61) and James Stewart (b. 1908) to portray his typically idealistic heroes, whose essential decency and belief in the American way enabled them to triumph over adversity and corruption. While such New Deal films as *Mr Deeds Goes to Town* (1936) and *Mr Smith* 65 *Goes to Washington* (1939) can be accused of populism and sentimentality, they were also satirical, sincere and intelligent, and had a good-humoured optimism that was noticeably muted in the later additions to the 'Capra-corn' canon *Meet John Doe* (1941) and *It's a Wonderful Life* (1946). Regularly collaborating with the scriptwriter Robert Riskin, Capra also excelled at screwball comedies, such as *Platinum Blonde* (1931), *It Happened One Night* (1934) and *You Can't Take It With You* (1938). His fascination with dialogue and performance engendered a relatively unobtrusive style whose adherents included John Ford, Yasujiro Ozu and Satyajit Ray.

64 Charles Vidor, *Gilda* (1946). Columbia's leading star of the Golden Age, Rita Hayworth epitomized the glamorous 'Love Goddess' which Hollywood publicists had exploited since the 1920s.

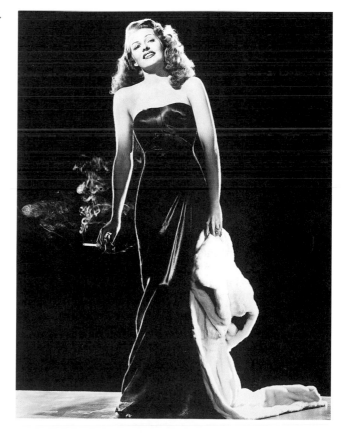

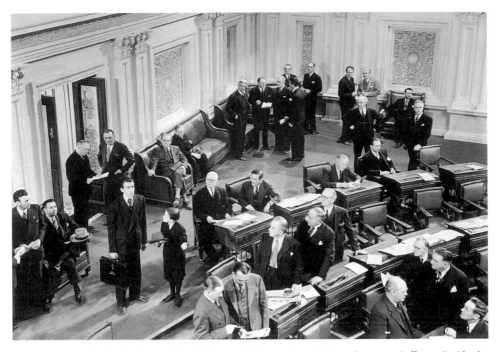

65 Frank Capra, *Mr Smith Goes to Washington* (1939). James Stewart as Jefferson Smith, the Boy Ranger leader who exposes graft at the centre of government. Shot in a meticulous reconstruction of the Senate chamber, the film made exceptional use of directional sound and metaphorical camera angles.

A descendant of the Mutual Film Corporation, Hollywood's newest and least conventional studio, RKO Radio Pictures, was in receivership from 1933 to 1939, in spite· of the success of Astaire and Rogers, and of *King Kong* (Merian C. Cooper and Ernest B. Schoedsack, 1933), with its remarkable stop-motion photography and special effects by Willis O'Brien. The studio possessed stars of the calibre of Katharine Hepburn and Irene Dunne, directors like George Stevens, a designer as distinguished as Van Nest Polglase and producers as imaginative as Pandro S. Berman and Val Lewton. Yet besides literary adaptations, including *Little Women* (George Cukor, 1933), *Of Human Bondage* (John Cromwell, 1934), *Becky Sharp* (1935) and *The Hunchback of Notre Dame* (William Dieterle, 1938), RKO's most lucrative properties were those they distributed on behalf of Walt Disney and the independents Selznick and Goldwyn.

Goldwyn's fruitful association with William Wyler (1902–81), an accomplished adaptor of literary and theatrical material, yielded *These*

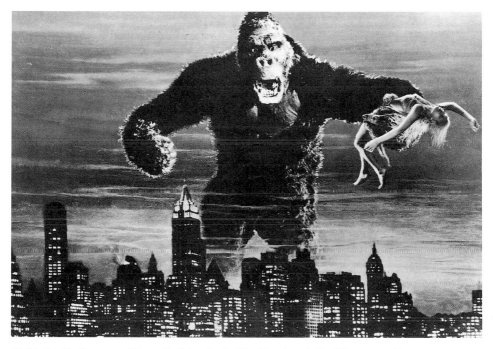

66 Merian C. Cooper and Ernest B. Schoedsack, *King Kong* (1933). Fay Wray grasped by the mighty ape (in fact an 18-inch model made of metal, rubber, cotton and rabbit fur). RKO re-released the film in 1938, less scenes of Kong crushing people and inquisitively removing Wray's clothing, to comply with the Production Code.

Three and *Dodsworth* (both 1936), *Dead End* (1937), *Wuthering Heights* (1939) and *The Little Foxes* (1941). Wyler, in turn, benefitted from his collaboration with the cinematographer Gregg Toland (1904–48), whose experiments with deep-focus photography were to reach their apogee in Orson Welles's audacious film debut, *Citizen Kane* (1941). 67

Welles (1915–85) was signed up by RKO in 1939 on the strength of such theatrical successes as a voodoo version of *Macbeth* and the nationwide panic caused by his radio adaptation of H. G. Wells's *War of the Worlds* on Halloween 1938. Assured complete artistic freedom even before he had so much as acted in a film, Welles proposed to shoot Conrad's *Heart of Darkness* with a subjective camera. However, anticipating exorbitance after just a few 'animatic' sequences, the studio intervened. Undeterred, Welles began to prepare a *film à clef* about the press baron William Randolph Hearst that he proposed to call *American*. In addition to assembling a technical team of Toland, the screenwriter Herman J. Mankiewicz, the composer Bernard

Herrman, the designer Perry Ferguson and the editors Robert Wise and Mark Robson, he also gathered a cast that contained many of his own Mercury Theatre company. Welles claimed that his only pre-production preparation was to watch *Stagecoach* forty times. But the film that was eventually to be called *Citizen Kane* obviously embraced a much wider range of genres, styles and techniques, amongst which the most readily discernible were those of Murnau, the *Kammerspielfilm* and the deep-focus poetic realism of Jean Renoir.

62
67

Beginning with Kane's death and a booming parody of a 'March of Time' newsreel, the film is (to use Jesse Lasky's term) a 'narratage', a series of interviews and flashbacks divided by lap dissolves which attempt to uncover the significance of the magnate's last word, 'Rosebud'. However, as Welles later said, 'the point of the picture is not so much the solution of the problem as its presentation' and much of *Kane*'s importance derives from its form.

Using high-intensity carbon arc lamps to achieve sharp-edged chiaroscuro lighting, Eastman Kodak's new ultrasensitive Super XX stock, and a portable BNC camera fitted with plastic-coated wide-angle lenses, Welles and Toland were able to bring an unprecedented diegetic and metaphorical depth to their compositions. These were enhanced by the inclusion of set ceilings and a careful deployment of props and performers. Electing to shoot in long takes (or sequence shots) to eliminate the need for excessive narrative editing, they were able to obtain considerable intra-frame movement thanks to dramatic crane shots and a technique of Toland's invention called 'pan focus-ing'. Welles also established screen space by his exceptional use of sound. Drawing on his radio experience, he fashioned the 'lightning mix' of 'swish pans' and overlapping sounds, which devolved responsibility for the logic of the images to the soundtrack.

Re-using old RKO sets throughout and footage from *Son of Kong* at the start of the picnic scene, the film cost just $839,727 to make. Yet, owing to the pressure exerted by a furious Hearst, it was a com-mercial flop and earned Welles a reputation not as America's first true Expressionist, but as a political and financial risk. Following its art-house revival during the 1950s, *Kane* became a key text in the *auteur* debate and has ever since consistently topped 'all-time greatest' polls of critics and film-makers alike.

Welles's second RKO film, *The Magnificent Ambersons* (1942), extended many of *Kane*'s techniques, but while he was on location in Mexico it became the subject of keen front office attention. Forty-four minutes were cut from the original and a happy ending, shot by

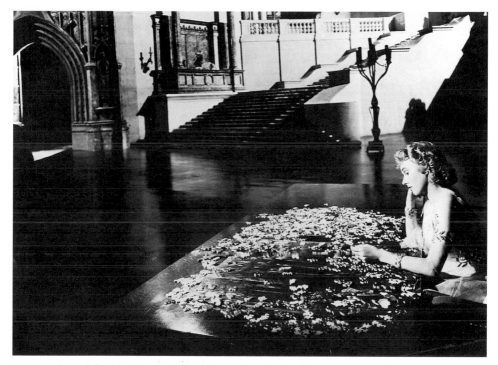

67 Metaphorical depth in Orson Welles's *Citizen Kane* (1941). Kane's second wife, Susan Alexander (Dorothy Comingore), struggles with a jigsaw puzzle (itself a metaphor for the mystery of identity at the core of the film) in the cavernous grandeur of Xanadu, emphasizing her isolation and incongruous presence in both Kane's home and his life.

the production manager Freddie Francis, was appended. As with von Stroheim's *Greed*, the strength of the *mise-en-scène* allowed the director's vision to transcend the emasculation, but Welles was on thin ice and with the failure of *Journey into Fear* in 1943 his contract was terminated. Forced to accept roles in other directors' films to finance his personal projects, Welles continued to explore his characteristic themes – lovelessness, betrayal and the corrupting influence of power and ambition – in what François Truffaut considered to be such 'flawed classics' as *The Lady from Shanghai* (1948), *Macbeth* (1948), *Othello* (1952), *A Touch of Evil* (1958) and *The Chimes at Midnight* (1966). A victim of the studio system, Welles – ironically – anticipated in his first two films the widescreen and stereophonic developments that the system itself was to employ in an attempt to bolster its flagging post-war fortunes.

Colour has been employed to enhance the visual impact of moving images since the earliest lantern slides. Paint was applied by hand to Edison's Kinetoscope reels as early as 1894 and two of the films shown at the premiere of the Vitagraph in 1896 contained colour sequences. Tinting and toning processes were widely used during the silent era: Méliès, for example, used tints to heighten fantasy; Griffith equated tint with emotional tone in The Birth of a Nation (1915); and Eisenstein tinted the red flag raised on board The Battleship Potemkin (1925).

The principles of colour photography may have been established as early as 1855, but it was not until 1906 that G. A. Smith patented the first feasible cinematographic process, Kinemacolor. Several two-colour additive rivals appeared over the next quarter-century, among them Biocolour (1908), Prizma Color (1917), Cinecolor (1925), British Raycol (1929), Vovolor (1932) and Omnicolor (1933). The first three-colour additive process, Chronochrome, was demonstrated by Léon Gaumont in 1912. Once more a variety of alternatives emerged, including Horst (1926), Franchita (1931, known as Opticolor in the USA), Hérault Trichrome (1926) and Dufaycolor (1934).

Subtractive colour had first been proposed by Louis Ducos du Hauron in 1868. As with additive colour, the first practical applications had been two-colour systems, the earliest of which was Arturo Hernandez-Mejia's Cinecolorgraph (1912). A wealth of derivatives were developed in the U.S. – Kodachrome (1916), Kesdacolor (1918), Multicolor (1928), Vitacolor (1930), Magnacolor (1931), Coloratura (1931) and Trucolor (1946) – and in Europe: UK – Polychromide (1918) and Chemicolor (1931); Holland – Sirius Color (1929); Germany – Ufacolor (1930); and France – Harmonicolor (1936). The most successful two-colour subtractive process, however, was Technicolor, which was first employed for Toll of the Sea in 1922. The prototype three-colour subtractive process was patented as Zoechrome by T. A. Mills in 1929, shortly to be followed by two French systems, Splendicolor (1929) and Chimicolor (1931). However, Technicolor again came to dominate the market with the introduction of a three-strip camera, which was used to shoot Disney's animated Flowers and Trees in 1932 and the live-action short La Cucaracha two years later. The introduction of multilayered stocks like Gasparcolor (1933, Hungary) and Agfacolor (1936, Germany) prompted Technicolor to develop its own monopack in 1940, although it was

gradually replaced during the 1950s by Eastmancolor, which formed the basis of such processes as Warnercolor, Metrocolor, Pathecolor and De Luxe. Similarly, Agfacolor was the inspiration for Sovcolor (1942, USSR), Gevacolor (1947, Belgium), Ferraniacolor (1952, Italy) and Ansco Color (1953, USA). The Japanese Fujicolor negative–positive process appeared in 1955.

Notwithstanding the development of colour cinematography, the majority of features were shot in monochrome until the 1950s, although serious or realistic topics continued to be filmed in black-and-white well into the next decade. Initially, owing to its expense, colour was employed primarily for its novelty or decorative value, with producers urging the extravagant use of bold hues in costumes and scenery. However, directors soon began to exploit the aesthetic possibilities of colour in their compositions, placing objects in warm shades like red, yellow and orange against backgrounds of cooler blues, greens and purples to highlight them or to achieve the illusion of depth.

Film-makers like Ozu, Visconti, Minnelli, Powell and Pressburger, Lean and Rohmer stand among the cinema's leading colour stylists, but while Nicholas Ray, Sirk, Fassbinder and Almodóvar have made symbolic use of colour, formal experimentation in the mainstream has been curiously rare. Among the most notable examples are Ivan the Terrible (Eisenstein, 1942), Moulin Rouge (Huston, 1952), Gate of Hell (Kinugasa, 1953), South Pacific (Joshua Logan, 1958), Pierrot-le-fou (Godard, 1965) and Daisies (Chytilová, 1966). Perhaps the most celebrated instance is Antonioni's insistence in The Red Desert (1964) that natural and inanimate objects were painted to reflect the psychological states of his characters.

Although monochrome is occasionally used for flashbacks or the depiction of imaginary or spiritual worlds (notably Wenders's Wings of Desire, 1987, which reversed the convention established in The Wizard of Oz, 1939), the majority of feature films are now shot in colour. Indeed, an increasing number of black-and-white pictures are being colorized for video release. However, as films like Eraserhead (Lynch, 1976), Manhattan (Allen, 1979), Raging Bull (Scorsese, 1980), Down by Law (Jarmusch, 1986), Schindler's List (Spielberg, 1993) and Clerks (Kevin Smith, 1994) demonstrate, it is still possible to achieve commercial and critical success with monochrome.

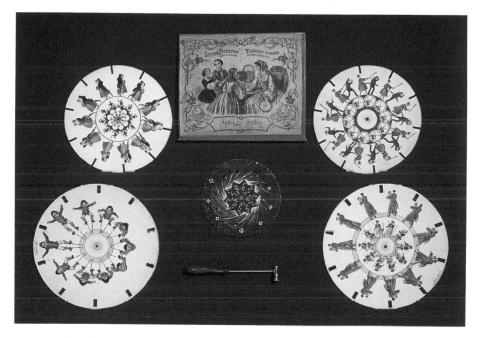

I A Phenakistoscope or Fantascope disc (*c.* 1833), manufactured by Ackerman & Co.

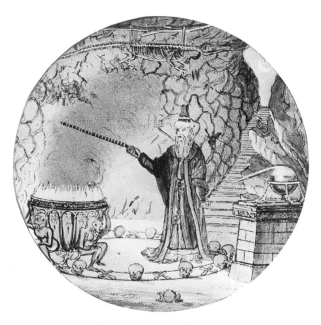

II A magic lantern slide (*c.* 1870).

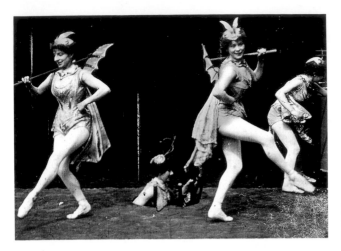

III Georges Demenÿ, *La Biche au bois* (1896). A hand-tinted film shot at the Châtelet Theatre, Paris.

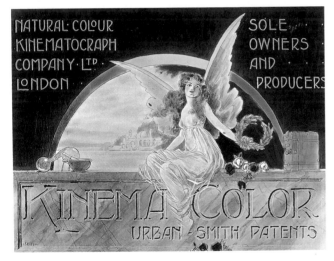

IV The Kinemacolor logo (*c.* 1910–11).

V A test shot in two-colour Kodacolor (*c.* 1922).

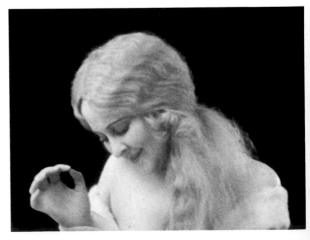

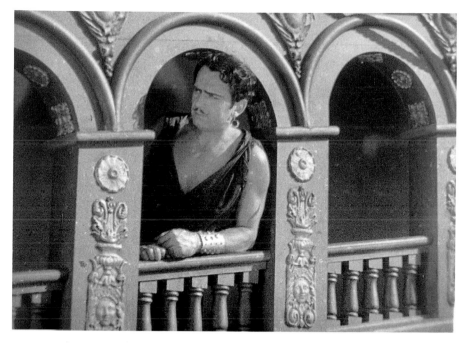

VI   Albert Parker, *The Black Pirate* (1926). Two-colour Technicolor.

VII   *The Last Days of Pompeii* (1926), coloured by the Pathécolor stencil process.

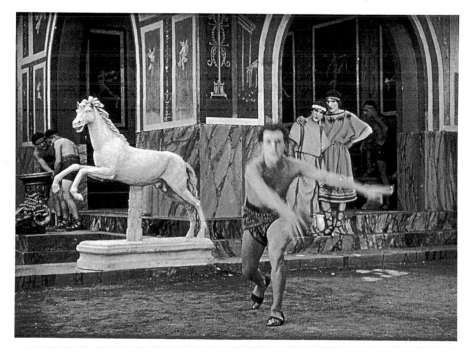

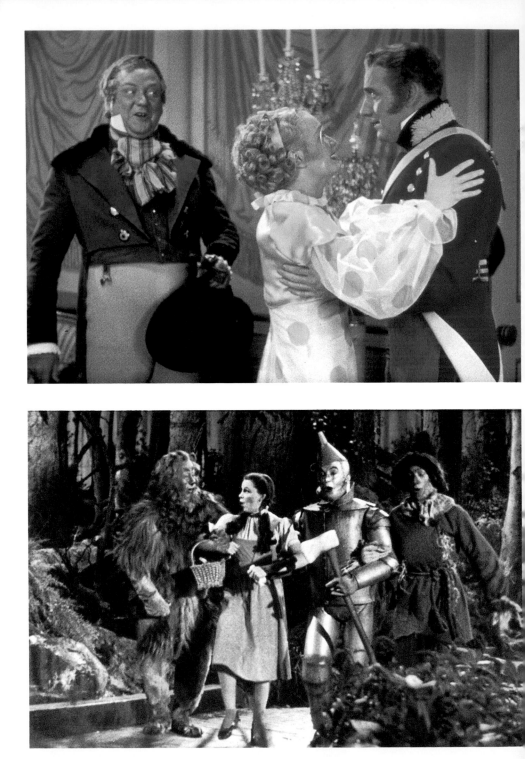

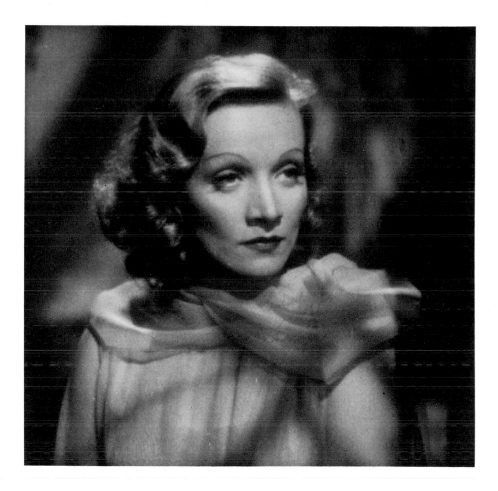

VIII   Rouben Mamoulian, *Becky Sharp* (1935), the first feature shot in three-colour Technicolor.

IX   Victor Fleming's *The Wizard of Oz* (1939) made rare use of an expensive, light-intensive Technicolor process, in which 3 strips of monochrome film were exposed through a prism to segregate the primary colours.

X   Shot in Technicolor, Richard Boleslawski's *The Garden of Allah* (1936), with Marlene Dietrich, won a special Oscar for its achievement in colour cinematography.

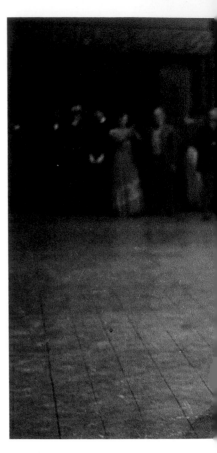

XI Josef von Baky, *The Adventures of Baron Münchhausen* (1943). A lavish Agfacolour spectacle made to celebrate the silver jubilee of Ufa.

XII John Huston, *Moulin Rouge* (1952), a bold experiment in Technicolor and tinting.

XIII Laurel and Hardy in *Way Out West* (James Horne, 1937), colorized for video release in 1984.

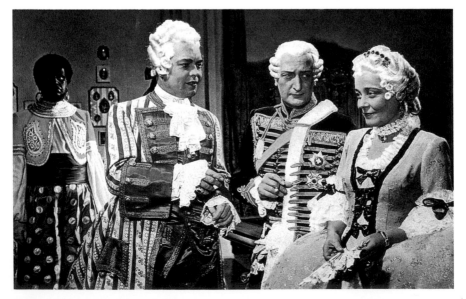

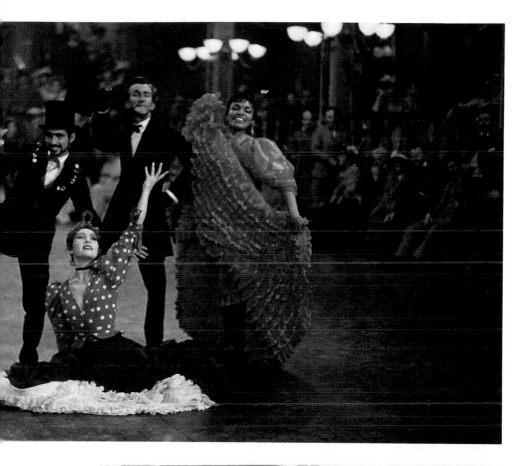

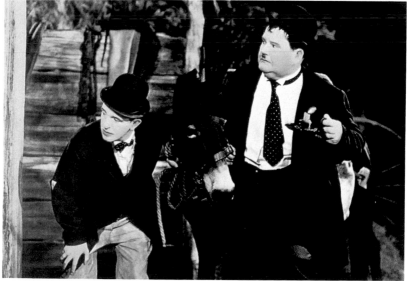

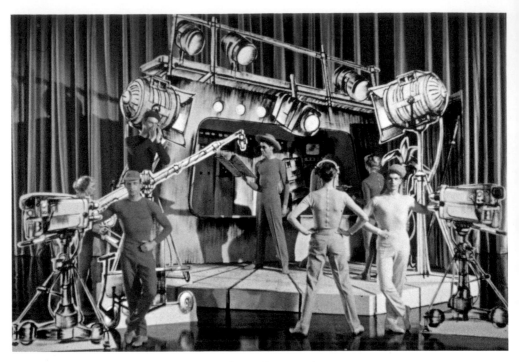

XIV   Guy Hamilton, *Charley Moon* (1956), shot in Eastmancolor.

XV   Luchino Visconti, *The Damned* (1969), shot in Eastmancolor.

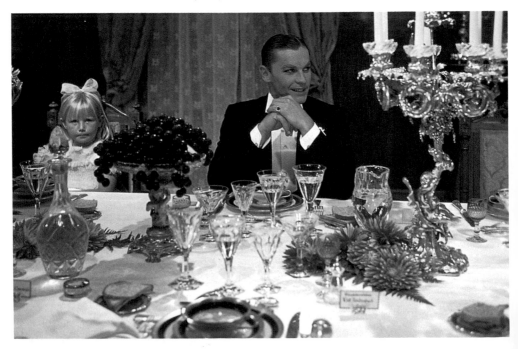

CHAPTER FIVE

The Emergence of National Cinemas 1930–45

Long subjected to Hollywood saturation by the universal appeal of the silents, non-English-speaking cinemas were given the opportunity to erect language barriers by the coming of spoken dialogue. Yet the national film industry that was initially most rejuvenated by the advent of sound was Britain's. By the mid-1930s, despite remaining the biggest foreign market for American pictures, Britain ranked among the world's three largest film producers, although it enjoyed few international successes and much of its quota-driven, shoestring output was tailored for domestic consumption.

However, Michael Balcon, now director of production at Gaumont-British, astutely recognized the merit of pandering to popular tastes. Films featuring such musical entertainers as Gracie Fields and Jessie Matthews and music-hall comics like George Formby and Will Hay generated the revenue for him to indulge in higher profile ventures like George Arliss biopics. Widely regarded as the father of the British film industry, Balcon spurned the available exiled European directors in favour of nurturing such homegrown talent as Carol Reed (1906–76) and Michael Powell (1905–90). However, his most important protégé, by some way, was Alfred Hitchcock.

Formerly a designer and scriptwriter, Hitchcock had joined Balcon's Gainsborough Pictures in 1924 and worked on a number of Ufa co-productions before making his directorial debut in Munich with *The Pleasure Garden* (1925). Heavily influenced by Expressionism and the *Kammerspielfilm*, Hitchcock's best-known silent feature, *The Lodger* (1927), recalled Murnau's use of camera and *mise-en-scène*. However, by the time he made *Blackmail*, the first British talkie, for John Maxwell's British International Pictures in 1929, Hitchcock was already heightening suspense by means of montage. Originally a silent, *Blackmail* explored a key Hitchcockian theme of fear amidst the commonplace and was the first of his films to employ a famous landmark for its finale. Partially reshot and dubbed, it remains notable for its expressive use of naturalistic and contrapuntal sound and the camera's relentless pursuit of significant detail. Although *Murder* (1930), scripted

68

by his wife Alma Reville, included the screen's first improvised speeches and an audacious 360° pan during a dialogue sequence, it was not until he was reunited with Balcon at Gaumont that Hitchcock began to produce some of his finest work.

Fatalist, moralist and obsessive stylist, Hitchcock created a world unmistakably his own through an apparently effortless blend of comedy, romance and suspense that belied a highly complex technique. Constructing meticulous storyboards of each shot and making inspired use of naturalistic sound, musical motifs and audiovisual juxtapositions, he generated tension through an understated manipulation of décor, props and performers, which was intensified by means of unerring camera placement and precise editing.

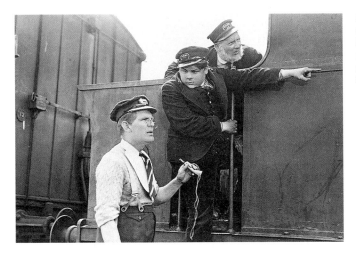

68 Will Hay, Graham Moffat and Moore Marriott in *Oh, Mr Porter* (Marcel Varnel, 1937), on the track of smugglers posing as ghosts at their sleepy Irish station.

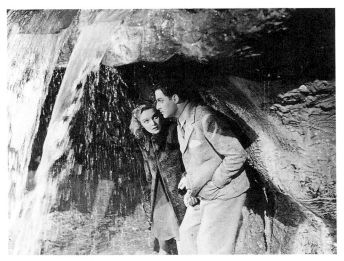

69 Alfred Hitchcock, *The 39 Steps* (1935). Robert Donat on the run from the police and on the track of a spy-ring while handcuffed to Madeleine Carroll.

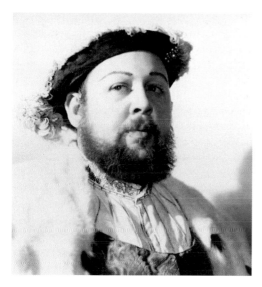

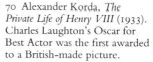

70 Alexander Korda, *The Private Life of Henry VIII* (1933). Charles Laughton's Oscar for Best Actor was the first awarded to a British-made picture.

The sinister, Expressionist *The Man Who Knew Too Much* (1934) was followed in 1935 by an adaptation of John Buchan's spy novel *The 39 Steps*. Brisk, amusing and packed with classic Hitchcock moments, this superbly structured film (turning on another of the director's favoured themes, that of false accusation) could almost be called a 'screwball mystery'. In stark contrast were his two 1936 films, the morally ambiguous *Secret Agent*, adapted from Somerset Maugham's 'Ashenden' stories, and *Sabotage*, a brutal updating of Conrad's novel *The Secret Agent*. Hitchcock returned to a breezier style for his last two British thrillers, *Young and Innocent* (1937), which contained a virtuoso 145-foot track to focus on a guilty man's twitching eye, and the assured, inventive *The Lady Vanishes* (1938), which earned him a contract with Selznick.

Exploiting Hollywood's superior technical facilities, Hitchcock largely abandoned montage in favour of extended takes and camera fluency for his first American film, *Rebecca*, which won the Academy Award for Best Picture of 1940. A brooding psychological drama based on Daphne du Maurier's bestseller, the film also introduced a new depth of characterization into Hitchcock's films. Two further subtle, suspenseful personality studies, *Suspicion* (1941) and *Shadow of a Doubt* (1943), followed each side of the minor espionage entertainments *Foreign Correspondent* (1939) and *Saboteur* (1942). The nature of

69

motivational forces was to become a recurrent theme during the second half of Hitchcock's career, in which he also became increasingly preoccupied with experimental shooting techniques and the manipulation of screen space and audience response.

Unlike Balcon, Britain's other leading commercial producer, Alexander Korda (1893–1956), consciously aimed to capture a corner of the international market. An outspoken critic and wunderkind director in his native Hungary, Korda had made films in Vienna, Berlin, Paris and Hollywood before coming to Britain in 1931. He founded London Films the following year and, buoyed by the worldwide success of *The Private Life of Henry VIII* (1933) – a Lubitsch-like pageant, starring Charles Laughton – he embarked on an ambitious expansion programme. A co-production deal was signed with United Artists, up-to-date new studios were constructed at Denham, and film-makers like René Clair, Jacques Feyder, Robert Flaherty, Paul Czinner and Josef von Sternberg were invited to undertake prestigious projects. Korda sought to reproduce his winning formula with a series of historical spectacles, including *Catherine the Great*, *The Scarlet Pimpernel* (both 1934) and *Rembrandt* (1936); imperial adventures such as *Sanders of the River* (1935), *Elephant Boy* (1937) and *The Four Feathers* (1939); and H. G. Wells adaptations like *Things to Come* and *The Man Who Could Work Miracles* (both 1936). However, audiences failed to respond. By 1938 Korda was on the verge of bankruptcy and not even an extension of the quota was able to prevent a dramatic drop in production throughout the rest of the industry. Only the British documentary movement continued to prosper.

Even before John Grierson (1898–1972) made *Drifters* for the Empire Marketing Board (EMB) in 1929, Britain was renowned for the quality of its documentaries. However, this dignified study of the North Sea fishing industry, with its 'creative treatment of reality', was to transform the nature of documentary cinema. Grierson was placed in charge of the EMB's new film unit, which was to produce more than a hundred films over the next three years. In 1932, the unit was transferred to the General Post Office, where Grierson gathered around him a group of young left-wing film-makers, who were permitted to embrace journalistic, dramatic or poetic styles, providing they presented institutions and contemporary affairs 'in a fashion which strikes the imagination and makes observation a little richer'.

Although Paul Rotha (*The Face of Britain*), and Edgar Anstey and Arthur Elton (*Housing Problems*, both 1935) attempted to establish a cinema of social purpose, commercial sponsorship often curtailed

70

71

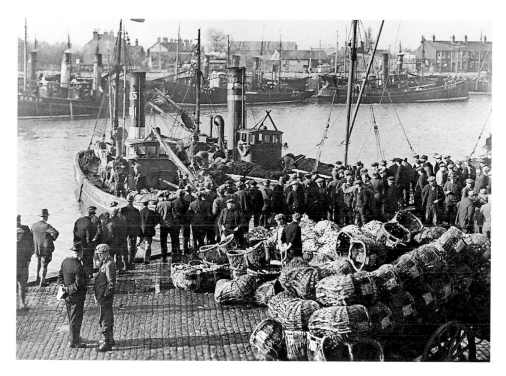

71 John Grierson, *Drifters* (1929). Written, directed, edited and partly photographed by Grierson himself, this 40-minute silent study of the North Sea fishing fleet recalled the insight of Flaherty and the energy of Eisenstein.

opportunities for in-depth analysis. However, form was less subject to approval than content and British documentaries during the 1930s were frequently experimental to the point of being avant-garde. Basil Wright adopted a symphonic structure for *Song of Ceylon* (1934), a combination of commentary, direct sound and lyrical montage, while for *Night Mail* (co-directed by Harry Watt, 1936), he used verses by W. H. Auden and a score by Benjamin Britten to accentuate the rhythms of the London–Glasgow Postal Special. Britten also collaborated with the Brazilian-born Alberto Cavalcanti on *Coal Face* (1936), a 'film oratorio' that combined simple images with industrial sound effects and choral music. Len Lye and Norman McLaren, on the other hand, usually preferred jazz soundtracks for their abstract animations, which were achieved by applying paint directly onto the celluloid.

Around the time Grierson left to superintend the foundation of the National Film Board of Canada in 1939, the influence of the

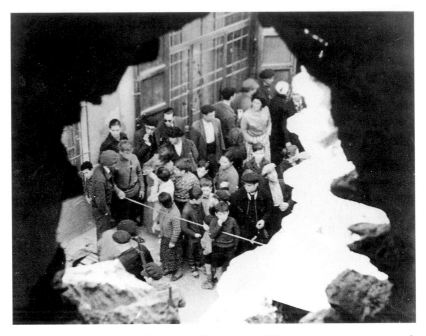

72 Joris Ivens (1898–1989), *The Spanish Earth* (1937). With a commentary written and spoken by Ernest Hemingway, this scathing indictment of Fascist war atrocities stands amongst Ivens's finest work. Combining montage, lyrical Impressionism and dramatic reconstruction, Ivens's documentaries were noted for their provocative juxtaposition of sound and image.

72 documentary movement became increasingly discernible in the consciously realistic settings of a number of British features, including *The Edge of the World* (Michael Powell, 1937), *They Drive By Night* (Arthur Woods, 1938) and *The Stars Look Down* (Carol Reed, 1939). However, the magnitude of Grierson's legacy would only become fully apparent during the Second World War.

While Britain was experiencing its brief renaissance, France was entering a golden age. Initially, it had seemed as though sound could only bring about the ruination of the French cinema. The visual experimentation of the avant-garde Impressionists ceased almost immediately, while the system of small-company production that had accommodated them collapsed as Western Electric and Tobis-Klangfilm made extortionate demands for rights to their sound processes. Eager to exploit the French market, Paramount set up a colossal studio at Joinville for the production of multilingual versions, while Tobis established a similar, but smaller, concern at Epinay-sur-Seine. It was here, however, that René Clair shot the three delightfully inventive musical comedies that were not only to revive the French film but also to alert the entire industry to the expressive potential of sound.

In *Sous les toits de Paris* (1930), advertised as 'the most beautiful film ever made', Clair made merely provisional use of sound in boldly integrating asynchronous effects with typically sophisticated images. However, for *Le Million* (1931) he 'conceived that it would be possible to recapture the unreality of light comedy by replacing words with music and songs'. Using operetta, recitative, ballet and slapstick to circumvent dialogue, Clair heightened the sense of ethereal illusion by the placement of gauze between the performers and the sets, and the almost Surrealist addition of contrapuntal sounds. Elsewhere in his book *Cinema Yesterday and Today* (1970), Clair wrote that 'to laugh is to dream, to laugh is to be free, to laugh is to take revenge, to laugh is to possess everything we lack in reality', and this sentiment clearly informs *A Nous la liberté* (1932), a biting satire on industrialization and the impossibility of freedom within society. In spite of its thematic gravity and Lazare Meerson's chillingly dehumanizing sets, Clair retained the musical-comedy format, but the film proved a commercial failure, as did *The Fourteenth of July* (1933) and *The Last Millionaire* (1934). Increasingly persecuted by the right-wing press, Clair left France to make *The Ghost Goes West* for Korda in 1935. On the outbreak of war he migrated to Hollywood, where he made such comic fantasies as *I Married a Witch* (1942) and *It Happened Tomorrow* (1944).

Every bit as enterprising as Clair was Jean Vigo (1905–34), hailed by the American critic James Agee as 'one of the few real originals who have ever worked on film'. The combination of comedy, lyricism and Surrealism that had characterized Vigo's documentaries *A Propos de Nice* and *Taris* (1931) was again to the fore in *Zéro de conduite* (1933, banned until 1944), the story of a revolt by provincial schoolboys against their tyrannical masters that is suffused with the militancy of Vigo's anarchist father and memories of his own unhappy childhood. An iconoclast in form as in content, Vigo selected unusual angles and perspectives to subvert traditional screen dimensions and used the sensations of his characters to establish metaphorical space. However, the disjointed continuity was less calculated. Vigo had exceeded the agreed running time and was forced to adopt a poetic

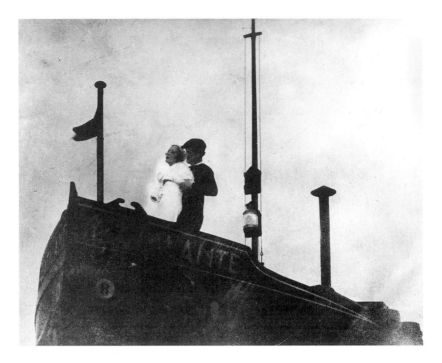

unity that drew on the inner logic of the action. Full of references to Chaplin, Gance and Emile Cohl, the film also incorporated an atmospheric score by Maurice Jaubert, which he achieved by alternating the direction of the soundtrack during recording.

73   Largely shot on location, Vigo's next film, *L'Atalante* (1934), a romance set on a river barge, was to be his last. Blending exaggerated characterization with moments of surreal fantasy, it harked back to the Impressionism of the 1920s, but its lyricism, understated imagery and realistic evocation of daily life anticipated the Poetic Realism which was to infuse French cinema for the remainder of the decade.

The French critic Georges Sadoul identified in this style 'the influence of literary naturalism and Zola, certain traditions of Zecca, Feuillade and Delluc, certain lessons also from René Clair and Jean Vigo'. Poetic Realism divided into two distinct periods – the first (1934–37) exuding national optimism at the rise of the Popular Front, the second (1938–40) reflecting despair at that government's collapse and the unremitting onset of Fascism. However, it was united by the regular contributions of the writers Charles Spaak and Jacques Prévert, designers like Lazare Meerson and Alexandre Trauner, and such per-

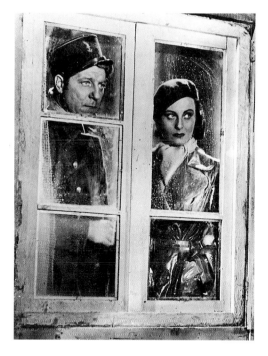

73 Jean Vigo, *L'Atalante* (1934). Jean Dasté and Dita Parlo as the newly-weds on board the eponymous river barge that soon becomes a prison from which she must escape.

74 Jean Gabin and Michèle Morgan in Marcel Carné's *Quai des brumes* (1938). Influenced by von Sternberg and the studio realism of the *Kammerspielfilm*, this tale of a trapped army deserter was perhaps the most infamous example of poetic fatalism.

formers as Jean Gabin (whose doomed anti-heroes came to personify receding French esteem), Michel Simon, Raimu, Pierre Fresnay, Louis Jouvet, Harry Baur, Françoise Rosay, Arletty, Michèle Morgan and Dita Parlo.

Among the leading Poetic Realist directors was Jacques Feyder, who worked with Spaak and Meerson on *Le Grand Jeu* (1934), *Pension Mimosas* (1935) and, most notably, *La Kermesse héroïque* (1935), a period satire on conquest and collaboration, widely referred to as a 'living museum' for the way in which it brought to life the paintings of Brueghel, Memlinc, Hals and Vermeer. Spaak also scripted *La Bandera* (1935) and *La Belle équipe* (1936) for Julien Duvivier (1896–1967), who made eight other Popular Front pictures, although his best-remembered film is *Pépé-le-Moko* (1937), written by Henri Jeanson in homage to Hawks's *Scarface*. Telling how the gangster Jean Gabin is lured by love from the Casbah to his death, this deeply pessimistic film, with its muted violence, is a classic of Poetic Realism's fatalist tendency.

However, its finest practitioner was Marcel Carné (b. 1909). After *Jenny* (1936) and the atypically bizarre comedy *Drôle de drame* (1937), Carné made two of the most despondent films of the period. Produced in association with Prévert and influenced by the work of Murnau, 74

Lang, von Sternberg and Lupu Pick, *Quai des brumes* (1938) and *Le Jour se lève* (1939) were slow, brooding, introspective studies of decent people inexorably drawn to destruction by fate. Simultaneously metaphysical and realistic, *Le Jour se lève* was undeniably demoralizing, yet it was *Quai des brumes*, an excursion in gloomy studio realism, that was to be held responsible by some in the Vichy government for France's capitulation to the Nazis, although Carné was quick to counter that the storm was not the fault of the barometer.

In spite of his penchant for 'canned theatre', Marcel Pagnol's *populisme* placed him on the fringe of Poetic Realism. A firm believer that film was a performer's medium, Pagnol (1895–1974) concentrated on dialogue and characterization, but many of his vigorous, involving films benefitted from location shooting, notably the Provençal tales *Merlusse* (1935), *Regain* (1937) and *La Femme du boulanger* (1938) and

the Marseilles trilogy of *Marius* (1931), *Fanny* (1932) and *César* (1936). Sacha Guitry (1885–1957), on the other hand, saw film as a means of recording his performances in his own plays. Yet even he was capable of moments of cinematic invention, such as *The Story of a Cheat* (1936), which was played entirely in dumbshow with an accompanying non-diegetic commentary.

Of all the directors to work in the Poetic Realist style, the most influential was undoubtedly Jean Renoir. Following an erratic silent career, Renoir, who always maintained 'I am not a director – I am a storyteller', matured into a genuine artist of the cinema with the coming of sound. Expertly dissecting both human relationships and Europe's decaying social and political structures, he imbued his work with a humanistic fatalism that unerringly stripped away superficial gaiety to reveal underlying melancholy. Renoir's richly literate, yet austerely realistic films combined intricate diegetic and intellectual parallels with a complex irony that was conveyed in expertly lit deep-focus images, which both generated the meaning of the narrative and controlled its tone.

Following his sound debut, *On purge bébé* (1931), Renoir made two more assaults on bourgeois susceptibilities, both starring Michel Simon – *La Chienne* (1931) and *Boudu Saved from Drowning* (1932). However, they failed commercially, as did his version of Flaubert's *Madame Bovary* (1934), which attempted to recreate the symbolism of the novel's substructure in purely cinematic terms. In 1935, he was invited by Pagnol to shoot *Toni* on location in Marseilles. Using unknown leads and a non-professional supporting cast and, for the first time, composing in depth, Renoir aimed to make this story of immi-

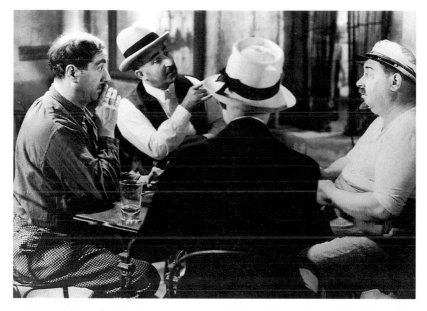

75 *Marius* (Alexander Korda, 1931), part one of Marcel Pagnol's Marseilles trilogy. His popular realism has reached new audiences thanks to Claude Berri's *Jean de Florette* and *Manon des sources* (both 1986) and Yves Robert's *Le Chateau de ma mère* (1990) and *La Gloire de mon père* (1991).

grant workers 'as close as possible to a documentary'. The resultant film simultaneously recalled Soviet realism and foreran Italian Neo-Realism.

After the studio realist parable *The Crime of Monsieur Lange* (1936), with its advocacy of Popular Front collectivism, Renoir supervised *La Vie est à nous* (1936), a piece of election propaganda for the French Communist Party that mixed newsreel footage and dramatic reconstruction to warn against the menace of Fascism. Following an adaptation of Maupassant's *Une Partie de campagne* (1936) that clearly bore the influence of his father's painting, and a version of Gorky's *The Lower Depths* (1936), Renoir returned to the theme of Europe's perilous situation in *La Grande Illusion* (1937). 76

Co-written with Charles Spaak and set amid the prison camps of the First World War, this 'statement of men's brotherhood beyond political borders' attempted to demonstrate the futility of conflict and the redundancy of a class system that could only precipitate the

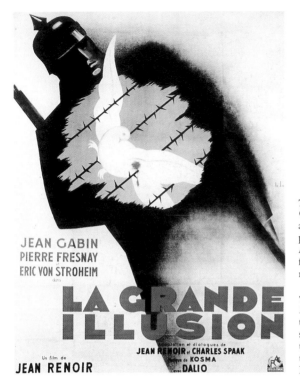

JEAN GABIN
PIERRE FRESNAY
ERIC VON STROHEIM
dans

LA GRANDE
ILLUSION

adaptation et dialogues de
JEAN RENOIR et CHARLES SPAAK
Un film de
JEAN RENOIR
musique de KOSMA
avec DALIO

76 A poster for Jean Renoir's *La Grande Illusion* (1937). The Nazis attempted to destroy all European prints but a negative was found by American troops in Munich in 1945, from which the film was painstakingly reconstructed.

77 Jean Renoir and Nora Grégor in *La Règle du jeu* (1939). Renoir's culturally rich, technically innovative and structurally complex feature invoked the spirit of Impressionist painting and the theatrical tradition of Musset and Beaumarchais.

collapse of civilization. Furthering his earlier experiments with deep-focus photography, Renoir constructed much of the film out of moving sequence shots which eschewed traditional editing techniques and which drew their dramatic tension from his precise deployment of figures and metaphorical objects on different spatial levels within the frame. André Bazin considered *La Grande Illusion*'s simple, eloquent style to be 'photographed realism', yet it also had a sonic authenticity thanks to Renoir's insistence that each nationality speak in its native tongue. Branded 'cinematographic enemy No. 1' by Goebbels, the film also owed much of its power to the superbly nonchalant performances of a cast that included Jean Gabin, Pierre Fresnay, Marcel Dalio and Erich von Stroheim.

A disappointing French Revolutionary drama, *La Marseillaise* (1938), and an updating of Zola's *La Bête humaine* (1938) were followed by Renoir's most ambitious and, at the time, controversial film, *La Règle du jeu* (1939). Returning to the theme of civilization 'dancing

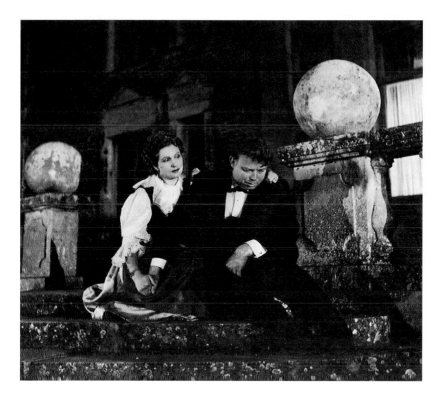

on a volcano', Renoir chose to adopt the structure of the eighteenth-century farces of Marivaux and Beaumarchais, although throughout the shooting of this largely improvised film he was torn between a 'desire to make a comedy out of it and the wish to tell a tragic story. The result of this ambivalence was the film as it is.' In his auto-biography, *My Life and My Films* (1974), Renoir wrote: 'It is a war film, and yet there is no reference to the war. Beneath its seemingly innocuous appearance the story attacks the very structure of our society.' In depicting the parallel lives of the above and below stairs inhabitants of a country chateau, Renoir aimed not only to show that 'for every game, there are rules. If you don't play according to them, you lose', but also to expose the rigidity, prejudice and decadence of contemporary France.

Forced to abandon plans to make the film in Technicolor, Renoir extended his pioneering use of long takes and depth of field, thus enabling the constantly moving camera to lend structural unity to plot development and maintain dramatic relationships in continuous temporal and spatial flow. Although witty and elegant, *La Règle du jeu* had an overriding pessimism that was encapsulated in the famous rabbit hunt, the horror and metaphorical emphasis of which was reinforced by Renoir's rare employment of montage. In spite of the removal of thirteen minutes of footage at the request of the distributors, the film nearly provoked a premiere-night riot and not even another twenty minutes-worth of cuts could prevent it from being banned by the censors. As Renoir later wrote, the film's fate had been sealed by the public's recognition of its own role in the disintegration of France: 'People who commit suicide do not care to do it in front of witnesses.'

Renoir left Europe in 1941, producing only two films of any marked quality over the next decade: *The Southerner* (1945), a Poetic Realist study of American dustbowl agriculture, and *The River* (1951), his first colour film, which he shot in India. He returned home preoccupied with the theatricality that was to inform *The Golden Coach* (1952), *French CanCan* (1954) and *Eléna et les hommes* (1956), but his later career was plagued by inconsistency. An independent throughout his forty-six years as a director, Renoir retained his deeply personal vision and his delight in experimentation to fashion the style that was to profoundly influence, among others, Orson Welles, the Neo-Realists and the *auteurs* of the French New Wave.

Sound came late to an Italian cinema already deep in the throes of a crisis precipitated by the influx of German and American silents. Only fifteen features were made in Italy in 1925, prompting Stefano Pittaluga (1887–1931) to merge Italy's three major studios – Italia, Cines and Palatina – into the Società Anonima Stefano Pittaluga (SASP), with the aim of establishing a national cinema based on the Hollywood model. In 1927, Mussolini granted SASP exclusive distribution rights to the films made by L'Unione Cinematografica Educativa (LUCE), the state newsreel and documentary service that he himself had founded in 1924 to exploit the power of what he considered to be 'the strongest weapon' of the century. However, with Pittaluga's death in 1931 the Italian cinema once more found itself in danger of submersion beneath the swelling tide of imports.

Persuaded by Pittaluga of the economic and cultural importance of a national film industry, Mussolini began to reorganize its structure, starting with the creation of the Ente Nazionale Industrie Cinematografice (ENIC) in 1934, which was designed to control distribution and exhibition throughout the country. The following year he set a quota on Hollywood films and to boost domestic production

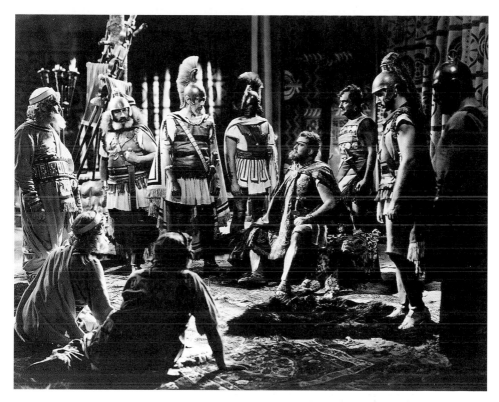

78 Carmine Gallone, *Scipione l'Africano* (1937). Exploiting the Italian genius for 'sword and sandal' spectacle, propaganda pictures like this sought to boost national pride by glorifying heroic deeds of the past

sanctioned the construction of the vast Cinecittà studios near Rome. Also in 1935, Mussolini established the world's second film school, Centro Sperimentale. The director Luigi Chiarini and his assistant Umberto Barbaro were accorded considerable latitude in their teaching methods, and Centro could soon boast such alumni as Roberto Rossellini, Luigi Zampa, Pietro Germi, Giuseppe de Santis and Michelangelo Antonioni.

In return for his subsidies and incentives, Mussolini was rewarded with a commercial cinema of enormous popular appeal that rivalled Hollywood in terms of narrative and stylistic sophistication. As experimentation and the discussion of serious topics were prevented by strict censorship, the result was a proliferation of escapist entertainments like the glamorous *'telefono bianco'*, or 'white telephone' melodramas, 'canned' operas and comedies of manners. Equally, there was little cinematic merit in calligraphism, a form of decorous literary adaptation that spawned the likes of *A Pistol Shot* (Renato Castellani, 1942) and *Jacob, the Idealist* (Alberto Lattuada, 1943). Overt propaganda was kept to a minimum. Barely detectable in historical spectacles like *1860* (Alessandro Blasetti, 1934) and *Scipione l'Africano* (Carmine Gallone, 1937) and the fictional documentaries of Francesco de Robertis and Roberto Rossellini (including *The White Ship*, 1942), it was even handled discreetly in such deliberate exercises in Fascist glorification as Giovacchino Forzano's *Black Shirt* (1933) and Blasetti's *The Old Guard* (1934).

While rarely inspired, the work of the leading Italian directors Blasetti (*Sun*, 1929, and *Mother Earth*, 1931) and Mario Camerini (*Rails*, 1929, released 1931, and *Figaro and His Big Day*, 1931) has been largely ignored because of its contemporaneity with Mussolini's regime. Even greater ignominy has been the fate of those film-makers who chose to pursue their careers inside the Third Reich. The Nazi cinema produced little of artistic significance but it should not be presumed that all the films of an industry as firmly rooted in escapism as its Italian counterpart were vehement avowals of National Socialism or incitements to racial hatred. Indeed, of the 1250 or so films produced during this period, markedly less than a quarter contained overt propaganda.

Although Josef Goebbels, Hitler's Minister of Propaganda and Public Enlightenment, declined to nationalize the German cinema until 1942, he did subject it to considerable regimentation. In 1933 he established the Reichsfilmkammer (Reich Film Chamber), which not only passed the Reichlichtspielgesetz (Reich Cinema Law, 1934) outlawing Jewish participation in the German film industry, but also began denouncing films like Pabst's *Westfront 1918* and *Kameradschaft* as the work of 'degenerate artists'. Curiously, Pabst was to return to Germany in 1939 to spend the war in the production of historical epics, yet his later career was devoted to such virulently anti-Nazi pictures as *The Last Ten Days* (1955).

Fritz Lang was another key silent director to earn the 'degenerate' tag for his 1931 film *M*, a brooding study of evil, corruption and decay that made exceptional use of parallel editing, asynchronous sound, silence and the physical presence of its star, Peter Lorre, in the role of a child murderer. Arriving in Hollywood in 1935, Lang directed twenty-three films over the next quarter of a century, but with the exception of *Fury* (1936), *You Only Live Once* (1937) and *The Big Heat*

(1953), he never quite managed to regain the impetus of his German period.

The mediocrity of Nazi cinema owed much to the fact that many pre-eminent Weimar film-makers were imprisoned and others had left because of the Parufamet Agreement in 1926. Robert Wiene, Billy Wilder, Robert Siodmak, Richard Oswald, Douglas Sirk, Curtis Bernhardt, Anatole Litvak, Max Ophüls, Paul Czinner, Lotte Reiniger and Leontine Sagan were among those who eventually managed to follow Lang into exile. The majority of those who remained, including Werner Hochbaum (*Die ewige Maske*, 1935), Willi Forst (*Maskerade*, 1934), Helmut Kautner (*Romanze in Moll*, 1943) and Luis Trenker (*Condottieri*, 1937) were reliable but uninspired craftsmen. Best known for light comedies, Herbert Selpin was no more inspired, but he managed habitually to dilute the ideological content of his films, until Goebbels finally had him murdered during the shooting of *Titanic* in 1943. Among the many others to join the exodus were the performers Peter Lorre, Conrad Veidt, Fritz Kortner, Albert Basserman, Oscar Homolka and Anton Walbrook, as well as the producer Erich Pommer, the cinematographer Eugene Schüfftan and the composer Franz Waxman.

Almost of equal import was Goebbels's predilection for trivial escapism, boasting lavish production values and attractive stars: operettas in the tradition of such early sound films as *Congress Dances* (Erik Charrell, 1931); musical comedies like *Amphytrion* (Reinhold Schünzel, 1935); fantasies, including Josef von Baky's *The Adventures of Baron Münchhausen* (1943), and a series of detective thrillers and romantic melodramas. The Party line was, however, more in evidence in newsreels and such *Staatsauftragsfilme* as the historical epics *Bismarck* (Wolfgang Liebeneiner, 1940) and *Frederick the Great* (Veit Harlan, 1942), and the Nazi venerational *S. A. Mann Brandt* (Franz Seitz, 1933) and *Hitler Youth Quex* (Hans Steinhoff, 1933). But the most forceful and eloquent propaganda pieces of the period were undoubtedly Leni Riefenstahl's *Triumph of the Will* (1935) and *Olympia* (1938).   79

Personally selected by Hitler on the strength of her work in mountain films, Riefenstahl (b. 1902) was presented with thirty cameras, a crew of more than 120, unlimited financial resources and the guaranteed co-operation of the Nazi hierarchy in order to record the 1934 Party rally at Nuremberg. Special elevators, platforms, ramps and tracks were provided so that the cameras would miss nothing of the spectacle choreographed by Albert Speer. The result of eight months' editing, *Triumph of the Will* blended the architecture of the city, the

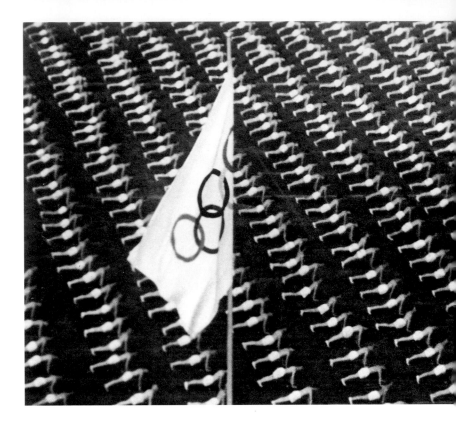

rally arena and the Congress Hall with mass human geometric patterns to convey the power and universality of Nazism, while cleverly angled close-ups enhanced the messianic status of the Führer.

Making innovative use of telephoto lenses and slow motion, and with eighteen months in post-production, *Olympia* was an account of the 1936 Berlin Olympic Games that played down the cult of personality in favour of that of the physique, itself a key tenet of Nazism. Clearly, Riefenstahl's films stand in stark contrast to the crudely propagandist features made during the war. Nevertheless, her detractors insist that she was politically committed to her work, although she always maintained that she was simply a film-maker engaged in the production of art.

Soviet film-makers were caught in a similar form-versus-content dilemma throughout the 1930s as a result of Stalin's insistence on the cinema of Socialist Realism. Its imposition coincided with the arrival of sound, and opportunities for experimentation were thus greatly

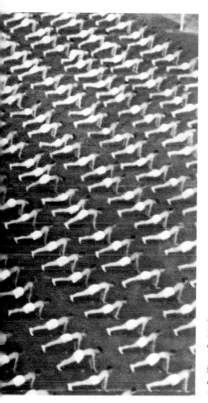

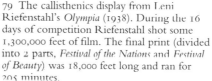

79 The callisthenics display from Leni Riefenstahl's *Olympia* (1938). During the 16 days of competition Riefenstahl shot some 1,300,000 feet of film. The final print (divided into 2 parts, *Festival of the Nations* and *Festival of Beauty*) was 18,000 feet long and ran for 205 minutes.

reduced, although most of the great directors of the silent era made accomplished transitions: Kuleshov – *The Great Consoler* (1933); Vertov – *Enthusiasm* (1931) and *Three Songs for Lenin* (1933); Pudovkin – *A Simple Case* (1932) and *Deserter* (1933); and Dovzhenko – *Ivan* (1932).

The majority of Soviet film theatres were denied sound until 1938, by which time more than one-third of annual production was being banned or withheld by the Kremlin. As in other totalitarian states, escapism (*Jazz Comedy*, Grigori Alexandrov, 1934) and historical reconstruction (*Peter the First, Parts I & II*, Vladimir Petrov, 1937–9) were encouraged. Similarly, there were a number of features lionizing Party heroes – fictional ones in *Chapayev* (the Vasiliev Brothers, 1934), *Schors* (Alexander Dovzhenko, 1939), *We from Kronstadt* (Yefim Dzigan, 1936) and *Baltic Deputy* (Alexander Zharki and Josef Heifitz, 1939); and actual ones in Mikhail Romm's *Lenin in October* (1937) and *Lenin in 1918* (1939). Films justifying government policies were also sanctioned, such as Friedrich Ermler's *Peasants* (1932) and *The Great Citizen* (1934), which attempted to legitimize collectivization and the purges respectively.

Before Eisenstein's rehabilitation in 1938, films of genuine quality were rare, with the exceptions of Kozintsev and Trauberg's witty Maxim trilogy – *The Youth of Maxim* (1935), *The Return of Maxim* (1937) and *The Vyborg Side* (1939) – with its striking compositions and sprightly episodic structure, and Mark Donskoy's three-part adaptation of Gorky's autobiography – *The Childhood of Maxim Gorky* (1938), *My Apprenticeship* (1939) and *My Universities* (1940) – which was acclaimed for its humour, humanity and period authenticity.

Since 1930 Eisenstein had been in Hollywood studying sound techniques and developing a number of film treatments for Paramount, including *The Glass House*, *Sutter's Gold* and *An American Tragedy*. When nothing came of these he agreed, at Chaplin's suggestion, to join the novelist Upton Sinclair in the production of *Que Viva Mexico!*, an ambitious study of the Mexican revolutionary spirit. Dismissed after a feud with Sinclair during the late stages of filming in 1932, Eisenstein returned home to teach at the VGIK. For the next six years, Boris Shumyatsky, motivated by personal animosity, offered Eisenstein nothing but humiliating assignments while refusing permission for such cherished projects as a history of Moscow and biographies of Pushkin and the Haitian statesman Toussaint L'Ouverture. When he did finally receive a project, *Bezhin Meadow*, a combination of serious illness, Shumyatsky's obduracy and dramatic changes in government policy forced him to abandon it, though near completion, in 1937.

The publication of the retractive pamphlet *The Mistakes of Bezhin Meadow* did much to restore Eisenstein in the eyes of the Party bureaucracy, and following the execution of Shumyatsky early in 1938, he was awarded the prestigious production *Alexander Nevsky*. His first sound film, this staunchly anti-Nazi tract was conceived in operatic terms, with Sergei Prokofiev's score alternately complementing and contradicting the visual images. Painstakingly composed with a precise and symbolic use of light, mass and space, *Alexander Nevsky* told of the repulsion by the ruler of thirteenth-century Novgorod of an invading army of Teutonic knights. Complete with swish pans and a buffeting camera style that placed the viewer at the centre of the action, the 'Battle on the Ice' remains among the director's finest achievements.

Prevented from making a trilogy about life in the Central Asian desert, a film about Spain and a history of the Red Army, Eisenstein

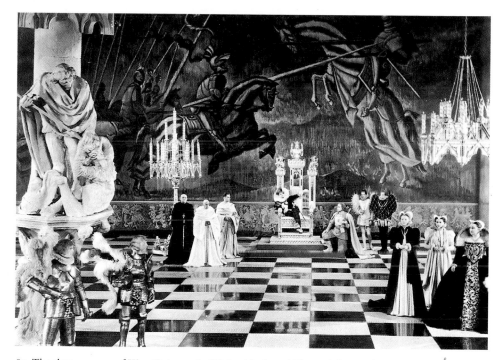

80 The throne room of King Sigismond of Poland in Sergei Eisenstein's *Ivan the Terrible* (1944). Inspired by El Greco, I. Chpinel's sets and Andrei Moskvin's lighting were essential to a film whose meaning was dependent on design rather than montage.

returned to the theatre in 1939. Here, while mounting a Bolshoi production of Wagner's *Die Walküre*, he became increasingly fascinated with synaesthesia, a kind of sensory domino effect that was to have a conspicuous influence on his last features, *Ivan the Terrible: Part I* (1944) 80 and *Part II: The Boyar's Plot* (1946).

Originally intended as a trilogy, *Ivan the Terrible* was two years in pre-production and filmed in strict accordance with the storyboards that also served as the sole inspiration for Prokofiev's score. Eisenstein later wrote that 'the grandeur of our theme necessitated a grandiose design' and, consequently, he abandoned montage in favour of functional editing and a concentration on the *mise-en-scène*, to which the cast, led by Nikolai Cherkasov, contributed with their highly expressive and angular performances. Complete with a colour sequence shot using Agfacolor stock confiscated from the German army, *Part I* lacked pace and was often pictorialist, yet it was still awarded the Stalin Prize. *The Boyar's Plot*, however, with its allusions to murderous tyranny, was accused of historical error and the four completed reels of *Part III: Ivan's Struggles* were destroyed. Demonstrating that film can import elements from other art forms and still retain its aesthetic integrity, *Ivan the Terrible* was a courageous experiment and one of the finest films made within the constraints of Socialist Realism. Eisenstein died still hopeful of negotiating acceptable amendments.

Elsewhere in Eastern Europe, sound was enabling a number of national cinemas to consolidate against total Hollywood domination. Aided by a quota system and import taxes, the Czech film industry had witnessed a rise in annual production from just seven features in 1930 to more than forty by the time it was appropriated by the Nazis. Responsible for *Ecstasy* (Gustav Machaty, 1933), the most notorious film of the period on account of its flashes of a naked Hedy Kiesler (later Lamarr), the Czech cinema was also noted for its experimental animation, versatile directors like Karel Lamač, Martin Frič and Otakar Vávra, and the Barrandov studios that stood comparison with any on the Continent.

Poland did not get its first studio until 1920, although location realism was an integral part of the social purpose films made by Aleksander Ford, Wanda Jakubowska, Josef Lejtes, Jerzy Bossak and other members of START, the Society of the Devotees of Artistic Film. Their style was to have a profound influence on the new Polish cinema of the 1950s. In spite of possessing the world's first national-ized film industry (at the turn of 1919), Hungary's contribution throughout the ensuing decades was limited by strict censorship to the theoretical writings of Béla Balázs, the light–space experiments of the photographer László Moholy-Nagy and the documentaries of George Hoellering. Mention should also be made of Vassil Gendov and Boris Grazhov, whose literary adaptations accounted for many of the fifty-five films made in Bulgaria between 1915 and 1950.

Among Asian countries, India's fifteen major languages, diverse dialects, and a unique musical system presented her regional cinemas with the means to resist foreign competition. Escapist musical melo-dramas (complete with diegetically significant song-and-dance rou-tines) accounted for the bulk of production in both the Hindi-speaking All-Indian cinema and the different local centres, although a number of Bengali directors, including Debaki Bose (*Chandidas*, 1932) and P. D. Barua (*Devdas*, 1935), favoured social realism. In spite of similar linguistic heterogeneity, Chinese cinema failed to make such a smooth transition to sound. Yet, in the face of mounting internal and external pressures, it was soon able to demonstrate a keen social and political awareness in *Wild Torrent* (Cheng Bu-kao, 1932) and the 1934 films *The Goddess* (Wu Yonggang), *The Big Road* (Sun Yu) and *The Song of the Fishermen* (Tsai Chu-shen). However, studios fell into Japanese hands during the 1937 invasion and Chinese film-makers were prevented from embracing truly national themes until the end of the civil war in 1949.

Retaining much of its poise and poignancy throughout the 1930s, Japanese cinema manifested little of the nation's increasingly evident militarism. Indeed, it even went so far as openly to criticize the central government in the socialist 'tendency' films instigated by Daisuke Ito. Apart from Ito's violent *jidai-geki*, including *Man-Slashing, Horse Piercing Sword* (1930), the majority of tendency films were *shomin-geki*, such as Teinosuke Kinugasa's *Before Dawn* (1932), Heinosuke Gosho's *Everything That Lives* (1936) and Tomu Uchida's *The Naked Town* (1937). However, following the imposition of strict censorship by the Ministry of Propaganda in 1937 such films were banned, and one tendency director, Sadao Yamanaka (*Humanity and Paper Balloons*, 1937), was sent to his death in the Chinese war.

Sound was introduced into Japan in 1931, sparking a series of business wars that culminated in the foundation of three (later five) *zaibatsu*, or production companies, which, with the exception of the custom of directorial tutelage, were essentially replicas of the Hollywood majors. Coincidental was the emergence of a number of important sub-genres within the *gendai-geki*, including the *haho-mono* (the mother-film), the *nansensu* (nonsense comedy) and the *sarariman* ('salaryman' drama). However, the most striking development during this period was the willingness of film-makers to experiment, whether with combinations of Western dramaturgies and Japanese poetic conventions or with visual styles. Although adhering to continuity editing, the Japanese delighted in breaching the 180° axis. Similarly, they made greater use of location shooting, oncoming action, dislocated camera movement, wide-angle lenses and deep space. Two film-makers in particular, Kenji Mizoguchi (1898–1956) and Yasujiro Ozu (1903–63), advanced these techniques to forge their own highly individualistic styles.

Mizoguchi, who made ninety features in his thirty-four-year career, began with painterly thrillers and literary adaptations, but his best films dealt with the conflict between ancient tradition and modern lifestyle, and the role of women within society. Although he often worked in the *gendai-geki*, his 1936 films *Osaka Elegy* and *Sisters of the Gion* had contemporary settings and each demonstrated a growing preference

81

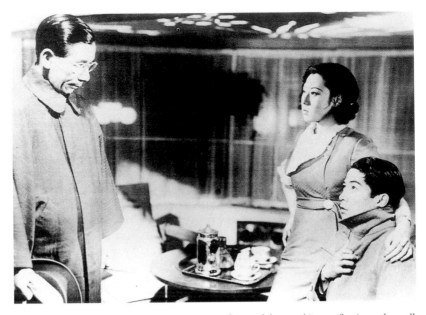

81 Kenji Mizoguchi, *Osaka Elegy* (1936). Influenced by *emakimono* (horizontal scroll painting), Mizoguchi's diagonal compositions invited the viewer to explore the world beyond the frame. The first of his markedly feminist films, *Osaka Elegy* has been compared stylistically to the 1930s work of Renoir and von Sternberg.

for compositional depth, a static camera and the extended take. Long into the sound era Mizoguchi was to continue to use angles, *mise-en-scène* and metaphorical camera movement in order to give visual expression to internal sensation.

Influenced by the Italian superspectacle, by Griffith and Lubitsch, Ozu none the less began his career in *nansensu*, before choosing to specialize in *shomin-geki* (*Passing Fancy*, 1933, and *A Story of Floating Weeds*, 1934) and its *haha-mono* (*The Only Son*, 1936) and *sarariman* (*I Was Born, But . . .*, 1932) sub-genres. Almost minimalist in style, Ozu's films on the routines and family relationships of the lower middle classes were notable for their unique approach to diegetic and temporal logic. Often decentring narrative events by means of ellipsis, he relied on depth of characterization and strong dialogue to sustain the action, which was invariably recorded from a low angle in long takes with a static camera. But it was his inspired manipulation of on- and off-screen space that made his films so remarkable.

Ozu pioneered the use of off-centre framing, a technique that exploited the centrifugal force of an image to guide the viewer to the edges of the frame and thus the conclusion that a real world existed beyond them. In order to achieve this he devised a fully circular filmic space around which he could construct alternative axes of action and thus create totally new spatial contexts throughout a scene. Although requiring painstaking graphic matching and disallowing even the most basic pans, this method ensured the complete integration of action with location.

Off-screen space was also fashioned through the 'curtain' or 'pillow' shots Ozu used as transitions. Devoid of figures, these 'empty scenes' were usually lingering 'still lifes' of urban landmarks or objects in the *mise-en-scène* – in other words, poetic digressions, which, virtually meaningless in terms of theme and narrative, prompted the viewer to contemplate the nature of events already occurring elsewhere in the film's world. Similarly, Ozu conveyed the impression of simultaneous action through a combination of static camera and contrapuntal sound, while in his later films he achieved added realism by having characters involved in an off-screen activity venture into the frame in its pursuit.

Anthropomorphism, Zen aestheticism and a revolt against Hollywood classicism have been variously cited as the inspiration for Ozu's unique and, to some critics, 'unreasonable' style. Essentially a conservative, in spite of his individuality, he was among the most influential of the Japanese film-makers whose work emerged at the end of the Second World War.

Since the First World War, when the potential of cinema had been woefully underexploited, governments worldwide had come to appreciate its propaganda value and no similar mistake was made between 1939 and 1945. But it was not until the end of the Phoney War, in the spring of 1940, that the film industries of Europe were placed on a full war footing.

In Britain, a reduction in quantity coincided with a marked improvement in quality. The GPO Film Unit became the Crown Film Unit inside the Ministry of Information, which, in addition to the public service shorts of Richard Massingham, sponsored the production of what might be called fictional documentaries, such as Harry Watt's *Target for Tonight* (1941), Charles Frend's *San Demetrio, London* (1943) and Pat Jackson's *Western Approaches* (1944). The most skilled exponent of these features was Humphrey Jennings (1907–50), considered by the critic and director Lindsay Anderson to be 'the only real poet the British cinema has yet produced'. Making inspired use of audiovisual juxtapositions, Jennings perceptively captured the spirit of wartime Britain in such films as *Listen to Britain* (1941), *Fires Were Started* (1943) and *A Diary for Timothy* (1945).

82

Realism continued to inform British fictional features, whether those dealing with the actual conflict – *In Which We Serve* (Noël Coward and David Lean, 1942), *The Way Ahead* (Carol Reed, 1944) and *The Way to the Stars* (Anthony Asquith, 1945); or the home front – *Went the Day Well?* (Cavalcanti, 1942), *Next of Kin* (Thorold Dickinson, 1942) and *Millions Like Us* (Frank Launder and Sidney Gilliat, 1943). On the other hand, period nostalgia like *The Life and Death of Colonel Blimp* (Michael Powell and Emeric Pressburger, 1943), *This Happy Breed* (David Lean, 1944) and *Henry V* (Laurence Olivier, 1944) was also immensely popular.

Having resisted Nazi reorganization, the cinema of Vichy France produced some two hundred largely escapist films, including such thrillers as *Goupi mains-rouges* (Jacques Becker, 1943), nostalgic pieces like *Nous les gosses* (Louis Daquin, 1940), and numerous musicals and historical melodramas. Working within this 'safe' genre, Marcel Carné still managed to make the impudent Occupation allegories *Les Visiteurs du soir* (1942) and *Les Enfants du paradis* (1945), the latter also being a complex, almost novelistic investigation of the relationships between life and art, reality and illusion. However, not all subversive depictions of the Occupation were as readily understood, particularly when couched in terms of fatalist Poetic Realism. *Le Corbeau* (1941), for example, a bitter story of poison-pen letters, earned the director Henri-Georges Clouzot and the star Pierre Fresnay punishment as collaborators after the liberation.

83

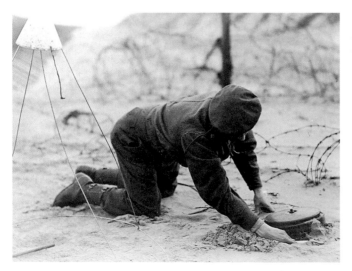

82 Humphrey Jennings, *A Diary for Timothy* (1945). Written by E. M. Forster and blending documentary realism, humanist narrative and impressionistic imagery, this complex work was a portrait of Britain on the verge of peace.

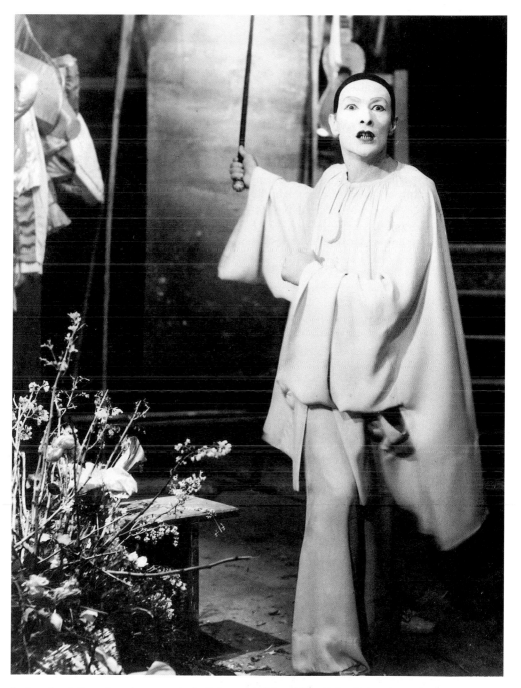

83 Jean-Louis Barrault as the pantomimist Debureau in Marcel Carné's *Les Enfants du paradis* (1945). A tribute to the theatre and France's indomitable spirit, the film took over 2 years to complete because of Nazi sabotage, the arrest of cast members, the need for secrecy with performers in the Maquis and Carné's determination to show his epic in a free France.

Wartime Soviet cinema was sustained by historical epics like *Ivan the Terrible* and Socialist Realist accounts of heroism. The 'Great Patriotic War' also revived the spirit of the documentarists of the 1920s: compilation films like *A Day in the New World* (1941), the monthly *Fighting Film Album* collections of information and reconstruction, and Dovzhenko and Yulia Solnitseva's 1943 poetic reportage piece, *Battle for the Ukraine*, were among the best Soviet productions of the period.

Similarly, the documentaries that were sponsored by various American governmental and military offices have retained their reputations, most notably Frank Capra's seven-part compilation series *Why We Fight* (1942–4), Stuart Heisler's *The Negro Soldier* (1944), and the graphic battle despatches (*Report from the Aleutians* (John Huston, 1943), *The Battle of Midway* (John Ford) and *Memphis Belle* (William Wyler, both 1944).

84

While Hollywood's leading directors justified or reported the war, its stars did their bit by enlisting, morale-boosting at the front, serving at the Hollywood Canteen, selling war bonds or simply providing escapist entertainment on the screen. Although productions dropped by 40 per cent, the Second World War was a boom time for Hollywood. Full employment meant people had money to spend and, with an entertainment tax making going to the movies seem patriotic, attendances rose to a weekly eighty-five million.

Hollywood began the war with a series of crude flagwavers, depicting the enemy as cowardly incompetents, but such sentiments were soon abjured and the studios began to produce more responsible features, like *Watch on the Rhine* (Herman Shumlin) and *Keeper of the Flame* (George Cukor, both 1943), and *The Hitler Gang* (John Farrow) and *Lifeboat* (Alfred Hitchcock, both 1944). However, the convincing depiction of occupied Europe continued to elude Hollywood, with even Renoir's *This Land Is Mine* and Lang's *Hangmen Also Die* (both 1943) guilty of confusing courage with sentimentality. Battle films did mature in the course of the conflict, with *Bataan* (Tay Garnett, 1943) and *Guadalcanal Diary* (Lewis Seiler, 1944) among the films to reproduce authentically the horror of warfare.

Of all warring powers, Germany was alone in resorting to such overtly belligerent propaganda as the anti-British *Ohm Krüger* (Hans Steinhoff, 1941) and the notoriously anti-Semitic *Jew Süss* (Veit Harlan) and *The Eternal Jew* (Fritz Hippler, both 1940). Unconvinced of the efficacy of propaganda, Goebbels continued to place his trust in escapism, although a number of impressive compilation films were

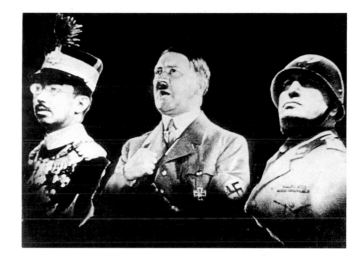

84 Frank Capra, *Why We Fight* (1942–4). Combining newsreel, feature excerpts, reconstructions, stills, maps, captions and animated sequences by Disney, the 7 films in this intricately composed series belied the fact that Capra had no prior documentary experience.

produced, including Hippler's *Campaign in Poland* (1940) and *Victory in the West* (1941).

Japanese film-makers had been encouraged to extol national fighting prowess since 1937, although the first films commissioned by the Ministry of Propaganda, including *Five Scouts* (Tomotaka Tasaka, 1938) and *The Story of Tank Commander Nishizumi* (Kimisaburo Yoshimura, 1940), were distinctly pacifist in tone. A strict production code was imposed in the wake of Pearl Harbor in an effort to ensure that fictional documentaries like *The Suicide Troops of the Watch Tower* (Tadasi Imai, 1942) were not alone in promoting war aims. However, many directors chose to remain silent rather than conform; Ozu, for example, made just two films in the decade from 1937, *The Brothers and Sisters of the Toda Family* (1941) and *There Was A Father* (1942). Others, like Mizoguchi (*The Story of the Late Chrysanthemums*, 1939) and Akira Kurosawa (b. 1910) (*The Judo Story*, 1943), chose to work in a *jidai-geki* sub-genre, the *Meiji-mono*, although Mizoguchi was later compelled to make the more militaristic two-part *chambara* ('swordfight film') *The Forty-Seven Loyal Ronin* (1941–2). The hostilities eventually took their toll, however, and shortage of resources limited each of the three major *zaibatsu* to the production of just two features per month, with the resultant closure of some 1650 theatres.

Italy, the final member of the Axis, continued to benefit from the state interventions of the 1930s, and produced 119 features in 1942 alone. This year was to prove of even greater significance for the emergence of a movement that was to have an incalculable impact on international cinema – Neo-Realism.

CHAPTER SIX

Facing Realities 1946–59

'The ideal film', wrote Cesare Zavattini (1902–89), the leading theorist and scenarist of Neo-Realism, 'would be ninety minutes of the life of a man to whom nothing happens.' In 1942, he urged Italian film-makers to repudiate the star system, studio artifice and plot contrivance that had bolstered the escapism, spectacle and rhetoric of the Fascist era, and focus solely on the contemporary realities facing ordinary people in their daily lives. Reiterating Zavattini's proposals in an article published early the following year, the critic Umberto Barbaro labelled this fresh approach 'Neo-Realism', endorsing French Poetic Realism as its exemplar.

Although links with nineteenth-century *verismo* literature and Soviet revolutionary realism can be identified, Neo-Realism did, indeed, draw on recent French cinema as its primary source of technical, intellectual and aesthetic inspiration. Yet Neo-Realism remained firmly rooted in the poverty and pessimism of its immediate historical context, deriving its most vital impetus from its adherents' desire both to reflect the socio-economic impact of authoritarianism and war and to revolt against the constraints that had prevented meaningful cinematic expression for some two decades. There is, therefore, a certain irony in the fact that the Fascist film industry not only trained many Neo-Realists in their craft but also anticipated several of the movement's characteristic elements, particularly in its wartime semi-documentaries.

Ossessione (1942) has been traditionally acknowledged as the prototype Neo-Realist film, yet its director Luchino Visconti (1906–76) consciously neglected the political commitment of the Zavattini-Barbaro manifestos, instead employing Neo-Realism as a stylistic device capable of conveying the melodramatic brutality and psychological power of James M. Cain's thriller *The Postman Always Rings Twice*. *La Terra trema* (1948) similarly testified to Visconti's highly personal interpretation of the mode, for in spite of being largely improvised on location by a non-professional cast speaking its own Sicilian dialect, it also incorporated an elaborate *mise-en-scène*, stately camera

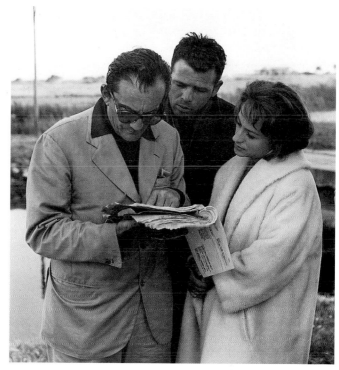

85 Luchino Visconti on the set of *Rocco and His Brothers* (1960). A major influence on directors like Fassbinder, Bertolucci and Scorsese, he has been called 'the most Italian of internationalists, the most operatic of realists, and the most aristocratic of Marxists'.

movements and rhythmic editing. Although he made further tonal use of monochrome in *Rocco and His Brothers* (1960), Visconti became increasingly preoccupied, in historical dramas such as *Senso* (1954) and *The Damned* (1969) and literary adaptations like *The Leopard* (1963), *The Stranger* (1967) and *Death in Venice* (1971), with the expressive use of colour and stylized décor that reflected his dual passion for theatre and opera.

85

XV

It was not until the last days of the war that a more authentic Neo-Realist style began to emerge, as film-makers were forced onto the streets following the partial destruction of Cinecittà during the liberation of Rome. The scarred city served as their *mise-en-scène* and its citizens, often cast according to typage, became their 'stars'. Allowing their non-professionals to improvise, film-makers adopted a flexibility of framing and camera movement, shooting in available light and adding dialogue in post-production to attain a documentary-like spontaneity.

Based on actual events and shot on location on stock spliced together from fragments bought from street photographers, Roberto Rossellini's *Rome, Open City* (1945), the first in his war trilogy, achieved a surface documentarism that came closer to the prescribed Neo-Realist style than *Ossessione*. Yet for all its social commitment, visual authenticity and technical ingenuity, the film still relied on a melodramatic narrative, conceptual framing, montage and star performances (by Anna Magnani and Aldo Fabrizi) to explore the experience of the Nazi occupation. Also scripted by Rossellini, Sergio Amidei and Federico Fellini, *Paisà* (1946), a series of six vignettes capturing the spirit of Italy during the Liberation, similarly exploited Neo-Realist techniques to create what James Agee called 'the illusion of the present tense', but its depth of characterization betrayed an increasing divergence from the movement's basic tenets.

The concluding part of Rossellini's trilogy, *Germany, Year Zero* (1947), bore out André Bazin's contention that Neo-Realism was an ontological not an aesthetic position, the employment of whose 'technical attributes like a recipe do not necessarily produce it'. Considering the film a failure, Rossellini (1906–77) abandoned Neo-Realism, and in films like *The Miracle* (1948) and the six features starring Ingrid Bergman, developed a detached, ironic approach to his paradoxical, elliptic narratives that, like the more traditional dramas of Visconti, made extensive use of long takes shot with zoom lenses. The final phase of his career saw the production for French and Italian television of a number of colour docudramas, including *The Rise to Power of Louis XIV* (1966) and *The Age of the Medici* (1972), that were remarkable for their historical authenticity and *mise-en-scène*.

Zavattini himself scripted the features of Neo-Realism's other major director, the ex-matinee idol Vittorio De Sica (1901–74), yet not even these adhered strictly to his fundamental precepts – if, indeed, did any Neo-Realist film. *Shoeshine* (1946), a spontaneous, episodic story of corrupted innocence in Nazi Rome that disdained neat optimism, perhaps came closest, although it was their next collaboration, *Bicycle Thieves* (1948), that excited greater attention. A parable of modern urban life exploring the response of everyday people to the overwhelming societal forces relentlessly shaping postwar Italy, the film adopted a 'flow of life' structure comprising vignettes of contrasting emotional tones, each one of which traced a further stage in the search by a father (Lamberto Maggiorani) and son (Enzo Staiola) for the stolen bicycle on which the family's livelihood depended. De Sica's roaming camera achieved a powerful poetic

86

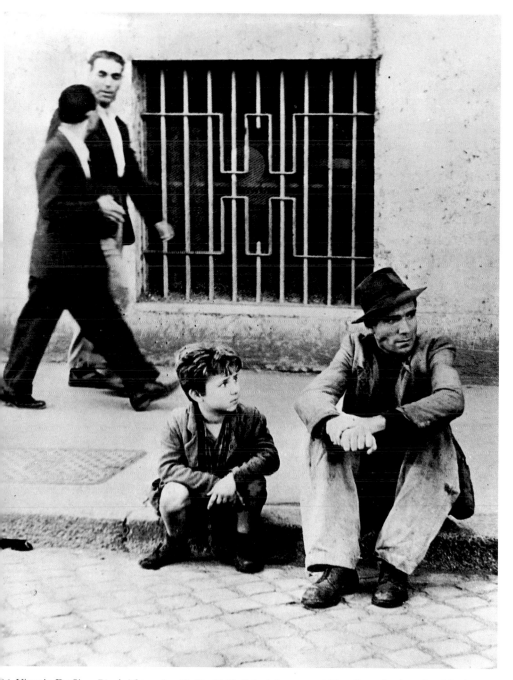

86 Vittorio De Sica, *Bicycle Thieves* (1948). David O. Selznick proposed Cary Grant for the role of the impov-
erished Antonio but De Sica selected a factory-worker, Lamberto Maggiorani, and Enzo Staiola as his son.

purity through its facial close-ups and ironic observation of the *mise-en-scène*'s intricately composed symbolism, but he was unable to prevent melodramatic sentimentality from intruding on the delineation of the central relationship. A similar charge was levelled against *Umberto D* (1952), an almost Chaplinesque tale of old age, which is usually considered the movement's last significant film, although De Sica later made both *The Roof* (1957) and *Two Women* (1960) in a distinctly Neo-Realist vein. With the exception of the remarkable *The Garden of the Finzi-Continis* (1971), De Sica's final films were invariably romantic melodramas or sex comedies, like *Yesterday, Today and Tomorrow* (1963) and *Marriage, Italian Style* (1964).

Alberto Lattuada, Luigi Zampa, Renato Castellani, Luciano Emmer, Carlo Lizzani and Pietro Germi all made valuable contributions to the Neo-Realist canon, before Giuseppe De Santis's *Bitter Rice* (1948) heralded a return to more overt commercialism with its blend of agrarian realism, sensational eroticism and star glamour. In spite of its international appeal, Neo-Realism had received a mixed critical and commercial reception at home and was already in decline when the protectionist Andreotti Law of 1949 attempted to prevent the production of films that failed to serve the 'best interests of Italy' by withholding state subsidies and export licences. Increasingly formal, psychological and stereotypical, Neo-Realism ultimately fell victim to the economic recovery which eroded its ideological basis and thematic resources and which financed the resumption of studio production.

Notwithstanding its brevity, Neo-Realism had a long-lasting effect not only on the Italian film industry (where its legacy continues to inspire or infuriate), but also on the French New Wave (*see* Chapter 7) and on established and nascent cinemas worldwide. Surprisingly, Hollywood was one of its chief beneficiaries, with filmmakers recognizing in it a means of exploring the concerns afflicting a disillusioned nation, and studio heads a way of reducing production costs while still guaranteeing quality entertainment.

Few would have anticipated the need for such parsimony in 'Tinsel Town' in the immediate post-war period, however. Commercially, 1946 was the most successful year in Hollywood history, with approximately a hundred million Americans visiting the movies each week, returning record annual receipts of $1.7 billion. Moreover, there was an unprecedented demand for current and backlist pictures from the war-torn nations of Europe and South-East Asia. Yet within months Hollywood was plunged into crisis by a coincidence of diverse social,

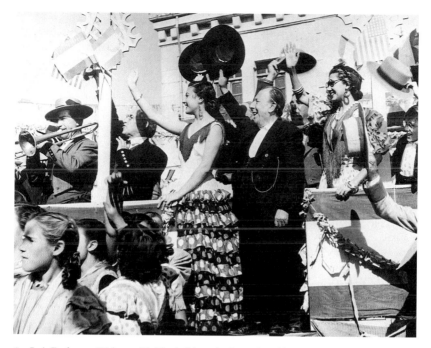

87 Luis Berlanga, *Welcome, Mr Marshall* (1952). Co-scripted by Berlanga and Juan Antonio Bardem, this Neo-Realist comedy, about a poor Castilian town trying to elicit aid from Marshall Plan commissioners, was one of the most successful films of the Franco era.

economic and political factors, many of whose impact had been fore-stalled only by the war.

Cinema going had been an American pastime for some thirty years. But, as the wartime emotional dependence on it receded, and as urban populations began to drift into the suburbs away from the downtown and neighbourhood theatres, it became increasingly obvious that the habit was now just one of many leisure options competing for consumers' dollars. Concurrent with audience decline was a rise in production costs fomented by nationwide inflation and the 25 per cent pay award that had settled the 1945 studio strike. Then, in 1947, Britain, Hollywood's biggest overseas customer, imposed a 75 per cent tariff on imported films, prompting a retaliatory export boycott.

Matters worsened in 1948 when the verdict in the government's anti-trust case against the film industry was returned. The Paramount

Decrees ruled that the system of vertical integration was monopolistic and gave the studios three years to divest themselves of their theatre chains. The end of block-booking drove minors like Rainbow, Liberty and Eagle Lion into liquidation and even the majors were forced to economize. Prestige productions were postponed in favour of tautly scripted, meticulously planned projects which bore the influence not only of Neo-Realism, but also of the wartime documentaries. Unfettered by studio overheads, independent production became the norm, reinvigorating American cinema by at last giving its film-makers the opportunity to explore controversial contemporary issues in an adult manner.

In an optimistic exploration of the American response to the horrors of war, William Wyler's *The Best Years of Our Lives* (1946) demonstrated the customary Hollywood reluctance to confront social realities. Within a year, however, a new generation of film-makers was exposing the nation's sinister, cynical underside in a cycle of 'problem pictures'. Often melodramatic in tone, these films were nevertheless remarkable for the candour with which they addressed such topics as anti-Semitism (*Crossfire*, Edward Dmytryk, 1947); racism (*Home of the Brave*, Mark Robson, 1949); alcoholism (*The Lost Weekend*, Billy Wilder, 1945); delinquency (*Knock on Any Door*, Nicholas Ray, 1949); political corruption (*All the King's Men*, Robert Rossen, 1949); prison injustice (*Brute Force*, Jules Dassin, 1947); rigged sport (*The Set-Up*, Robert Wise, 1949) and post-war reintegration (*The Men*, Fred Zinnemann, 1950).

Stylistically linked to the social-consciousness feature were several semi-documentary case studies, including *The House on 92nd Street* (Henry Hathaway, 1945), *Boomerang!* (Elia Kazan, 1947) and *The Naked City* (Dassin, 1948), that restaged true-life crimes in their actual milieux using a mix of contract players and non-professionals. However, both genres asserted that social duplicity could be remedied by traditional American values, an ingenuous idealism that was notably absent from the brutal, pessimistic pictures dubbed *films noirs* by the French in 1946.

Although some critics have traced *film noir's* origins back to *The Maltese Falcon* (John Huston, 1941), it is generally accepted that its prototypical style was established by Wilder's *Double Indemnity* (1944), which demonstrated a preoccupation with the basest human instincts and a conviction of the inevitability of moral corruption. Essentially a 'cinema of moral anxiety', *noir* manifested a number of key influences, including Freudianism, 'hard-boiled' detective fiction, German

88

156

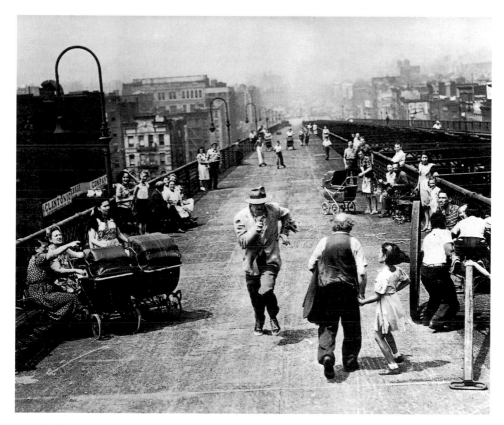

88 Jules Dassin, *The Naked City* (1948). Employing over 100 locations throughout New York, this tautly directed docudrama was shot largely from a van fitted with a one-way mirror by William Daniels.

Expressionism, French fatalism and post-war cinematic realism, as well as the intrinsic saturninity of the period. While *noir* films were made across the generic range, its most effective vehicle was undoubtedly the crime melodrama populated by any combination of *femmes fatales*, hapless veterans, petty racketeers, lowlife detectives and debased members of the establishment.

Film noir's themes were reinforced by an expressive visual style that owed much to the preponderance of exiled Ufa directors and cinematographers working within it. Aided particularly by the development of higher speed lenses and finer grain stocks, they utilized angular, depth-of-field photography, wide-angled distortion, low-key lighting and 'night-for-night' shooting to achieve *noir*'s unique sense of psychological dislocation. Rejuvenating the careers of several long-time stars by compelling them to play against type, *film noir* represented something of a counter-tradition in Hollywood history. It fostered numerous popular classics, including *Farewell, My Lovely* (Edward Dmytryk, 1945), *The Postman Always Rings Twice* (Tay Garnett, 1946), *Cry of the City* (Robert Siodmak, 1948), *White Heat* (Raoul Walsh, 1949), *Night and the City* (Jules Dassin, 1950) and *Kiss Me Deadly* (Robert Aldrich, 1955).

However, the nihilistic impression given of American society by post-war cinema proved unacceptable to right-wing elements within the nation's hierarchy, many of which sought to punish Hollywood for its acquiescence in New Deal liberalism and its production of pro-Soviet wartime propaganda. In September 1947, the House Un-American Activities Committee (HUAC) began its investigation into 'communism in motion pictures' by subpoenaing forty-one witnesses, many of whom, like Jack Warner, Louis B. Mayer, Walt Disney, Ronald Reagan, Adolphe Menjou and Gary Cooper, were prepared to identify colleagues they considered to be leftist sympathizers. However, ten 'unfriendly' witnesses – the screenwriters Alvah Bessie, Lester Cole, Ring Lardner, Jr, John Howard Lawson, Albert Maltz, Samuel Ornitz, Adrian Scott and Dalton Trumbo, and the directors Herbert Biberman and Edward Dmytryk – refused to co-operate and were jailed for contempt of Congress.

Prominent film liberals formed the Committee for the First Amendment to champion the cause of the 'Hollywood Ten', but its support dwindled in the face of the 'Waldorf Statement' (issued in November 1947 by the film industry's principal governing bodies), which introduced a blacklist of socialist sympathizers. A brief hiatus followed, during which the studios resumed the production of sanitized escapism, but in 1951, a second HUAC inquiry began insisting that witnesses 'name names' of Party members and fellow travellers. By the conclusion of the third hearing in 1952, 324 artists had been blacklisted, including Joseph Losey, Jules Dassin, Paul Muni, John Garfield and Dorothy Parker, while dozens of others had been marginalized. The fact that both Carl Foreman's anti-HUAC parable *High Noon* (Fred Zinnemann, 1952) and Budd Schulberg's pro-McCarthy apologia *On the Waterfront* (Elia Kazan, 1954) were able to win Academy Awards gives some indication of the divisiveness of the witch-hunt. The tensions engendered by political paranoia pertained until 1960 when Otto Preminger openly hired Dalton Trumbo

89

92

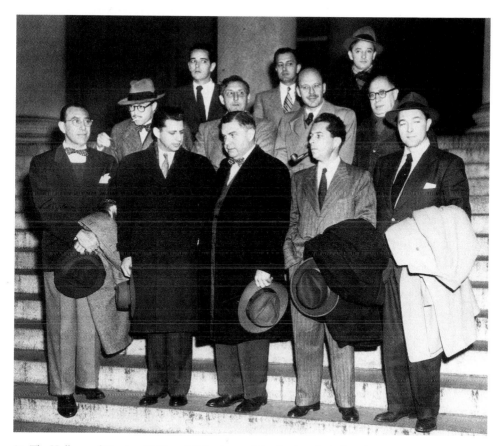

89 The Hollywood Ten (1948). From left, back row: Ring Lardner, Jr., Edward Dmytryk, Adrian Scott; middle: Dalton Trumbo, John Howard Lawson, Alvah Bessie, Samuel Ornitz; front: Herbert Biberman, the lawyers Martin Popper and Robert W. Kenny, Albert Maltz and Lester Cole

(whose script for *The Brave One* had pseudonymously won the 1956 Oscar for Best Original Screenplay) to write *Exodus*, but in the interim its reverberations cruelly dissipated Hollywood's confidence and artistic vitality as it fortified itself to meet the challenge of television.

Ten years after the National Broadcasting Corporation (NBC) had begun regular daily broadcasts in 1939, there were a mere one million television sets in use across the United States, but within a decade there were fifty million and cinema attendances had slumped. Having lost to the radio networks in their attempts to secure station franchises in the late 1940s, and having failed to lure back audiences with theatrical telecasts, the studios sought to exact retribution by refusing to allow the new medium even to promote their stars, let alone screen their features. The snub proved financially detrimental and eventually the front offices had to capitulate. By 1956 the major television networks had not only bought or leased much of Hollywood's pre-1948 catalogue, but they were also broadcasting such shows as *MGM Parade*, *Twentieth Century-Fox Hour* and *Screen Directors Playhouse*. The truce had not been reached without a fight, as Hollywood sought to counter the attraction of small-screen, monochrome entertainment with widescreen, full-colour, stereophonic spectacle.

Whereas in 1947, 88 per cent of all Hollywood features were made in black and white, within a decade more than half were being shot in colour. The transition was facilitated by an anti-trust suit against
XIV Technicolor and the introduction in 1950 of Eastmancolor. Based on
XV the German Agfacolor process, this multilayered stock was compatible with conventional cameras, economic to process and capable of outstanding resolution and colour contrast. Monochrome remained popular, however, for subjects of a sinister or semi-documentary nature.

As with sound, the technique of widescreen projection had been available long before it was commercially adopted: Abel Gance's Polyvision and Paramount's Magnascope were among the systems tried in the 1920s. The studios had been reluctant to speculate during the Depression, but by the 1950s they were willing to try almost anything in order to alleviate their financial predicament.

The first of the new widescreen processes to appear was Cinerama. Originally called Perisphere, it had been demonstrated by the inventor Fred Waller at the 1939 World's Fair in New York as a training device for aerial gunnery. Cinerama required three synchronized cameras interlocked in an arc in order to record, and the images were projected at six times the industry standard onto a curvilinear screen. Exploiting peripheral vision and directional stereo sound to contrive the illusion of depth, films such as *This is Cinerama* (1952) placed the viewer at the centre of the action, but, while visually exhilarating, the process proved of limited narrative value. Despite inducing audiences back to the movies, Cinerama ultimately became prohibitively expensive for producer and exhibitor alike.

Stereoscopic three dimensionality (3-D), which similarly attempted to reproduce depth of vision, also hailed from an earlier cinematic era. Inspired by the stereopticon viewer, both William Friese-Greene and the Lumières had pioneered anaglyphic processes in which film strips, tinted red and blue-green, were projected simultaneously for viewing through spectacles with corresponding lenses. *The Power of Love*, the first feature to utilize monochromatic synthesis, was released in 1922, but with the development of polarized filters by Edwin Land in the 1930s, it was not long before full-colour 3-D films were being produced, initially in Germany and Italy. Shot in Natural Vision, *Bwana Devil* (Arch Oboler, 1952) began Hollywood's flirtation with the process, although the success of *House of Wax* (André de Toth, 1953) hinted at the possibility of a more permanent relationship as all the majors quickly released 'depthies' of their own. Sixty-nine 3-D features, predominantly action and horror films, were made over the next eighteen months, but by late 1954, pictures like Hitchcock's *Dial M for Murder* were being distributed in 'flat' print only. Largely incongruous with serious themes, 3-D failed less because of its inability to overcome the problem of stratified depth or the unpopularity of its polarized glasses, than because of its concomitance with CinemaScope.

Developed by Fox on the basis of the 'Hypergonar' lens, patented by Henri Chrétien for use in tank periscopes during the First World War, CinemaScope compressed in a 2:1 ratio its wide-field image into a standard 35mm frame. This was then 'unsqueezed' during projection by means of a cylindrical compensatory lens. Previously, the traditional aspect ratio of the cinema screen had been 4:3 (or 1.33:1), but Scope increased it to 8:3 (approximately 2.55:1, later reduced to 2.35:1), thus distending the picture and offering enhanced peripheral vision when cast onto a wraparound screen. Following the success of *The Robe* (Henry Koster, 1953), which also boasted four-track stereo sound, Fox made its anamorphic process available to its competitors and by the end of the year all but Paramount had purchased licences.

Equivalent systems soon began to appear around the world, notably Franscope and Dyaliscope (France), Ultrascope and Colorscope (Italy), Tohoscope and Daieiscope (Japan), Sovscope (USSR) and Agascope (Sweden). However, all eventually fell victim to Panavision, an anamorphic process invented by Robert E. Gottschalk that offered virtually distortion-free definition by means of a variable prismatic lens.

Paramount opted for a non-anamorphic process called VistaVision, which ran film through the camera horizontally in order to produce a double-negative that was twice the width and marginally taller than the standard 35mm frame. This was then optically rotated during printing to enable traditional vertical projection. Producing sharp,

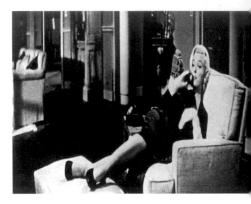

90 Jean Negulesco, *How to Marry a Millionaire* (1953). Marilyn Monroe 'squeezed' onto 35mm film by an anamorphic CinemaScope lens and 'unsqueezed' in projection.

bright pictures, VistaVision, complete with its Perspecta sound system, was popular with exhibitors and audiences alike. Yet it too succumbed to Panavision in 1961, although it is still widely used to achieve special optical effects.

Despite its hegemony in the 1950s, CinemaScope was not without its drawbacks. Distortion was common in close-ups, tracks and lateral movements across the frame, while there were frequent inconsistencies in clarity, colouring and definition. The independent producer Mike Todd was among the first to recognize that wide-gauge stock was more proportionate to dilated photographic fields, and he enjoyed phenomenal succes with *Oklahoma!* (Fred Zinnemann, 1955), which employed both wide-angle lenses and a 70mm strip called Todd-AO. Similar systems followed, including Panavision-70, which produced unsqueezed 65mm negatives, and MGM Camera 65 (later Ultra-Panavision), which produced images of a 2.75:1 aspect ratio by combining both wide-gauge and anamorphic principles.

While assimilating the aesthetic potential of widescreen production, Hollywood followed the precedent set in the early sound era and began to exploit the novelty value of its new technology. Commencing with *War and Peace* (King Vidor, 1956), the studios issued many long, opulent, but statically photographed, 'blockbuster' epics set in biblical (*The Ten Commandments*, Cecil B. De Mille, 1956) and ancient times (*Ben-Hur*, William Wyler, 1959, and *Spartacus*, Stanley Kubrick, 1960). They also produced historical biographies (*El Cid*, Anthony Mann, 1961, and *Lawrence of Arabia*, David Lean, 1962), musicals (*South Pacific*, Joshua Logan, 1958, and *The Sound of Music*, Robert Wise, 1965) and literary adaptations (*Around the World in*

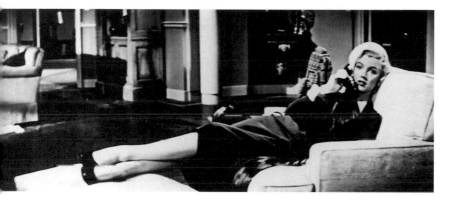

Eighty Days, Michael Anderson, 1956). Commanding unprecedented budgets, these grandiose pictures were increasingly made as 'runaways' in Europe as a means of releasing frozen studio assets, but they soon turned to 'box-office poison' and were largely abandoned after the calamitous *Cleopatra* (Joseph L. Mankiewicz, 1963).

As widescreen's purely technical tribulations were overcome, so was the problem of fusing intimacy and compositional balance with visual magnitude. Film-makers gradually came to appreciate that the wider field's capacity for focal depth enabled them to integrate character more closely with environment and stage dialogue sequences without resort to shot–reverse-shot cutting. Widescreen also encouraged longer takes, thus promoting the aesthetic of *mise-en-scène*, with its emphasis on composition in width and depth rather than montage. Identifiable in the films of Feuillade, von Stroheim, Murnau, Renoir and the Neo-Realists, as well as Griffith and Welles (who employed both techniques), *mise-en-scène* was first championed by the Hollywood veteran Henry King in 1955 and its most influential theoretician was André Bazin. While acknowledging that editing would remain the chief form of filmic assemblage, Bazin endorsed *mise-en-scène* for its ability to preserve the integrity of time and space through the linkage of several focal planes in one shot, thus heightening a scene's 'authenticity', as well as its 'creative' and 'democratic' perspective. The full potential of *mise-en-scène* remained unrealized, however, until the advent of the French New Wave (*see* Chapter 7).

Hollywood, in the meantime, was exceedingly fortunate to enter the widescreen era with so much innovative talent at its disposal, capable of exploiting the new aesthetic in films of all genres. A natural storyteller and keen student of human foible, John Huston (1906–87) had been a screenwriter before making his directorial mark with *The Maltese Falcon* (1941), *Key Largo* and *The Treasure of the Sierra Madre* (both 1948), all starring Humphrey Bogart, with whom he reunited for *The African Queen* (1951). Following the classic *noir* caper *The Asphalt Jungle* (1950), he made a pseudo-documentary version of Stephen Crane's *The Red Badge of Courage* (1951) and subsequently demonstrated a predilection for adaptations, invariably managing to evoke the atmosphere of the original source, whether literary (*The Man Who Would Be King*, 1975, and *The Dead*, 1987) or pulp (*Heaven Knows, Mr Allison*, 1957, and *Prizzi's Honour*, 1985). Another proficient writer-turned-director was Joseph L. Mankiewicz (1909–93), whose credits included *A Letter to Three Wives* (1949), *All About Eve* (1950) and *The Barefoot Contessa* (1954).

Already a feted stage director, Elia Kazan (b. 1909) rapidly established himself as one of Hollywood's leading Neo-Realists with a number of distinguished *noir* and problem pictures in the late 1940s. Throughout the following decade, his work increasingly began to reflect his association with the Actors' Studio (which he helped found in 1947), assisting students of the 'Method', like Marlon Brando (*A Streetcar Named Desire*, 1951, *Viva, Zapata!*, 1952, and *On the Waterfront*, 1954) and James Dean (*East of Eden*, 1955), to discover the 'psychological truthfulness' of their characters. In all, Kazan directed twenty-three Oscar-nominated performances, including nine winners. Following *Baby Doll* (1956), *A Face in the Crowd* (1957) and *Splendor in the Grass* (1961), his projects were of a markedly more personal nature.

Nicholas Ray (1911–79) first began to explore his characteristic themes of isolation and disaffection in the emotionally compact *films gris*, *They Live by Night* (1948) and *Knock on Any Door* (1949) and *noirs*, *In a Lonely Place* (1950) and *On Dangerous Ground* (1951). The evils of conformity also informed his widescreen pictures *Rebel without a Cause* (1955), which made metaphorical use of colour and established James Dean as the archetypal teenage anti-hero, and *Bigger Than Life* (1956). Both films revealed the fine appreciation of space and horizontal line that Ray had developed while a student of the architect Frank Lloyd Wright. Later, after the failure of his blockbusters of the early 1960s, Ray spent much of his life teaching film.

Samuel Fuller (b. 1911), like Ray a cult figure among the critics of *Cahiers du cinéma*, employed an energetic and uniquely personal style that was almost tabloid in sensibility despite the powerful symbolism

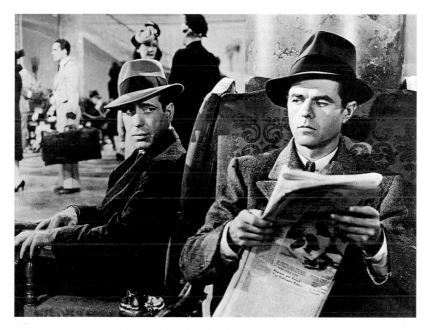

91 John Huston, *The Maltese Falcon* (1941). Humphrey Bogart as the private eye Sam Spade and Elisha Cook, Jr. as the psychotic hoodlum Wilmer Cook in the third film version of Dashiell Hammett's novel.

of its visual imagery. Usually in such traditional genres as the Western (*Forty Guns*, 1957), crime (*Pickup on South Street*, 1953) and war films (*The Steel Helmet*, 1950), Fuller's work had a violence and moral ambiguity that were particularly courageous in view of the blacklist. Equally eclectic were Don Siegel (1912–91) – *Riot in Cell Block 11* (1954), *Invasion of the Body Snatchers* (1956), *Baby Face Nelson* (1957), *Dirty Harry* (1971) and *The Shootist* (1976); and Fred Zinnemann (b. 1907) – *The Men* (1950), *High Noon* (1952), *From Here to Eternity* (1953), *The Nun's Story* (1959) and *A Man for All Seasons* (1966).

Douglas Sirk (1900–87) is best remembered for such colourful, stylized, melodramatic Ross Hunter productions as *Magnificent Obsession* (1954), *All That Heaven Allows*, *Written on the Wind* (both 1956) and *Imitation of Life* (1959), with their ambivalent analysis of middle-class propriety. Yet he was also responsible for impressive war pictures like *A Time to Love and a Time to Die* (1958), which made powerful contrasts between life on the battle and home fronts.

92

165

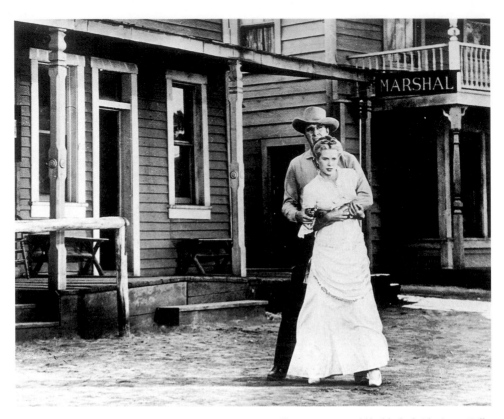

92 Fred Zinnemann, *High Noon* (1952). Killer Ian MacDonald holds the bride Grace Kelly hostage during his feud with her marshal husband, Gary Cooper. The film is often cited as the first 'adult Western' of the 1950s.

Like Sirk an exiled European, Otto Preminger (1906–86) merits consideration as much for his intrepidity as for his film-making. Not content with confounding the blacklist by hiring Dalton Trumbo in 1960, he also played a leading role in the breach of the Production Code. In clearing Roberto Rossellini's *The Miracle* of charges of blasphemy in 1952, the U.S. Supreme Court overturned its decision in the 1915 *Mutual* case which had excluded motion pictures from categorization in the media and thus denied them the right to free speech under the First Amendment. Amidst the following influx of foreign-language films, immune to the strictures of the Code, Preminger produced a succession of pictures on deliberately controversial themes: extra-marital sex (*The Moon is Blue*, 1953); drug addic-

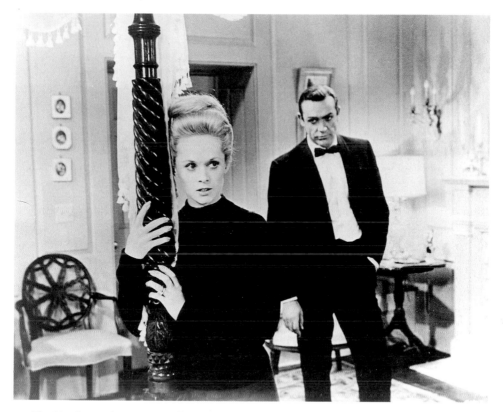

93 Tippi Hedren and Sean Connery in Alfred Hitchcock's *Marnie* (1964). Almost a summation of Hitchcock's stylistic and thematic preoccupations, the film made symbolic use of the colour red, abstract backdrops and inferior back projections to convey Marnie's disturbed state of mind.

tion (*The Man with the Golden Arm*, 1955); rape (*Anatomy of a Murder*, 1959); and political corruption and homosexuality (*Advise and Consent*, 1962). Hopelessly discredited, the Code was abandoned altogether in 1968 in favour of a ratings system ranging from general audience to adult only.

Among the other key directors working in anamorphic widescreen were Robert Aldrich, Stanley Kramer, Robert Rossen, Laszlo Benedek and the veterans Raoul Walsh and George Stevens. Only Alfred Hitchcock chose to work regularly in VistaVision.

After the success of his two immediate post-war films, *Spellbound* (1945) and *Notorious* (1946), Hitchcock began to explore the potential of the long take. However, *Rope* (1948), *Under Capricorn* (1949) and

Stage Fright (1950) all suffered dramaturgically as a result and he felt obliged to restore his reputation with the more obviously commercial *Strangers on a Train* (1951), *I Confess* (1953) and *Dial M for Murder* (1954), although each in its turn was an exceptional example of, respectively, characterization, location shooting and staging in depth.

Having made an uncomfortable comparison between voyeurism and cinema-going in *Rear Window* (1954), Hitchcock produced a string of films in VistaVision, including *To Catch a Thief*, *The Trouble with Harry* (both 1955), a remake of *The Man Who Knew Too Much* (1956) and *Vertigo* (1958). His most psychologically disturbing and technically accomplished film, *Vertigo* employed stylized colour, subjective camera movements (including track-zoom effects) and 360°, or vortical, editing to depict the obsessional attempts of an acrophobic (James Stewart) to transform a shopgirl (Kim Novak) into his supposedly deceased lover. Hitchcock responded to its critical and commercial failure with a classic pursuit thriller, *North by Northwest* (1959), before embarking on his blackest and most cynical and manipulative film, *Psycho* (1960).

Alternately cutting and travelling to deceive the viewer, Hitchcock dispensed a number of perfectly timed visual shocks, not least of which was the infamous 87-shot, 45-second shower sequence, which, with the shrieking violins of Bernard Herrmann's score, came to rival the 'Odessa Steps' as the prime example of cinematic montage. Following
93
The Birds (1963) and *Marnie* (1964), the latter considered by Truffaut to be one of the 'greatest flawed films', Hitchcock's work became increasingly inconsistent. A fatalist and a moralist (in spite of his frequent misogyny), Hitchcock was also a perfectionist, whose preoccupation with form made possible a unique interpretation of the anxieties of his age.

If divestiture and television had prompted the technical experiments of the 1950s, fear of blacklisting was largely responsible for the new directions taken within the Hollywood genres. Comedy struggled to accommodate the widescreen format and besides the films
94
of Judy Holliday and Marilyn Monroe, the manic farces of Dean Martin and Jerry Lewis and the wholesome screwballs of Doris Day and Rock Hudson, there was little of any quality. With Capra and Sturges in decline, the most significant comic talent was Billy Wilder (b. 1906), who cynically explored a range of social, moral and institutional themes in such *comédies noirs* as *Sunset Boulevard* (1950) and *The Seven Year Itch* (1955).

94 Billy Wilder, *Some Like It Hot* (1959). Marilyn Monroe as Sugar Kane, Tony Curtis as Josephine and Jack Lemmon as Daphne performing on board a train with Sweet Sue's Society Syncopaters.

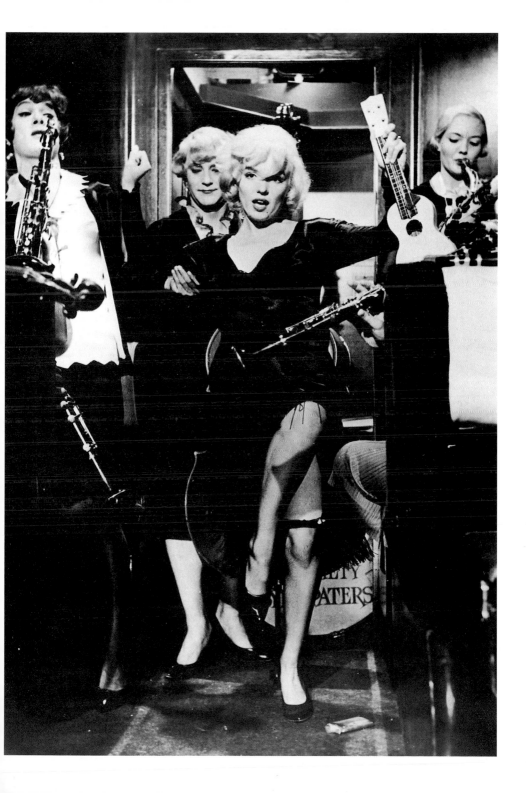

Wilder's 1959 classic *Some Like It Hot* was a spoof of the gangster movie, which had undergone something of a revival in the post-war era. Rooted firmly in *film noir*, 1940s pictures like *I Walk Alone* (Byron Haskin, 1947) and *Force of Evil* (Abraham Polonsky, 1948) had concentrated on the hoodlum in isolation, while the emphasis in the 50s shifted to syndicated crime – for example, *The Enforcer* (Bretaigne Windust, 1950) and *The Big Combo* (Joseph Lewis, 1955). Besides a number of Prohibition mobster biopics, a distinctive sub-genre emerged – the anti-Communist film, most notoriously *My Son John* (Mervyn LeRoy, 1952).

America's post-war crisis of identity was reflected in such 1950s Westerns as *Shane* (George Stevens, 1953), which challenged the idealized frontierism of Ford to present a grimmer view of the violence and values that had actually shaped the West. Developing the theme of the individual at odds with society, the 'psychological' Westerns of Anthony Mann (*Winchester '73*, 1950; *Bend of the River*, 1952, and *The Naked Spur*, 1953) and Budd Boetticher (*The Tall T*, 1957, and *Ride Lonesome*, 1959) – starring James Stewart and Randolph Scott respectively – made exemplary use of the wide screen to augment the genre's topographical symbolism.

First recognized as a distinct genre in the 1950s, science fiction (sci-fi) also explored contemporary issues in a metaphorical manner. Boasting state-of-the-art visual effects by George Pal and Ray Harryhausen, sci-fi had initially speculated on the feasibility of space travel (*Destination Moon*, Irving Pichel, 1950), before coming to reflect mounting Cold War fears of invasion and nuclear obliteration in such films as *The Day the Earth Stood Still* (Robert Wise, 1951), *When Worlds Collide* (Rudolph Maté, 1951), *Invaders from Mars* (William Cameron Menzies, 1953) and *Invasion of the Body Snatchers* (Don Siegel, 1956).

Christian Nyby's *The Thing* (1951) sparked a cycle of 'creature features', in which aliens or monstrous mutations threatened the future of civilization. Produced on shoestring budgets and invariably screened as double-bills or 'drive-in' specials, these movies became the staple of such exploitation studios as Allied Artists and American International Pictures (AIP). Besides Bert Gordon, AIP's most important director was Roger Corman (b. 1926). In addition to sci-fi quickies, Corman was also responsible for the run of Poe adaptations starring Vincent Price that, along with the producer Val Lewton's gothic chillers like *Cat People* (Jacques Tourneur, 1942), were the period's only noteworthy contributions to horror.

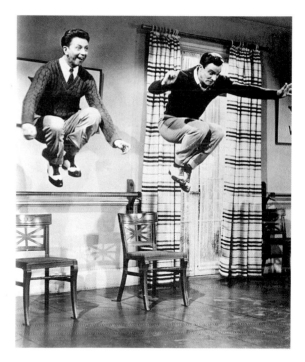

95 Donald O'Connor and Gene Kelly in the 'Moses Supposes' routine from *Singin' in the Rain* (1952), Kelly and Stanley Donen's affectionate spoof of the early days of talkies.

Similarly subjected to budgetary constraint were the small, literate films in the American *Kammerspiel* tradition. Almost Neo-Realist in look, films such as *Marty* (Delbert Mann, 1955) and *Twelve Angry Men* (Sidney Lumet, 1957) were adapted from original 'teleplays' and gave directors such as Richard Brooks, John Frankenheimer and Sam Peckinpah their start in features.

In stark contrast to these dollarwise movies were the high-production value musicals produced by Arthur Freed's unit at MGM. Meticulously using colour, light and décor to establish perspectival space and convey the kinetic energy of the dance, the films of Vincente Minnelli (1903–86) – *Meet Me in St Louis*, 1944; *The Pirate*, 1948; *An American in Paris*, 1951, and *Gigi*, 1958 – and Gene Kelly (b. 1912) and Stanley Donen (b. 1924) – *On the Town*, 1949; *Singin' in the Rain*, 1952, and *It's Always Fair Weather*, 1955 – were notable for their variety of dance styles and their use of numbers to develop character and plot. By 1955, however, musical costs had become so prohibitive that studios were reluctant to consider anything other than Broadway transfers like *The King and I* (Walter Lang, 1956), *West Side Story* (Robert Wise, 1962) and *My Fair Lady* (1964). With the notable later

95

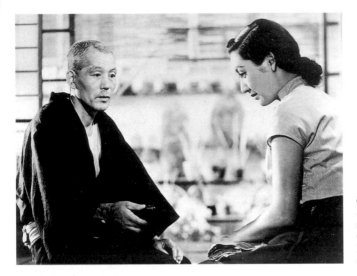

96 Yasujiro Ozu, *Tokyo Story* (1953). Noted for their restraint and naturalism, Chishu Ryu and Setsuko Hara were regular members of Ozu's ensemble.

exceptions of *The Sound of Music* (1965) and the films of Bob Fosse, which displayed a more realistic approach to adult themes (including *Cabaret*, 1972), the musical has rarely since attained such heights.

U.S. forces occupied Japan for seven years after its surrender in 1945, during which time there was an influx of Hollywood films, the *zaibatsu* were purged of war criminals and the proscription of *jidai-geki* meant that some 550 films were confiscated, many of which were destroyed. However, several pre-war film-makers were permitted to resume their careers, Mizoguchi (*The Life of Oharu*, 1952; *Ugetsu*, 1953, and *Sansho the Bailiff*, 1954) and Ozu (*Late Spring*, 1949; *Tokyo Story*, 1953, and *Good Morning*, 1959) in particular producing work of the highest calibre.

Japanese cinema remained largely unknown, however, outside South-East Asia. Showered with prizes at film festivals worldwide, *Rashomon* (Akira Kurosawa, 1950) radically altered the situation. Exploring the relativity of truth, *Rashomon* presented four equally credible accounts (each in a visual style appropriate to its narrator) of a forest encounter between a married couple and a samurai which results in the husband's death. Using incessant and often subjective tracking shots, compositional depth and precision editing, Kurosawa consciously structured the action to challenge accepted notions of perceived reality and filmic truth.

The satirical *shomin-geki Ikiru* (1952) was followed in 1954 by Kurosawa's *jidai-geki* masterpiece, *Seven Samurai*. Spectacular, yet humanistic in its depth of characterization, this 'tapestry of motion'

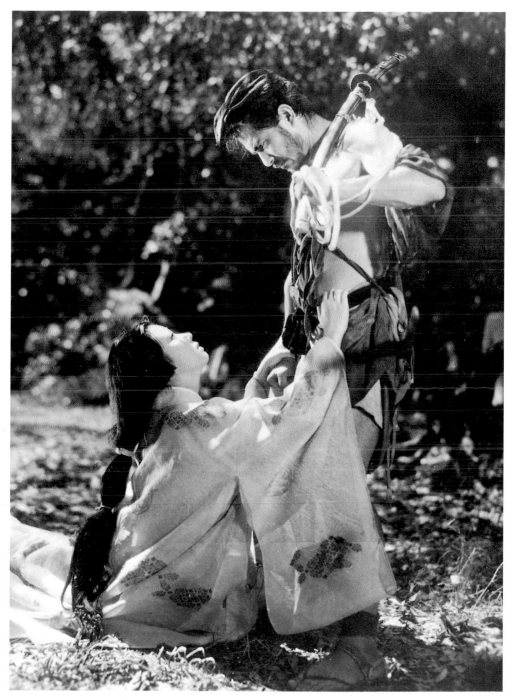

97 Toshiro Mifune as Tajomaru, the bandit, and Machiko Kyo as Masago, the wife, in Akira Kurosawa's *Rashomon* (1950).

again employed complex tracking and editing strategies, particularly in the final battle between the samurai and the bandits, in which Kurosawa combined deep-focus photography, dramatic angles, severe close-ups and variegated audiovisual speeds. The film was remade in Hollywood as *The Magnificent Seven* (John Sturges, 1960) and Kurosawa's later samurai picture, *Yojimbo* (1963), was to have a profound influence on the 'spaghetti' Westerns of Sergio Leone. Kurosawa's final film in the genre, *Kagemusha*, was released in 1980.

While adept at handling original material like *Red Beard* (1965), *Dodes'kaden* (1970) and *Dersu Uzala* (1975), Kurosawa excelled at literary adaptation, using visual symbolism faithfully to recreate the atmosphere of Dostoevsky's *The Idiot* (1951), Gorky's *The Lower Depths* (1957) and Shakespeare's *Macbeth* and *King Lear*, reworked as *Throne of Blood* (1957) and *Ran* (1985) respectively. Involved at every stage of his productions, which were indebted equally to the samurai ethic of *bushido*, Western art and the cinema of John Ford, Kurosawa paved an international path for such film-makers as Teinosuke Kinugasa, Keisuke Kinoshita, Tadashi Imai, Kon Ichikawa, Kaneto Shindo, Masaki Kobayashi and even the 'creature feature' specialist Ishiro Honda.

Besides Kurosawa, at least three other major *auteurs* came to prominence during the 1950s through the proliferation of 'art-house' cinemas and international film festivals like Venice (begun 1932), Cannes (1946) and Berlin (1951): Satyajit Ray (1921–92), a former student of painting under Rabindranath Tagore; Ingmar Bergman (b. 1918), the son of the Lutheran chaplain to the Swedish court; and Luis Buñuel, who returned to film-making fifteen years after the production of his Surrealist documentary *Las Hurdes* (1932).

Satyajit Ray's primary cinematic influences, Renoir and Neo-Realism, were both evident in the films with which he made his name – *Pather Panchali* (1955), *Aparajito* (1957) and *The World of Apu* (1959). Tracing the rites of passage of a poor Bengali boy, the 'Apu trilogy' had a simple, direct narrative style that belied the complexity of its many themes: poverty, the clash of Western and Indian values, the contrast of human cupidity with the constancy of nature and the inevitability of suffering and death. Relying heavily on reaction close-ups and occasional montage sequences to convey emotional or intellectual concepts, Ray also incorporated classical Indian soundtracks by Ravi Shankar to underscore the dramatic tension. His use of non-professionals in an industry firmly founded on a star system, and the discussion of serious themes, when contemporaries like Bimal Roy,

98

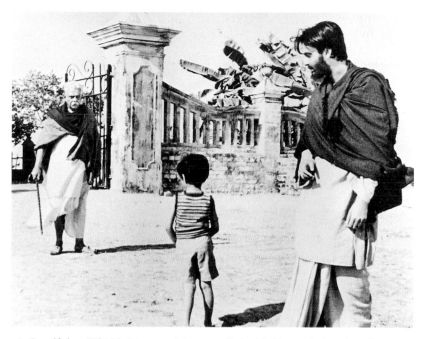

98 Grandfather (Dhirish Mazumder) is reconciled with his son-in-law Apu (Soumitra
Chatterjee) and grandson Kajol (Alok Chakravarty) at the conclusion of *The World of Apu*,
the final part of Satyajit Ray's Apu Trilogy (1955–8).

Guru Dutt, Meboob Khan and Raj Kapoor were concentrating on
traditional escapist musical melodramas, called *masala* socials, and
mythologicals, ensured that the films were never as well received at
home as they were abroad.

Throughout the 1960s, Ray focused on personal relationships and
Bengali culture in such films as *The Goddess* (1960), *The Big City*
(1963), *The Lonely Wife* (1964) and *Days and Nights in the Forest* (1970).
Rebuked for neglecting India's socio-economic and religious prob-
lems, he later demonstrated an increased political commitment in *The
Adversary* (1971), *Distant Thunder* (1973), *The Middleman* (1979) and *An
Enemy of the People* (1989).

Trained in opera and theatre, Ingmar Bergman began his film career
as a scriptwriter. In the immediate post-war decade, he directed a
series of thirteen Expressionist (and occasionally Neo-Realist) pictures
that recalled the themes of Ibsen and Strindberg and the tone of Stiller,

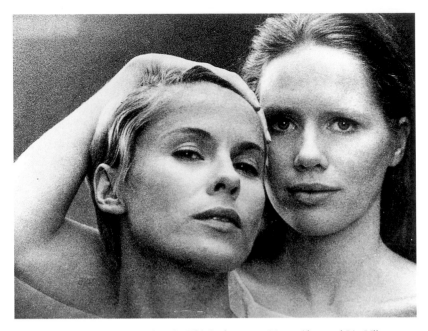

99 Ingmar Bergman, *Persona* (1966). Bibi Andersson as Nurse Alma and Liv Ullmann as the traumatized actress Elisabeth Vogler. Bergman conveyed the gradual transference of her anxiety by a repeated shot of their faces merging into one.

Sjöström and Dreyer. During the production of, among others, *Thirst* (1949), *Summer with Monika* (1952) and *Sawdust and Tinsel* (1953), Bergman established his customary practice of novelizing ideas before developing them into screenplays and forged long-lasting relationships with the lighting cameraman Gunnar Fischer and the performers Max von Sydow, Gunnar Björnstrand, Ingrid Thulin, Eva Dahlbeck, 99 Gunnel Lindblom, and Harriet and Bibi Andersson (also later Liv Ullmann and Erland Josephson).

After *Smiles of a Summer Night* (1955), a sophisticated sex comedy that shared many of the substratum preoccupations of *La Règle du jeu*, Bergman turned to more metaphysical questions. *The Seventh Seal* (1956), an allegory set in a medieval world of plague, sin and intolerance, exploited the visual power of the Swedish landscape and Expressionist lighting (as in the silhouetted 'dance of Death') to examine humanity's relationship to God and the value of life, a theme that recurred in *Wild Strawberries* (1957). Filling the unconscious mind of an elderly professor (Victor Sjöström) with chiaroscuro nightmares and radiant nostalgia as he travels to receive an honorary degree, *Wild Strawberries* was an odyssey through the darker side of the human condition to self-awareness. If these films, along with *Brink of Life* (1958) and *The Virgin Spring* (1960), offered some hope of the existence of God and the human propensity for good, the 'chamber play' trilogy – *Through a Glass Darkly* (1961), *Winter Light* and *The Silence* (both 1963) – was unrelieved in its pessimism.

The last film marked the beginning of Bergman's association with the cinematographer Sven Nykvist and with it a change of visual and thematic emphasis. Assimilating Nykvist's experimentalism, which derived largely from contemporary French and Italian cinema, Bergman's films demonstrated a new ellipticism thanks to the incorporation of alienation devices which disrupted spatial, temporal and causal unity. Ranging from identity and motivation to creativity and perception, his fresh themes were first explored in a second trilogy, comprising *Persona* (1966), *Hour of the Wolf* and *Shame* (both 1968), and subsequently in the intense drama of guilt and rage *The Passion of Anna* (1969), and the opulent study of recollection and compassion *Cries and Whispers* (1972), both of which made expressive use of colour, sound and telephotography.

Having analysed the disintegration of relationships in *Scenes from a Marriage* (1974) and *From the Life of the Marionettes* (1980), Bergman ended his directing career on an optimistic note with *Fanny and Alexander* (1982), which, like his script for Bille August's *The Best Intentions* (1992), contained numerous autobiographical references and suggested a restoration of the faith in illusion and creation that had lain dormant since *The Face* (1958).

Essentially a religious artist, Bergman considered the production of a film to be a collective enterprise similar to the construction of a medieval cathedral. Manifesting great integrity, courage and insight, his work revealed the cinema's ability to dissect the problems, emotions and ironies of life in a visually arresting and intellectually challenging way.

While Bergman invariably remained within the same state–subsidized environment, Luis Buñuel was an itinerant prepared to operate in more commercially oriented industries. After spells as a producer in Europe, war-documentary editor in New York and Spanish-version supervisor in Hollywood, he drifted to Mexico, where on the back of two popular comedies, he was offered the chance to direct *Los Olvidados* (1950). Disconcertingly combining Surrealism, Freudianism

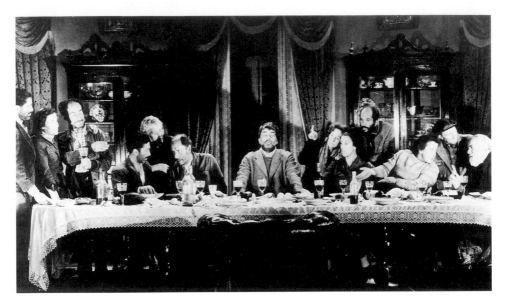

100 Parodying Leonardo's *Last Supper*, the beggars' banquet from *Viridiana* (1961), Luis Buñuel's savage satire on Fascism and Catholicism, was accompanied by excerpts from Handel's *Messiah*.

and austere realism, the film was as much a study of human baseness and malignancy as a portrait of inner city delinquency. Although it restored Buñuel's reputation, it did nothing to free him from the constraints of tight budgets and short production schedules under which he made *Susana* (1951), *Mexican Bus Ride* (1952) and highly individual adaptations of *Robinson Crusoe* (1952) and *Wuthering Heights* (1953).

Commuting between Mexico and Europe, Buñuel next entered a prolific period, during which he employed an almost unobtrusive visual style and varying degrees of satiric savagery to explore his most characteristic themes: the hypocrisy and invalidity of Catholicism (*El*, 1952; *Nazarín*, 1958; *Viridiana*, 1961, and *Simon of the Desert*, 1965); the tyranny of bourgeois conformity (*The Criminal Life of Archibaldo de la Cruz*, 1955, and *The Exterminating Angel*, 1962) and the evil of fascism (*Cela s'appelle l'aurore*, 1955; *Evil Eden*, 1956; *Republic of Sin*, 1960, and *The Diary of a Chambermaid*, 1964).

Made in France and linked by the themes of erotic infatuation (*Belle de jour*, 1967; *Tristana*, 1970, and *That Obscure Object of Desire*, 1977) and the intractability of convention (*The Discreet Charm of the Bourgeoisie*, 1972, and *The Phantom of Liberty*, 1974), Buñuel's later

100

films were significantly more complex in style and mellow in approach, yet they retained the unique blend of experiment, anarchy and morality that made him one of cinema's most original and subversive artists.

The same could not be said for J. Arthur Rank, whose organization was at the forefront of the post-war British obsession with breaking into the American market. However, Hollywood was far more adept at the production of novelettish melodramas and wartime reconstructions than Rank and Gainsborough, and only Alexander Korda managed to make any headway, courtesy of a series of co-productions and the sale of the London Films catalogue to network television. Ironically, the most successful films of the period were those that exploited British cinema's traditional predisposition for comedy and literary adaptation.   101

Produced by Michael Balcon and directed by Henry Cornelius (*Passport to Pimlico*, 1949), Robert Hamer (*Kind Hearts and Coronets*,   102 1949), Charles Crichton (*The Lavender Hill Mob*, 1951) and Alexander

101 Vivien Leigh and Claude Rains on the set of Gabriel Pascal's adaptation of George Bernard Shaw's *Caesar and Cleopatra* (1945).

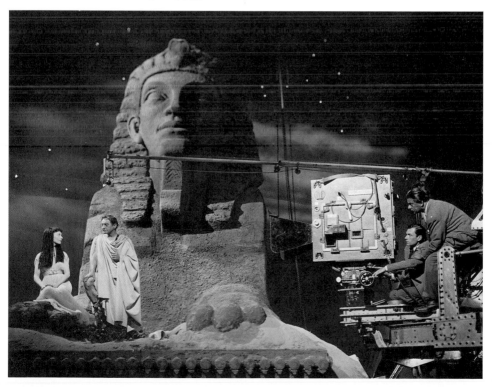

Mackendrick (*The Man in the White Suit*, 1951, and *The Ladykillers*, 1955), the Ealing comedies benefitted from their intelligent scripts, small scale and adroit playing, particularly by Alec Guinness.

Reverential and meticulously crafted, the era's adaptations were made by the country's most distinguished talents, Laurence Olivier (*Hamlet*, 1948, and *Richard III*, 1955), David Lean (*Brief Encounter*, 1945; *Great Expectations*, 1946, and *Oliver Twist*, 1948) and Anthony Asquith (*The Winslow Boy*, 1948; *The Browning Version*, 1951, and *The Importance of Being Earnest*, 1952). In spite of their more stylized visual approach, Thorold Dickinson (*The Queen of Spades*, 1949), Carol Reed (*Odd Man Out*, 1946; *The Fallen Idol*, 1948, and *The Third Man*), and Michael Powell and Emeric Pressburger (*Black Narcissus*, 1946; *The Red Shoes*, 1948, and *The Tales of Hoffman*, 1951) were also considered key contributors to the staple.

Post-war French cinema suffered from a similar over-emphasis on adaptation. Indeed, the pictures within the 'Tradition of Quality' gave such precedence to the dialogue of scenarists like Charles Spaak, Jean Aurenche, Pierre Bost and Jacques Sigurd over visual symbolism that François Truffaut denounced them as writers' films twice over. Moreover, many of the directors operating within the 'Tradition' and contemporary *film noir* were so preoccupied with the stylistic representation of reality that they were frequently guilty of lapses into cold academicism.

Expertly played and meticulously constructed, French films at this time were, thus, largely made by commercial craftsmen rather than inspired artists. Claude Autant-Lara (*The Devil in the Flesh*, 1947) and Jacqueline Audry (*Huis Clos*, 1954) were the most competent adaptors, while Yves Allégret (*Such a Pretty Little Beach*, 1949), Henri-Georges Clouzot (*Wages of Fear*, 1953, and *Les Diaboliques*, 1954) and André Cayatte (*Let Justice Be Done*, 1950) were among the leading practitioners of *noir*.

Exhibiting marginally more individualism were René Clément (b. 1913), whose best films focused on the war (*The Battle of the Rails*, 1946; *Les Maudits*, 1947, and *Jeux interdits*, 1952), Jacques Becker, who specialized in psychological comedies (*Antoine et Antoinette*, 1947, and *Edouard et Caroline*, 1951) and thrillers (*Casque d'Or*, 1952, and *Grisbi*, 1953), and Jean-Pierre Melville (*Les Enfants terribles*, 1949, and *Bob le flambeur*, 1955), whose independent productions were to impress the New Wave.

However, Jean Cocteau (1889–1963), a leading exponent of the literate tendency, and the studio stylist Max Ophüls (1902–57) both

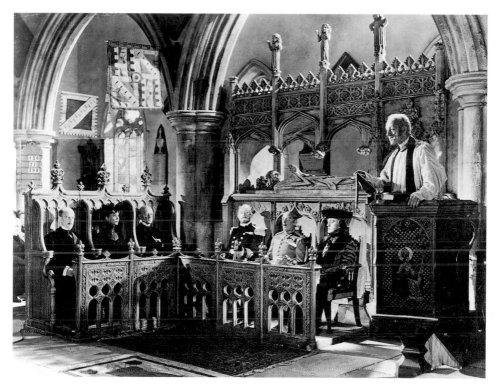

102 Valerie Hobson as the grieving widow and Alec Guinness as the surviving members of the d'Ascoyne family in Robert Hamer's *Kind Hearts and Coronets* (1949).

proved that personal visions were compatible with 'Quality'. In contrast to the claustrophobic realism of *Les Parents terribles* (1948), much of the rest of Cocteau's work revealed a fascination with formative expressionism, in other words, the method of cinematically reproducing imagined realities by means of material surfaces. Drawing its inspiration from the paintings of Vermeer, his allegorical retelling of *Beauty and the Beast* (1946) used luminous monochrome photography and Mélièsian trickery to explore contemporary morality. Comparable techniques were later employed to investigate the process of artistic inspiration in *Orphée* (1950) and the links between poetry, the subconscious and death in the confessional *Le Testament d'Orphée* (1959).

More nomadic even than Buñuel, Ophüls made his twenty-one films in six different countries. He arrived in France in 1950 after a fruitful spell in Hollywood that had yielded the compelling melo-

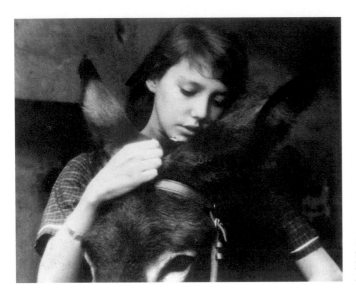

103 Anne Wiazemsky with the true star of Robert Bresson's charming parable, *Au Hasard, Balthazar* (1966).

drama *Letter from an Unknown Woman* (1948) and the 1949 *films noirs* *Caught* and *The Reckless Moment*. Renowned for his fidelity to period detail, graceful camera elaborations and genius for intra-frame composition (that owed much to both German Expressionism and French Impressionism), Ophüls imbued films like *La Ronde* (1950), *Le Plaisir* (1951) and *Madame De . . .* (1953) with the sociological insight of von Stroheim, the cynical wit of Lubitsch and the textural finesse of von Sternberg. His final picture was *Lola Montès* (1955), an achronological memoir of the celebrated nineteenth-century courtesan. Employing stylized tones and décor to convey the artificiality of human emotion, Ophüls kept Christian Matras's camera in constant circulatory motion throughout the lengthy takes, often framing through verticals to break the CinemaScopic space. The film was a perfectly executed exercise in widescreen *mise-en-scène*, but it was callously cut and re-edited by its producers after its failure at the box office.

Despite operating within what *Cahiers* critics called '*cinéma du papa*', Cocteau and Ophüls exerted considerable influence over the filmmakers of the New Wave. The latter were to be even more indebted to the films of Robert Bresson (1907–82), Jacques Tati (1908–82) and the 50s' documentary movement.

A former screenwriter, Bresson's wartime pictures, *Les Anges du péché* (1943) and *Les Dames du Bois de Boulogne* (1945) were very much in the scenarist tradition. However, with *The Diary of a Country Priest* (1950) and *A Man Escaped* (1956), his work began to exhibit an uncompromising psychological realism born of an ascetic approach to dialogue, performance and *mise-en-scène*. All with literary antecedents, precisely constructed films like *Pickpocket* (1959), *The Trial of Joan of Arc* (1962) and *Au Hasard, Balthazar* (1966) and the more pessimistic *A Gentle Creature* (1969), *Four Nights of a Dreamer* (1971) and *L'Argent* (1983) explored the nature of human spirituality through the crises of individuals in isolation. Thematically and stylistically similar to Dreyer, Bresson's oeuvre was much admired by Bazin for its coalescence of dialogue and silent-screen poetry.   103

There was something of the sophisticated silent clowning of Linder, Chaplin and Keaton in the restrained mime of Jacques Tati. Blending satire, slapstick and character comedy, *Jour de fête* (1948), *M. Hulot's Holiday* (1953), *Mon Oncle* (1958), *Playtime* (1967) and *Traffic* (1971) were all based on acute observation of human behaviour and an intel-   104

104 The English version of Jacques Tati's *M. Hulot's Holiday* (1953) opens with a caption reading: 'Don't look for a plot, for a holiday is meant purely for fun.' However, behind the inspired comedy was an audacious assault on the narrative conventions that had sustained the cinema since Griffith.

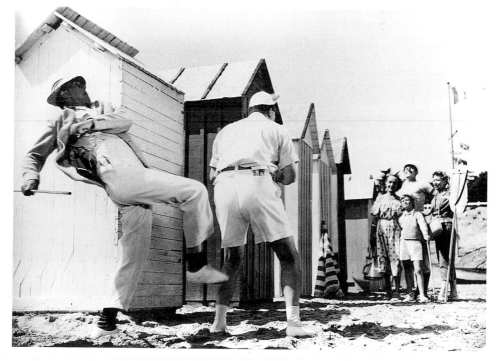

ligent appreciation of the absurdities and inefficiency of the modern world. Always given their own time and space in which to develop, Tati's gags belied their puntilious preparation and made inspired use of props and exaggerated sound. At the time of his death, he was working on another vehicle for his gangling, genial *alter ego* M. Hulot, which was to be called, aptly, *Confusion*.

The documentary movement was one of the New Wave's most significant stylistic influences. Jean Grémillon (*The Sixth of June at Dawn*, 1945), Georges Rouqier (*Farrebique*, 1946), Roger Leenhardt (*The Last Holiday*, 1948) and Alain Resnais (*Nuit et brouillard*, 1955) all made profound contributions, but the movement's most important film-maker was undoubtedly Georges Franju (1912–87). A co-founder (with Henri Langlois) of the national film archive, La Cinémathèque Française (1937), Franju drew on Expressionism and realism to achieve the blend of horror and lyricism that characterized such films as *The Blood of the Beasts* (1949), *Hôtel des Invalides* (1951) and his debut feature, the Surrealist semi-documentary, *The Keepers* (1958).

Harking back to the work of Vigo and the Poetic Realists, as well as anticipating the radicalism of the *Cahiers* generation, Franju's work can be seen as a vital link between traditional French cinema and the New Wave which, according to many critics, first broke in 1954 with Agnès Varda's *La Pointe courte*.

CHAPTER SEVEN

New Inspirations 1959–70

'A classic film cannot translate the real rhythm of modern life', wrote Alain Resnais. 'Modern life is fragmented, everyone feels that. Painting, as well as literature, bears witness to it, so why should the cinema not do so as well, instead of clinging to the traditional linear narrative.' In 1959, Resnais's *Hiroshima, Mon Amour* was one of three features, along with François Truffaut's *The 400 Blows* and Jean-Luc Godard's *Breathless*, to demonstrate the emergence of a new audio-visual language that permitted the kind of dramaturgical Impressionism that Resnais had envisaged.

Crucial to the evolution of 'a means of expression as supple and subtle as that of written language' was the concept of *caméra-stylo* ('camera-pen'), originally conceived by the critic and film-maker Alexandre Astruc in an article published in *L'Ecran français* in 1948. His contention that the director was the author of a film was christened '*la politique des auteurs*' by Truffaut in his 1954 assault on the 'Tradition of Quality', entitled 'A Certain Tendency in French Cinema'. According to '*auteur* theory', the most significant films were those that bore the 'signature' of their directors by proclaiming their personalities and key themes. Among those accorded a place in this *cinéma d'auteurs* were Gance, Vigo, Rossellini, Renoir, Cocteau, Ophüls and Bresson, as well as such Hollywood *metteurs en-scène* as Lang, Hawks, Ford, Hitchcock, Welles and Nicholas Ray.

Truffaut's essay had appeared in the film journal *Cahiers du cinéma*, which, under the joint editorship of André Bazin and Jacques Doniol-Valcroze, vigorously advocated the principles of *mise-en-scène* and *la politique des auteurs*. Among its other regular contributors were young *cinéphiles* like Claude Chabrol, Jean-Luc Godard, Jacques Rivette and Eric Rohmer, who, under the tutelage of Henri Langlois at the Cinémathèque Français, had come to appreciate the mastery of past *auteurs* and the inadequacy of contemporary main-stream cinema. Langlois encouraged them to put their theories into practice and, inspired by the critical acclaim of Agnès Varda's *La Pointe courte* (1954) and the commercial success of Roger Vadim's

And God Created Woman (1956), they completed a number of 16mm shorts, including *Le Coup de Berger*, directed by Rivette in 1956, *Les Mistons* (Truffaut, 1957) and *All Boys Are Named Patrick* (Godard, also 1957).

Reflecting all the New Wave's main aesthetic concerns, these early films also demonstrated many of the movement's most characteristic technical traits. Prime among them were location shooting (using natural light, direct sound and hand-held cameras), improvisation, homages to admired *auteurs*, private jokes and elliptical editing. These and uniquely cinematic devices such as irising, obtrusive camera movements, variegated speeds, sudden shifts in shot distance and jump cuts were consciously used by the New Wave *cinéastes* to disrupt the temporal and spatial continuity of the traditional narrative. In addition, they drew the audience's attention to the self-reflexivity of a film and the power of the *auteur* over its creation and even its perception. Indeed, so determined were they to convey the 'filmicness' of their work that many of them inserted shots of the very paraphernalia of production into the action. Technical innovation was complemented by dramaturgical experiment, with loose causal connections, disconcerting shifts in tone, digressions, ill-defined character motivations and ambiguous conclusions, all reinforcing the aesthetic distance between the viewer and the film.

Such was the initial impact of the New Wave that more than a hundred directors managed to raise funds for their debut features between 1959 and 1962. However, the *nouvelle vague* soon ceased to function as a collective phenomenon and the subsequent influence that a small group of its constituent members has continued to exert over French cinema derives wholly from the success of their own highly individual visions.

The most commercially successful of this coterie was François Truffaut (1932–84). Influenced by Renoir, Hitchcock, *film noir* and the Hollywood B movie, Truffaut had been the most caustic of the *Cahiers* critics. But in spite of giving the *nouvelle vague* its initial impetus – when *The 400 Blows* took the Best Direction prize at the 1959 Cannes Film Festival – he ultimately proved to be among its most traditional directors. Photographed by Henri Decaë, *The 400 Blows* was an austere account of adolescence that consciously evoked Neo-Realism, Vigo's *Zéro de conduite* and Murnau's camera subjectivity. Made for only $75,000, it marked the beginning of a semi-autobiographical series, comprising the *Antoine and Colette* episode from the portmanteau film *Love at Twenty* (1962), *Stolen Kisses* (1968), *Bed and*

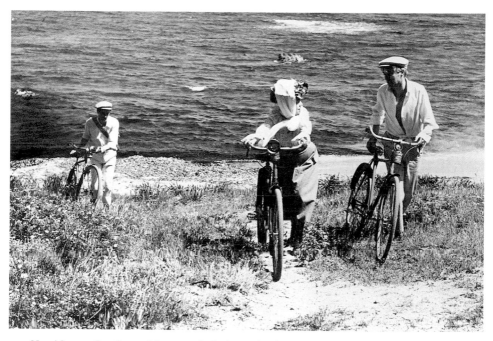

105 Henri Serre as Jim, Jeanne Moreau as Catherine and Oskar Werner as Jules in François Truffaut's *Jules et Jim* (1961). Alluding to all periods of cinema history and a wide range of artistic, literary, dramatic and musical sources, Truffaut's adaptation of Henri-Pierre Roché's novel was a triumphant synthesis of 'Tradition of Quality' and *nouvelle vague*.

Board (1970) and *Love on the Run* (1979), which featured Jean-Pierre Léaud as its central character, Antoine Doinel.

In keeping with his reputation as the scourge of the 'Tradition of Quality', Truffaut approached the task of adaptation, whether from literature or pulp fiction, as an *auteur* and not as a 'gentleman who added the pictures'. Full of visual puns and quotations from films across the Hollywood generic range, the gangster pastiche *Shoot the Pianist* (1960) was followed by *Jules et Jim* (1961), a tribute to Poetic Realism that owed much to its deft re-creation of period, a lyrical script and Edgar G. Ulmer's Western *The Naked Dawn* (1956). Expertly played by Jeanne Moreau, Oskar Werner and Henri Serre and shot by the leading New Wave cinematographer Raoul Coutard, the film made exceptional use of telephoto zooms, undercranking, freeze frames and anamorphic distortion to sustain its fatalism and explore a key Truffaut contention that 'monogamy is impossible, but anything else is worse'.

105

Later pictures, such as *The Wild Child* (1970), *The Story of Adèle H.* (1975), *The Green Room* (1978), *The Last Metro* (1980) and the Hitchcockian thrillers *The Bride Wore Black* (1967), *Mississippi Mermaid* (1969) and *Finally Sunday* (1983), were similarly derived from written sources and prompted some critics to accuse Truffaut of resorting to the mainstream stratagems he had sought so hard to discredit. However, each film demonstrated fully Truffaut's fluency in the cinematic language he had helped to formulate, although none was as bold as *Day for Night* (1973), his self-reflexive paean to film-making, in its blurring of the distinction between illusion and reality.

Markedly more radical in form and content than the work of Truffaut was that of Jean-Luc Godard (b. 1930), the most stylistically and ideologically militant of the *Cahiers* film-makers. 'The whole New Wave', he wrote, 'can be defined, in part, by its new relationship to fiction and reality', and Godard has devoted each of the four distinct phases of his career to redefining that relationship in order to exploit cinema's potential for intellectual, political and artistic expression.

Based on a Truffaut story, Godard's debut feature, *Breathless*, contained virtually every cinematic device associated with the *nouvelle vague* and is widely considered to be its most influential film. A homage to the fatalistic anti-heroes of Jean Gabin and Humphrey Bogart, it was dedicated to the U.S. B-movie studio Monogram and was the first of a number of pictures similarly modelled on *film noir* and the gangster genre – *The Little Soldier* (1960), *Band of Outsiders* (1964), *Alphaville* (1965), *Pierrot-le-fou* (1965) and *Made in U.S.A.* (1966).

106

While engaged in the production of these parodic tributes, Godard also contributed to seven portmanteau films and embarked on a sequence of 'critical essays', including *It's My Life* (1962), *Les Carabiniers* (1963), *A Married Woman* (1964), *Masculin/féminin* (1966), *Two or Three Things I Know About Her* (1966), *La Chinoise* (1967) and *Weekend* (1967). Increasingly political in tone and experimental in form, these self-reflexive exercises incorporated interviews, colloquies, speeches to camera, statistics, slogans, symbols and calligraphy into the most casual narrative structures in order to expose both the redundancy of traditional cinematic language and the decadence of Western capitalism.

With *Le Gai Savoir* (1968), Godard entered an even more radical phase. Rejecting his *auteur* status, he formed the Dziga-Vertov Group with the Maoist intellectual Jean-Pierre Gorin in order to make 'political films politically'. Although revolutionary in their use of audio-

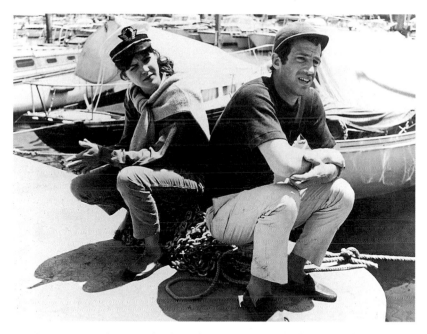

106 Anna Karina and Jean-Paul Belmondo in Jean-Luc Godard's *Pierrot-le-fou* (1965). An adaptation without a script of Lionel White's novel *Obsession*, Godard's 'completely spontaneous film' was a bold amalgam of pulp fiction, *hommage*, and literary and philosophical reference.

visual imagery to address a range of contemporary issues, the eleven 'essays' that resulted from this collaboration, among them *British Sounds* (1969), *Wind from the East* (1969) and *Tout va bien* (1972), tended to demonstrate that Godard's major preoccupations were with communication and the process of film-making rather than with political agitation.

Godard parted from Gorin in 1973 and began to investigate, in works like *Numéro deux* (1975) and *Six Times Two* (1976), the possibility of achieving fresh perspectives on cinematic reality through a combination of film and videotape. He resumed production for theatrical exhibition in 1980 with *Sauve qui peut (la vie)* and in subsequent features like *Passion* (1982), *First Name: Carmen* (1983), *Hail, Mary* (1984), *Detective* (1985) and *King Lear* (1987) he has attempted to acquire a fuller understanding of the nature and meaning of cinema by launching an assault on the assumptions of the New Wave itself.

Every bit as prolific as Godard, but considerably more conventional in subject and style, Claude Chabrol (b. 1930) had been the first *Cahiers* critic to make features. However, the failure of *Les Bonnes Femmes* (1960) to repeat the success of *Le Beau Serge* (1958) and *Les Cousins* (1959) consigned him to the production of mainstream thrillers for much of the next decade. Indeed, apart from a series of stylish Hitchcock *hommages* exploring Chabrol's key themes of obsession and compulsion (*Les Biches*, 1968, and *La Rupture*, 1970) and the impact of murder on small social groups (*The Unfaithful Wife*, 1968, *Killer!*, 1969, and *The Butcher*, 1970), his later career has been plagued by inconsistency. But the psychological insight and ironic detachment of his work have made Chabrol one of France's most popular directors.

Chabrol's production company, AJYM, financed the first film of his *Cahiers* colleagues Jacques Rivette (b. 1928) and Eric Rohmer (b. 1920). Truffaut claimed that the New Wave began 'thanks to Rivette' and *Cahiers* deemed his debut feature, *Paris Belongs to Us* (1960), 'the most significant and most resolutely modern work of the new cinema'. All the same, Rivette has struggled to find a niche for such long, stately and complex films as *La Religieuse* (1965), *L'Amour fou* (1968), *Céline and Julie Go Boating* (1974) and *La Belle noiseuse* (1991), in spite of their remarkable integrity and their insight into the mysteries of identity and the mechanics of the creative process.

If Rivette was the novelist of the New Wave, then Eric Rohmer, Bazin's successor as editor of *Cahiers du cinéma*, was its finest exponent of the short story. Rohmer considers his to be a 'cinema of thoughts rather than actions', dealing 'less with what people do than with what is going on in their minds while they are doing it'. His first cycle of wry, philosophical, yet uniquely cinematic chamber dramas, 'Six Moral Tales' (1962–72), explored the disruptive influence on personal identity of sexual attraction and began his long-term collaboration with the cinematographer Nestor Almendros. The equally talkative and intimate 'Comedies and Proverbs' sextet (1980–87) focused on the resilience of capricious youth in the face of emotional crisis, a theme which is shared by the later 'Four Seasons' cycle.

Rohmer was the last to make the transition from *Cahiers* critic to *auteur*, but not all the film-makers traditionally associated with the *nouvelle vague* trod the same path. Many were already working within the film industry when the New Wave came to prominence, among them members of the so-called 'Left Bank School' like Alain Resnais, Agnès Varda, Jacques Demy, Chris Marker and Louis Malle, who owed allegiance to neither camp.

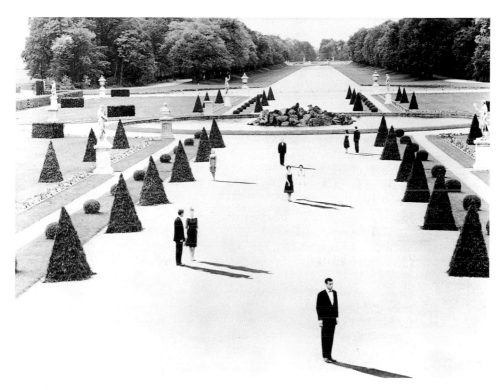

107 Alain Resnais, *Last Year at Marienbad* (1961). Shot in Dyaliscope by Sacha Vierny, this complex, modernist study of the nature of reality made symbolic use of tracking shots and rigid geometric compositions.

A former editor and documentarist, Alain Resnais (b. 1932) considered film-making to be a collective art and always worked closely with his screenwriters (invariably novelists such as Jean Cayrol, Marguerite Duras and Alain Robbe-Grillet) and the cinematographer Sacha Vierny in order to translate the written word into visual poetry. Heavily influenced by Henri Bergson's theories of time and 'creative evolution', Resnais produced complex, allusive and austere films in which he sought to compensate for his medium's lack of 'true syntax' by creating 'a form of cinema which would come near to the novel without having its rules'. His preoccupation with time and memory informed all his major films, including *Hiroshima, Mon Amour* (1959), *Last Year at Marienbad* (1961), *Muriel* (1963) and *The War Is Over* 1966), 107
and inspired such characteristic technical traits as the elliptical transition between the objective and subjective narrative modes and his use

of stylized tracking shots to present the past, present and future upon the same spatial and temporal plane. Resnais's attempt to fashion a 'cinema of pure association' by representing 'the complexity of thought and its mechanisms' on the screen earned him the reputation with 1960s audiences of being a 'difficult' director. However, with later films like *Stavisky* (1974), *Providence* (1977), *My American Uncle* (1980), *Mélo* (1986) and *Smoking/No Smoking* (1994) he achieved a degree of popular appeal more commensurate with his critical status.

The *Cahiers* critics often supported one another in the production of their earliest features, and Resnais offered similar encouragement to Chris Marker and Agnès Varda (b. 1928), for whom he edited *La Pointe courte* in 1954. While this film, with its blend of fiction and documentary, established Varda as a genuine *auteur* and 'the mother of the New Wave', she was unable to raise funds for another feature until 1961. Chronicling a singer's restless wait to discover if she has cancer, *Cleo from Five to Seven* focused on Simone de Beauvoir's maxim that 'one isn't born a woman, one becomes one', a theme that was to recur in *Le Bonheur* (1965), *One Sings, the Other Doesn't* (1977) and *Vagabonde* (1985), each of which was notable for its intellectual rigour and powerful natural imagery. In *Jacquot de Nantes* (1991), Varda recalled the childhood fascination with cinema of her husband Jacques Demy (1931–90), whose bittersweet homages to Ophüls and Gene Kelly – *Lola* (1961), *The Umbrellas of Cherbourg* (1964) and *The Young Girls of Rochefort* (1967) – remain among the most fondly remembered films of the entire New Wave.

While Resnais and Varda sought to explore the key Left Bank themes of 'the manipulation of time and the paradox of memory' through stylized narrative, Chris Marker (b. 1921) preferred to do so through the documentary. Primarily influenced by *cinéma-vérité* (a technique developed from the style of Vertov's Kino Pravda and Flaherty by Jean Rouch in the course of making *Chronicle of a Summer*, 1961, and *Punishment*, 1963), Marker combined visual poetry and radical politics in film essays like *Cuba, si!* (1961), *Le Joli Mai* (1963) and *Far from Vietnam* (1967), which he supervised for a Marxist collective.

Louis Malle (b. 1932) also began his career as a documentarist, co-directing *The Silent World* with the underwater explorer Jacques-Yves Cousteau in 1955. Although he had already established his reputation with *Lift to the Scaffold* (1957) and *Les Amants* (1958) before the *nouvelle vague* emerged, Malle has traditionally been associated with it, even though his films have a stylistic and thematic eclecticism that is hardly in keeping with *la politique des auteurs*. However, in films like *Zazie dans le métro* (1960) *Le Feu follet* (1963), *Dearest Love* (1971), *Lacombe Lucien* (1974), *My Dinner with André* (1981) to *Vanya on 42nd Street* (1994), Malle has consistently demonstrated the kind of cinematic ingenuity and restless intelligence that lie at the very heart of the New Wave.

Notwithstanding their thematic and stylistic diversity, the film-makers of the French New Wave shared a desire to demolish the conventions that had sustained the narrative film since Griffith and replace them with an audiovisual language sufficiently eloquent and malleable to provide anyone working within the art form with a rich and powerful means of self-expression. Such was the success of their undertaking that film industries worldwide felt the impact of the *nouvelle vague*, many experiencing 'new waves' of their own.

By the mid-1950s, the British cinema, like the French, had become hidebound by a bourgeois tradition of quality. Among its chief critics were Lindsay Anderson (b. 1923) and Karel Reisz (b. 1926), who as editors of the Oxford University film journal *Sequence* had ceaselessly accused producers like Korda and Rank of complacently allowing Britain to become an outpost of Hollywood. In 1954, they formed the Free Cinema movement with the intention of making personal film statements that reflected their 'belief in freedom, in the importance of

108 Laurence Harvey as Joe Lampton on the streets of Warnley in Jack Clayton's influential adaptation of John Braine's novel *Room at the Top* (1958).

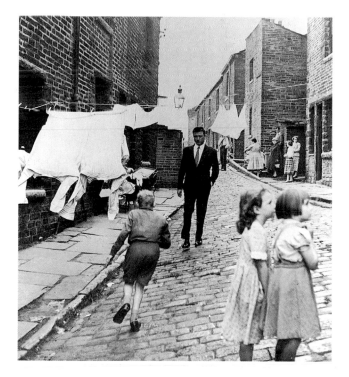

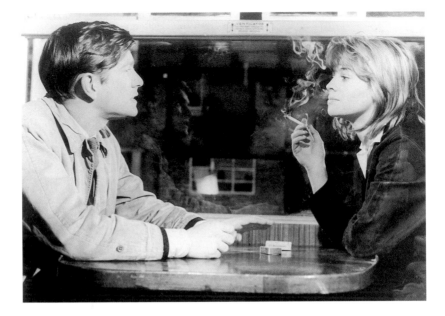

people and in the significance of the everyday'. Although Anderson's documentaries *O Dreamland* (1953) and *Every Day Except Christmas* (1957), and Reisz's *Momma Don't Allow* (with Tony Richardson, 1955) and *We Are the Lambeth Boys* (1958) played a significant role in the evolution of a social realist cinema, its real impetus came, ironically, from adaptations of the unceremonious studies of rebellious proletarian youth that had revolutionized late 1950s literature and theatre.

Shot on location against the grim backdrop of the industrial north, *Room at the Top* (Jack Clayton, 1958) and *Look Back in Anger* (Tony Richardson, 1959) were the first of these so-called 'kitchen sink dramas' to be filmed. Subsequent features like *Saturday Night, Sunday Morning* (Karel Reisz, 1960), *This Sporting Life* (Lindsay Anderson, 1963), Tony Richardson's *A Taste of Honey* (1961) and *The Loneliness of the Long Distance Runner* (1962), and John Schlesinger's *A Kind of Loving* (1962) and *Billy Liar* (1963) were markedly less mannered, particularly in their use of abrasive vernacular speech, and more indebted to the techniques of the Free Cinema and the *nouvelle vague*. However, the British New Cinema, like the French New Wave, began to disintegrate around 1963 to be succeeded by a brief vogue for films like *Darling* (John Schlesinger, 1965), *The Knack* (Richard Lester, 1965),

108

109

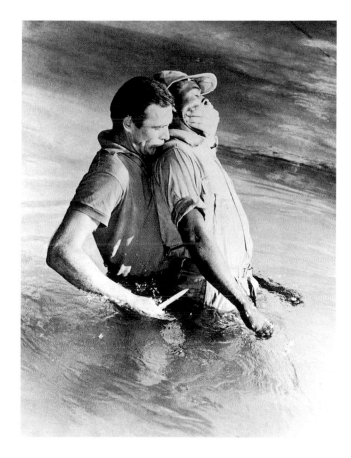

109 Julie Christie offers Tom Courtenay a tangible escape from his grim home town in swinging London in John Schlesinger's adaptation of Keith Waterhouse's *Billy Liar* (1963).

110 Terence Young, *Dr No* (1962). Sean Connery in the first of his 7 outings as agent 007, James Bond.

Alfie (Lewis Gilbert, 1966) and *Georgy Girl* (Silvio Narizzano, 1966), which centred on 'swinging London'. The majority of its members drifted into commercial production and only Anderson (*If. . .*, 1968, and *O Lucky Man*, 1973) persisted in making fiercely iconoclastic films.

Enticed by the commercial success of social realism and the cycle of James Bond adventures (that had begun with *Dr No* in 1962), 110 Hollywood began to invest heavily in British cinema, which initially responded with some of its most noteworthy achievements, including such literary adaptations as David Lean's *Lawrence of Arabia* (1962) and 111 *Dr Zhivago* (1965), Tony Richardson's *Tom Jones* (1963) and John Schlesinger's *Far from the Madding Crowd* (1967). Dozens of celebrated directors arrived to exploit the favourable conditions, but the only overseas film-makers to prosper were those already resident in the United Kingdom: Roman Polanski (*Repulsion*, 1965, and *Cul-de-Sac*, 1966); Joseph Losey, who in collaboration with Harold Pinter produced *The Servant* (1963), *Accident* (1967) and *The Go-Between* (1971); and Richard Lester, who adapted the techniques of the New Wave to capture the vibrancy of The Beatles in *A Hard Day's Night* (1964) and *Help!* (1965).

Another American who preferred to work in Britain was Stanley Kubrick (b. 1928). An ambitious film-maker with an insight into the darker side of human nature, Kubrick has spent his career redefining the boundaries of the traditional Hollywood genres: the blockbuster – *Spartacus* (1960); literary adaptation – *Lolita* (1962) and *A Clockwork Orange* (1971); the historical epic – *Barry Lyndon* (1975); horror – *The Shining* (1980); the war movie – *Full Metal Jacket* (1987) and science fiction – *Dr Strangelove* (1964) and *2001: A Space Odyssey* (1968). *2001* was remarkable not only for the special-effects photography of Douglas Trumbull, but also for Kubrick's attempt to produce an 'essentially nonverbal experience' that communicates 'more to the subconscious and to the feelings than it does to the intellect'.

111 Peter O'Toole as T. E. Lawrence and Omar Sharif as Sherif Ali in David Lean's 70mm epic adaptation *Lawrence of Arabia* (1962).

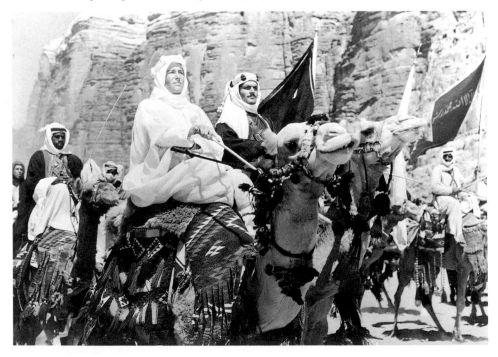

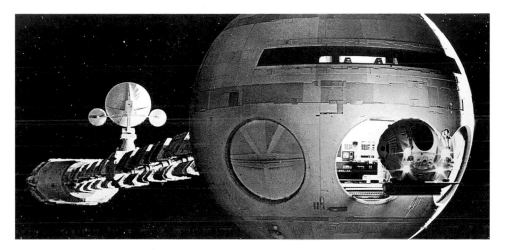

112 Stanley Kubrick, *2001: A Space Odyssey* (1968). Three years in production, *2001* cost $10.5 million, over 60 per cent of which was spent on special effects.

Ostensibly a study of the relationship between humanity and technology, it continues to defy definitive interpretation.

The Hollywood that Kubrick left behind in 1961 was beset with
problems more serious than any it had faced since the Depression.
Despite a drop in box-office receipts to a post-war low of $900 million
in 1962, the studios remained reluctant to accept the changing profile
of their typical audience and, disregarding the requirements of their
younger, better educated patrons, persisted with the 'universal appeal'
formula that had pertained since the industry's earliest days. Similarly,
they resisted the techniques of the *nouvelle vague* for fear that the
average viewer would have difficulty following such elliptical narratives as those already being produced by independents like John
Frankenheimer, Sidney Lumet and Sam Peckinpah. Commercially
and aesthetically, therefore, Hollywood was in dire need of rejuvena-
tion. The process began in 1967 with *Bonnie and Clyde*.

A potent blend of action, romance, comedy and political allegory,
David Newman and Robert Benton's shooting script for *Bonnie and
Clyde* was such a conscious *hommage* to the techniques of the New
Wave that both Truffaut and Godard were approached to direct
before Arthur Penn accepted the assignment. Initially dismissed by
American critics as an ostentatious gangster movie, the film provoked
outrage for its graphic depiction of violence and its anti-establishment

stance. Sam Peckinpah's brutal Western *The Wild Bunch* (1969), an exemplum about American involvement in Vietnam, was accorded a similar reception.

However, both films were huge hits with the baby-boom generation, and Hollywood, finally recognizing the constitution of its new audience, responded with a string of 'youth cult' pictures. Hurriedly made on shoestring budgets, the majority of these films were often risible, although a number later achieved cult status, notably *Easy Rider* (Dennis Hopper, 1969), *Medium Cool* (Haskell Wexler, 1969), *Alice's Restaurant* (Arthur Penn, 1969), and *The Strawberry Statement* (Stuart Hagmann, 1970), as well as the rock documentaries *Monterey Pop* (D. A. Pennebaker, 1969), *Woodstock* (Michael Wadleigh, 1970) and *Gimme Shelter* (Albert and David Maysles, 1971).

While *Bonnie and Clyde* disposed of the cinematic taboos surrounding violence and death, *The Graduate* (Mike Nichols, 1967) did much the same for sex. Explicit explorations of human sexuality like *Midnight Cowboy* (John Schlesinger, 1969) and *Carnal Knowledge* (Mike Nichols, 1971) and exploitation pictures like Russ Meyer's *Vixen* (1968) all benefitted from the increased potential for adult content offered by the rating system that replaced the Production Code in 1968. However, these films, in keeping with much of the output of the American New Wave, were radical merely in terms of content. Formal experimentation was largely the preserve of the documentary and underground movements.

Unanimous in their dismissal of the claim that *cinéma-vérité* consigned the 'truth' to film, American documentarists were divided on how best to employ its hand-held technique to achieve a purely observational style. In one camp were the advocates of 'direct cinema', whose prime exponents were the members of the Drew Associates production unit, who sought to reproduce the immediacy of photojournalism in such collective films as *Primary* (1960) and personal projects like *A Happy Mother's Day* (Richard Leacock, 1963), *Don't Look Back* (D. A. Pennebaker, 1967) and *Salesman* (Albert and David Maysles, 1969). Frederick Wiseman, on the other hand, considered his investigative method to be a form of 'reality fiction'. Focusing on the daily operation of traditional U.S. institutions, features like *Titicut Follies* (1967), *High School* (1969) and *Hospital* (1971) were noted for their elliptical structure and visual acuity. However, the new-found vitality of the documentary did little to persuade exhibitors of its box-office potential and throughout the 1960s it became increasingly dependent on television for an outlet.

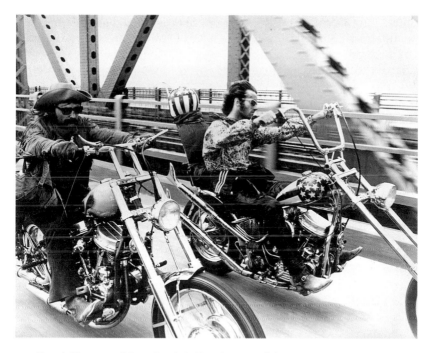

113 Dennis Hopper and Peter Fonda in Dennis Hopper's 'New Wave cowboy epic' *Easy Rider* (1969). Made for just $370,000, it grossed over $50 million.

The American underground, or avant-garde, had been cultivating its own circuit of cine-clubs since the silent era, in order to provide a forum for the work of such film-makers as James Sibley-Watson and Melville Webber (*The Fall of the House of Usher,* 1928), Robert Florey and Slavko Vorkapich (*The Life and Death of 9413 – A Hollywood Extra,* 1928), Ralph Steiner (*H2O,* 1929), Joseph Berne (*Dawn to Dawn,* 1934) and Maya Deren (*Meshes of the Afternoon,* 1943, and *Ritual in Transfigured Time,* 1946). However, in the immediate post-war period, it gained increased recognition and evolved into a distinct movement whose members became increasingly associated with one of four nebulous (and frequently overlapping) 'genres'.

The first, the film of pure form, which sought to explore the rhythms and configurations of moving patterns, had been pioneered by Hans Richter, Viking Eggeling, Fernand Léger and Oskar Fischinger in Europe in the 1920s. Undoubtedly their most important legatees were John and James Whitney, who experimented with paper cut-outs, optical printers, pantographs and colour filters in their earliest geometric ballets *Variations* (1941–3) and *Film Exercises 1–5* (1943–4). Working independently in the 1960s, they made exceptional use of images generated by analogue computers: James in *Lapis* (1963–6) and John in *Catalogue* (1961), although by the time John made *Permutations* (1970) and *Matrix* (1971), he had graduated to a digital machine. Among the other important choreographers of colour, light and shape to emerge in America in the 60s were Robert Breer (*Blazes*, 1961), Jordan Belson (*Phenomena*, 1965) and Scott Bartlett (*Offron*, 1967).

Similarly abstract were the films of the 'self-reflexive' genre, which explored not only the methodology of the cinema, but also its visual and psychological purpose. The most poetic of these film-makers was Stan Brakhage, who, in addition to his best-known photographic work *Dog Star Man* (1961–4), also produced a number of non-camera shorts by variously baking and scratching the celluloid strip, as well as covering it with natural debris (*Mothlight*, 1963) or handpainting it (*The Dante Quartet*, 1982–7). The structural film is often bracketed with the reflexive genre, on account of its rejection of the illusionist elements of cinema and its emphasis on film as material. Informal and inevitably controversial, George Landow's *Film in which there appear sprocket holes, edge lettering, dirt particles, etc* (1966), Hollis Frampton's *Zorns Lemma* (1970), the British film-maker Malcolm Le Gris's *Little Dog for Roger* (1967–8) and the Canadian Michael Snow's *Wavelength* (1967) and ↔ (1969, also known as *Back and Forth*) are among its most significant examples.

The final two genres were the satirical and the sexual. Although the work of Bruce Conner (*Marilyn x Five*, 1965) belongs firmly in the first category, the line of demarcation is more indistinct in the work of Mike (*Sins of the Fleshpoids*, 1965) and George Kuchar (*Hold Me While I'm Naked*, 1965), Kenneth Anger (*Fireworks*, 1947, and *Scorpio Rising*, 1962–4), Jack Smith (*Flaming Creatures*, 1963) and Andy Warhol. Warhol's earliest films, like *Sleep* (1963) and *Empire* (1964), were essentially minimalist extensions of his graphic art. However, with *Kiss* (1963) he began to experiment with the voyeuristic style that informed *My Hustler* (1965) and *Chelsea Girls* (1966) and such later pseudo-pornographic collaborations with Paul Morrissey as *Flesh* (1968) and *Trash* (1970).

American cinema was not alone in experiencing a pronounced increase in sexually explicit and graphically violent material in the

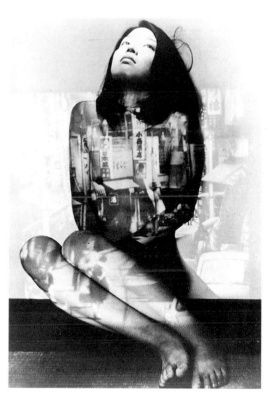

114 Demonstrating the influence of Godard and Dušan Makavejev, Nagisa Oshima's *The Man Who Left His Will on Film* (1970) used the conventions of the thriller to explore the failure of student radicalism in the late 1960s.

1960s. In its attempt to arrest audience decline the Japanese film industry devoted over half its total output in the decade after 1965 to the production of the sado-erotic *pinku-eiga*, or 'pink' film, and the brutal *yakuza-eiga*, or gangster movie. However, in their desperation to satisfy public demand, the struggling studios alienated a number of their most promising film makers, whose decision to go independent actuated the *nuberu bagu* or Japanese New Wave.

Violent, trenchant and despondent, the films of the *nuberu bagu*   114 focused on the problems wrought upon the post-war generation by the conflict between traditional Japanese values and the new social order. In spite of its thematic unity, this New Wave embraced a great diversity of styles: abstractionist – *Woman of the Dunes* (Hiroshi Teshigahara, 1964); theatrical – *The Red Angel* (Yasuzo Masumura, 1966); *cinéma-vérité* – *The Inferno of First Love* (Susumu Hani, 1968); historical – *Eros plus Massacre* (Yoshishige Yoshida, 1969); and commercial – *Tokyo Drifter* (Seijun Suzuki, 1966). Shohei Imamura adopted an almost anthropological approach for studies of economic desperation such as *Pigs and Battleships* (1961), *The Insect Woman* (1963), *Intentions of Murder* (1964) and *The Pornographer* (1966), while Masashiro Shinoda evoked the classical look of his master Ozu in *Pale Flower* (1963), *Assassination* (1964), *Punishment Island* (1966) and *Double Suicide* (1969).

Nagisa Oshima (b. 1932), the most militant and influential member of the New Wave, also possessed a highly distinctive style. His early films were uncompromising *yakuza-eiga*, but in 1968 he abandoned narrative in favour of the polemical dissertation in order to attack what he perceived to be a feudal revival in contemporary Japan. Echoing the essays of Godard and the avant-garde satires of the Yugoslav director Dušan Makavejev (see p. 217), films like *Death by Hanging* (1968), *The Diary of a Shinjunku Thief* (1968), *Boy* (1969) and *In the Realm of the Senses* (1976) invoked the mannerisms of the two prevailing commercial genres to underscore his vision of repression, intolerance and decay.

Just as Japanese cinema had retreated into commercialism after the passing of the era that had witnessed its rise to international prominence, so the Italian film industry had lapsed into escapism following the eclipse of Neo-Realism. In addition to sex comedies in the 'white telephone' manner, the most popular films with domestic audiences at this time were 'sword and sandal' spectacles like *Hercules* (1957), featuring the former Mr Universe Steve Reeves, the flamboyant horror films of Mario Bava and Riccardo Freda and the slow, pitiless and darkly humorous 'spaghetti' Westerns of Sergio Leone, which were among the period's most important contributions to an almost dormant genre. Notable for their disconcerting juxtaposition of long shots with abrupt, angular close-ups, the atmospheric soundtracks of Ennio Morricone and the inscrutable performances of Clint Eastwood, the films in Leone's 'Man with No Name' trilogy – *A Fistful of Dollars* (1964), *For a Few Dollars More* (1965) and *The Good, the Bad and the Ugly* (1966) – inspired imitations worldwide.

The prime movers in the 'second Italian film renaissance', Federico Fellini (1920–93) and Michelangelo Antonioni (b. 1912), had both begun their cinema careers as screenwriters for Roberto Rossellini. Fellini, a former cartoonist, had collaborated on a number of scripts, including *Rome, Open City*, *Paisà* and *The Miracle*, and his earliest films as a director, *Variety Lights* (co-directed by Alberto Lattuada, 1950) and *The White Sheik* (1952), were very much in the Neo-Realist tradition. *I Vitelloni* (1953) suggested the emergence of a more personal style and revealed the delight in autobiographical reference that would

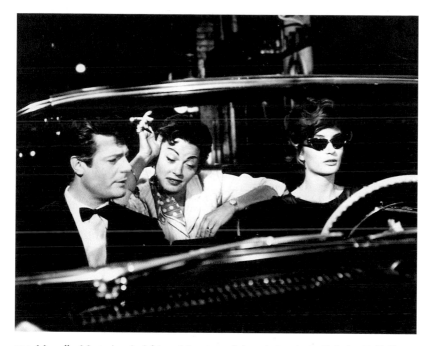

114

115 Marcello Mastroianni, Adriana Moneta and Anouk Aimée in Federico Fellini's *La dolce vita* (1959). Opening and closing with allusions to Dante's *Divine Comedy*, the film explored moral and spiritual decay in contemporary Italy.

underpin *8½* (1963), *Fellini's Roma* (1972), *Amarcord* (1973) and *Intervista* (1987). The critic Foster Hirsch has claimed that Fellini combined 'the two strains that have always dominated the Italian movies: the epic tradition, with its fondness for spectacle and the operatic gesture, and the humanist tradition, with its deep feeling for the outcast and the oppressed.' *The Swindlers* (1955) and the three films Fellini made with his then wife the actress Giulietta Masina were firmly in the latter category. Realistic in style, yet allegorical in content, *La Strada* (1954), *Nights of Cabiria* (1956) and *Juliet of the Spirits* (1965) all focused on the indomitability of women in the face of betrayal.

While sharing the theme of the 'mystery of identity', a significant proportion of Fellini's other work did, indeed, tend towards the epic. *La dolce vita* (1959), a sprawling, scathing satire on the hypocrisy of Catholicism and the decadence of contemporary Italy, established him as one of the world's most important widescreen *metteurs-en-scène*.

115

However, the burden of maintaining his reputation for flamboyant and controversial imagery sapped Fellini's inspiration, until he decided to make creative block the subject of his next film. A bewildering synthesis of reality and illusion, the imagined and the observed, 8½ starred Marcello Mastroianni as a director who retreats from his artistic frustrations into the surreal, fantasy world of his memories and obsessions in the hope of revelation, only to discover the intractability of his art.

Later features like *And the Ship Sails On* (1983), *Ginger and Fred* (1986) and *Intervista* were equally self-reflexive, while the lavish *Fellini Satyricon* (1969) and *Casanova* (1976), and the more modest *Orchestra Rehearsal* (1978) and *City of Women* (1980) recalled the savage social commentary of *La dolce vita*. Provocative, extravagant and often bizarre, Fellini's was a cinema of striking beauty and intellectual depth, which constantly strove to extend the potential of audiovisual language to explore the processes of creation, society and the mind.

Antonioni, an ex-critic on *Cinema*, had co-scripted the propagandist semi-documentary *A Pilot Returns* (1942) with the journal's editor and the dictator's son Vittorio Mussolini, before going to France to assist Marcel Carné with his anti-fascist allegory *Les Visiteurs du soir*. On returning to Italy, Antonioni directed *The People of the Po*, the first of seven short films made in the period 1943–7, but with the exception of *The Cry* (1957), he was never to return to their stringent Neo-Realism.

Whereas Fellini directed his invective at the inhabitants of the upper echelons of the bourgeoisie, Antonioni usually preferred (with the notable exception of *L'Avventura*) to concentrate on those striving to make headway in its lower-middle strata. His key themes of social displacement and urban alienation were first examined in a series of increasingly episodic films, including *Story of a Love Affair* (1950), *The Lady of the Camellias* (1953) and *The Girlfriends* (1955).

116   However, with *L'Avventura* (1959), he adopted a new style based on the use of widescreen deep focus and extended sequence shots, which enabled him both to relate his characters to their symbolic surroundings and to convey their overwhelming sense of ennui. This hugely innovative and influential film explored the unexplained disappearance of a rich woman from a volcanic island in the Mediterranean and the relationship that developed between her lover and her best friend during their search for her. 'My films are always works of searching', Antonioni revealed in a 1970 interview. 'I don't consider myself a director who has mastered his profession, but one

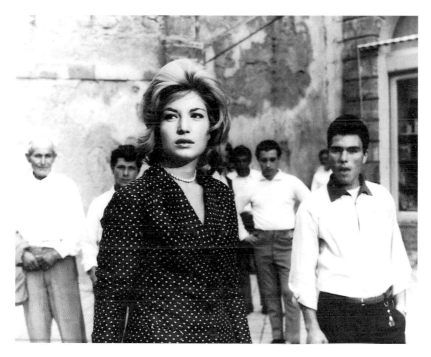

116 Monica Vitti as Claudia in Michelangelo Antonioni's *L'Avventura* (1959). She played similarly remote, anguished characters in the director's 'alienation' trilogy.

who is continuing his search and studying his contemporaries. I'm looking (perhaps in every film) for the traces of feeling in men, and of course in women, too, in a world where those traces have been buried to make way for sentiments of convenience and appearance: a world where feelings have been "public-relationized".'

He enlarged on his theme in the 'alienation' trilogy of *The Night* (1961), *The Eclipse* (1962) and *The Red Desert* (1964), which also witnessed a simplification of style as he attempted to bind his work more closely to 'the truth of our daily lives' rather than to logic. As he said after the completion of *The Night*, 'I believe I've managed to strip myself bare, to liberate myself from the many unnecessary formal techniques that are so common . . . I've rid myself of so much useless technical baggage, eliminating all the logical transitions, all those connective links between sequences where one sequence served as a springboard for the one that followed.'

Antonioni has devoted his career to proving his contention that 'film is not image: landscape, posture, gesture. But rather an indissoluble whole extended over a duration of its own that saturates it and determines its very essence.' In making inspired use of stylized colour and foreshortened perspective in *The Red Desert*, stills photography in *Blow-Up* (1968), natural imagery in *Zabriskie Point* (1970) and track-and-zoom shots in *The Passenger* (1975), he sought to reproduce on film the freedom of his abstract paintings. A complex and elusive film-maker, Antonioni has come as close as anyone to the composition of 'a cinematic poem in rhyme'.

Among the other Italian directors whose best work was produced during the New Wave were the satirists Pietro Germi (*Divorce Italian Style*, 1961, and *The Birds, the Bees, and the Italians*, 1966) and Elio Petri (*The Assassin*, 1961, and *Investigation of a Citizen Under Suspicion*, 1970) and the semi-documentarists Vittorio de Seta (*Bandits of Orgosolo*, 1961) and Gillo Pontecorvo (*The Battle of Algiers*, 1966, and *Quemada!*, 1969). A prolific documentarist in the 1950s, Ermanno Olmi combined both styles in a series of measured, elliptical Neo-Realist studies of working life that included *Il Posto* (1961), *The Fiancés* (1963), *One Fine Day* (1968) and *The Tree of Wooden Clogs* (1978).

The most politically committed film-maker of the Italian New Wave was the Marxist poet and essayist Pier Paolo Pasolini (1922–75), whom Susan Sontag considered 'indisputably the most remarkable figure to have emerged in Italian art and letters since the Second World War'. Pasolini's earliest films, *Accatone* (1961) and *Mamma Roma* (1962), were uncompromising examples of pure Neo-Realism, while his stunning interpretation of *The Gospel According to St Matthew* (1964) combined Neo-Realist techniques with a *cinéma-vérité* camera style. In contrast, the remainder of his 1960s output – *Oedipus Rex* (1967), *Theorem* (1968), *Pigsty* (1969) and *Medea* (1970) – employed an outrageous blend of myth, allegory and surrealism to proclaim his 'epical religious' vision of the sexual, political and spiritual hypocrisy of the bourgeoisie. Demonstrating considerable versatility, Pasolini fashioned yet another distinctive style for his 'trilogy of life', which comprised bawdy adaptations of *The Decameron* (1971), *The Canterbury Tales* (1972) and *A Thousand and One Nights* (1974) and for *Salò: The 120 Days of Sodom* (1975), an allegorical reworking of the writings of the Marquis de Sade set during the final days of Fascism.

The New Waves considered thus far were primarily formal departures from the traditional strategies of classical narrative cinema undertaken by film-makers who deemed them incapable of adequately

fulfilling their artistic, political and social goals. Each in its turn revital-
ized a stagnating commercial industry operating within a democratic
country. The new directions taken by the cinemas of Latin America
and Eastern Europe, on the other hand, while every bit as radical
aesthetically, owed their existence less to a conscious cultural choice
than to an unexpected revision of prevailing political conditions.

The first such instance in Latin America was the fall of the Peronist
government in Argentina in 1955 and the attendant collapse of censorship and the Hollywood-style studio system. The Buñuelian satirist
Leopoldo Torre-Nilsson (*The House of the Angel*, 1957; *The Fall*, 1959,
and *The Hand in the Trap*, 1961) and the Neo-Realist Fernando Birri
(*Throw a Dime*, 1958, and *Flood Victims*, 1962) were among the first to
exploit the new opportunities for freedom of expression. Inspired by
their example and that of the French New Wave, a group of younger
film-makers, calling themselves the '1960 generation', began to
fashion a *nuevo cine* (New Cinema). Yet in spite of the work of such
enterprising directors as Fernando Ayala (*The Candidate*, 1959) and
Manuel Antín (*The Odd Number*, 1961), Argentinian cinema was in
danger of returning to escapist formulaism before the emergence of
the *Cine Liberación* group in the late 1960s.

This militant phalanx functioned according to the principles of
'third cinema' laid down in a manifesto drafted by Fernando E. Solanas
and Octavio Getino. Dismissing the traditional narrative of 'first
cinema' and the *auteur* theory of 'second cinema', they called for a
radical new approach which would refute 'a cinema of characters with
a cinema of themes, one of individuals with one of the masses, one of
auteurs with one of operative groups, a cinema of neocolonial misin-
formation with a cinema of information, one of escape with one that
recaptures the truth, a cinema of passivity with one of aggression'.
Appropriately, *The Hour of the Furnaces* (1968), the most influential
work of this 'guerilla cinema', was directed by Solanas and Getino
themselves. Tracing the historic struggle of the Argentinian people for
manumission, this potent montage of newsreel, documentary footage,
slogans and dramatic reconstructions recalled the agit-prop technique
of Vertov.

Soviet revolutionary methods also provided the inspiration for the
New Cuban Cinema. Within three months of coming to power in
January 1959, Fidel Castro declared the cinema to be a national art and
founded the Instituto Cubano del Arte e Industria Cinematográficos
(ICAIC) to play a key role in his programme of Communist re-edu-
cation. Overcoming a severe lack of resources, the ICAIC succeeded

in producing 112 features, some 900 documentary shorts and over 1300 weekly newsreels between 1959 and 1985, the earliest of which were exhibited on lorries and boats called *cine-mobiles*, which toured both the Cuban mainland and the outlying islands in the manner of Soviet agit-trains. Among Cuba's leading film-makers during the 1960s were the documentarist Santiago Alvarez (*Hanoi, Tuesday the 13th*, 1967, and *LBJ*, 1968), Tomas Gutierrez Alea (*Death of a Bureaucrat*, 1966, and *Memories of Underdevelopment*, 1968), Manuel Octavio Gómez (*The First Charge of the Machete*, 1969) and Humberto Solás, whose *Lucía* (1969) earned international acclaim for its exploration of Cuban social attitudes in 1895, 1932 and 1969 through filmic styles germane to each year.

117

Pressure from Washington prevented these films from circulating widely around the rest of Latin America. Consequently, the new wave to exert the greatest influence over the area was *cinema nôvo*, which was born of the political instability that afflicted Brazil during the late 1950s. In calling on the Brazilian film industry to dispense with the *chanchada* musical comedies that were its staple, the movement's founder, Glauber Rocha, urged film-makers to harness the techniques of Neo-Realism and the *nouvelle vague* to indigenous folklore and Marxist principle in order to produce analyses of the nation's socioeconomic plight. In all, *cinema nôvo* passed through three distinct phases. The first, 1960–64, reflected popular optimism at the prospect of fundamental reform in such celebrations of proletarian revolt as *Barren Lives* (Nelson Pereira dos Santos, 1963), *The Guns* (Ruy Guerra, 1963) and Rocha's *Black God, White Devil* (1964). However, the failure of liberalism in the period 1964–8 induced despondency and Rocha's suitably entitled *Land in Anguish* (1967) was rare in its quality. Following the imposition on the country of a military junta, the movement entered its final, 'cannibal-tropicalist' phase (1968–74), during which political comment was confined to ingenious allegories like *Antonio das Mortes* (Glauber Rocha, 1969) and *The Gods and the Dead* (Ruy Guerra, 1970), and such caustic satires as Pereira dos Santos's *How Tasty Was My Little Frenchman* (1970).

The Marxist aesthetic of the Brazilian New Wave galvanized filmmakers throughout the continent, most notably the adherents of 'third cinema' in Argentina, the Bolivian Jorge Sanjinés (*Ukamau*, 1966, and *Blood of the Condor*, 1969) and the Chilean Miguel Littín (*The Jackal of Nahueltoro*, 1969). However, while Marxism was considered a doctrine of liberation by Latin American directors, it was identified with political and artistic repression by those working in Eastern Europe.

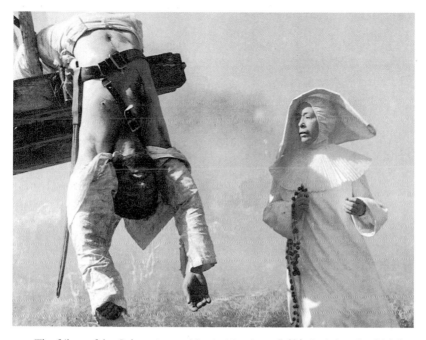

117 The failure of the Cuban 1895 uprising in Humberto Solás's *Lucía* (1969), which has been called 'an encyclopedia of progressive film in the sixties'.

In the immediate post-war period, Iron Curtain film industries were forced to conform to the tenets of Socialist Realism that had stifled Soviet cinema since the 1930s. Only semi-documentary accounts of life under the Nazi occupation presented directors with the opportunity to make serious statements, most notably the Poles Wanda Jakubowska (*The Last Stage*) and Aleksander Ford (*Border Street*, both 1948) and the Czechs Jiří Weiss (*Stolen Frontier*, 1947) and Otakar Vávra (*The Silent Barricade*, 1948). When the death of Stalin in 1953 was followed by a certain relaxation of Kremlin control over the Soviet bloc, film-makers took full advantage of it to explore a range of historical and contemporary themes.

In the USSR itself, the films of VGIK graduates like Tengiz Abuladze and Revaz Chkheidze (*Magdana's Little Donkey*, 1955), Mikhail Kalatozov (*The Cranes Are Flying*, 1957) and Grigori Chukrai (*The Ballad of a Soldier*, 1959) were judged among the nation's most enterprising since the coming of sound. Eastern Europe's lesser developed industries also fostered some interesting features: Romania – *Thirst* (Mircea Drăgan, 1960) and *Sunday at Six* (Lucian Pintilie, 1965); and Bulgaria – *On a Small Island* (Rangel Vulchanov, 1958) and *We Were Young* (1961), which was the debut of the Balkans' first woman director, Binka Zheliazkova.

The cinema of 'New Course' Hungary produced such capable directors as Károly Makk (*Liliomfi*, 1954), Felix Máriássy (*A Glass of Beer*, 1955) and Zoltán Fábri (*Professor Hannibal*, 1956), who would continue to be major figures long after the suppression of the November 1956 uprising. Similarly, a number of exceptional filmmakers comprised the 'Polish School' (1954–63), notably Andrzej Munk (*Man on the Track*, 1956; *Heroism*, 1958, and the posthumously released *The Passenger*, 1963), Jerzy Kawalerowicz (*Night Train*, 1959, and *Mother Joan of the Angels*, 1961) and Andrzej Wajda.

Wajda (b. 1926), like Munk and Kawalerowicz a graduate of the Lodz Film School, proved to be the most important artist of the three. Considered a 'romantic Neo-Realist', he first attracted international attention with his 'lost generation' trilogy – *A Generation* (1954), *Kanal* (1957) and *Ashes and Diamonds* (1958) – which examined the key Polish School theme of resistance to physical or ideological subjugation. Following *Lotna* (1959), Wajda made *Innocent Sorcerers* (1960), a controversial study of alienated youth that, like *Ashes and Diamonds*, featured Poland's James Dean, Zbigniew Cybulski. Cybulski's death in 1967, while boarding a train, reinforced his cult status and also pervaded Wajda's self-reflexive tribute to him, *Everything for Sale* (1968).

While Wajda's career was experiencing something of a downturn during the 1960s, a second generation of Lodz graduates, led by Roman Polanski (b. 1933) and Jerzy Skolimowski (b. 1938), came to the fore. Following the absurdist shorts *Two Men and a Wardrobe* (1958) and *Mammals* (1962), and his only Polish feature, the simmering study of sexual violence *Knife in the Water* (1962), Polanski elected to work abroad rather than endure repeated government censure. Subsequently something of an itinerant, he has continued to plumb the lower depths of human nature in films like *Rosemary's Baby* (1968), *Macbeth* (1971), *Chinatown* (1974) and *Tess* (1979). As government restrictions tightened, it was only a matter of time before the severity of Skolimowski's increasingly Godardian satires *Identification Marks: None* (1964), *Barrier* (1966) and *Hands Up!* (1967) would also force him to relocate. After *Le Départ* (1967), the best of his later films, *The Shout* (1978) and *Moonlighting* (1982), were produced in Britain.

118

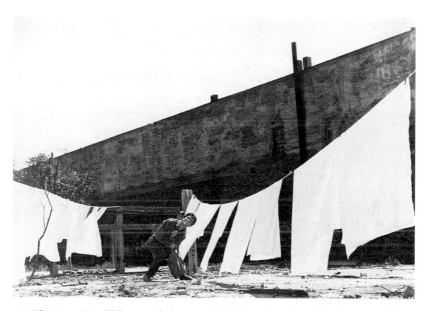

118 Zbigniew Cybulski's wounded assassin sheds blood on the pristine sheets symboliz-
ing post-war Poland before dying on a rubbish tip in Andrzej Wajda's assured exercise in
mise-en-scène, Ashes and Diamonds (1958).

With the stifling of Polish cinema came an unexpected political
thaw in Hungary which allowed for a resumption of its film renaissance. While pre-1956 cinema had been courageous in content, it had
remained formally traditional. However, in the course of the 1960s
András Kovács, István Gaál and Miklós Jancsó, all graduates of the
Budapest Academy for Dramatic and Cinematographic Art, each
developed an experimental style that fed into the radicalism of their
themes. Kovács was a disciple of *cinéma-vérité* and the immediacy of his
technique heightened the percipience of such exposés of Hungarian
bureaucratic, military and political inadequacy as *Difficult People*
(1964), *Cold Days* (1966), *Walls* (1968) and *Relay Race* (1970). While
Gaál's semi-autobiographical trilogy on the rural impact of Stalinism
– *Current* (1964), *The Green Years* (1965) and *Baptism* (1967) – revealed
his association with both Centro Sperimentale and the innovative Béla
Balázs Studio, his finest film, *The Falcons* (1970), a probing investigation into inter-war Hungarian Fascism, owed more to the fluid style
of Jancsó.

There was little atypical about the newsreels, documentaries and features that occupied Jancsó (b. 1921) during the first thirteen years of his career. However, with *Cantata* (1963), he began to demonstrate a sympathy with the psychological intensity, compositional depth and sequential shooting technique of Antonioni. *My Way Home* (1964) revealed a further refinement of his method as he introduced rhythmic tracking movements and zoom-lens shots to extend the duration of his already long takes. Subsequently, this fascination with his personal interpretation of the widescreen aesthetic has prompted Jancsó to reduce dramatically the shot content of his films, with *Winter Wind* (1969) and *Elektreia* (1974), for example, consisting of just 13 and 12 shots respectively. Invariably employing the metaphor of war and its aftermath to explore contemporary issues, films like *The Round-Up* (1965), *The Red and the White* (1967), *Silence and Cry* (1968), *Agnus Dei* (1970) and *Red Psalm* (1971) became increasingly abstract and austere. Yet through his complex choreography of figures on the sprawling Hungarian plains and his use of symbolic nudity, natural sound, folksongs and chants, and (since 1969) stylized colour, Jancsó has succeeded in producing some of the most visually arresting work of recent times.

119

119 Miklós Jancsó, *Red Psalm* (1971). Comprising only 30 shots taken with an incessantly moving camera, this 80-minute study of the nature of revolution was the culmination of Jancsó's experiments with widescreen *mise-en-scène*.

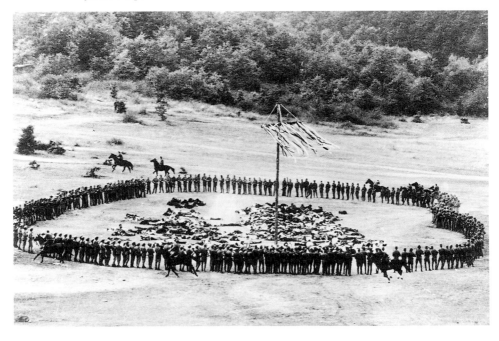

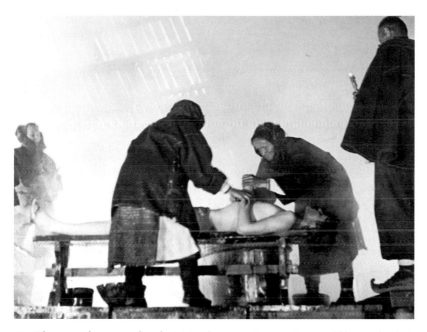

120 The monochrome used to depict Ivan's agony gives way to surreal blues and reds at the moment of his death. An example of the 'dramaturgy of colour' devised by Sergei Paradjanov for *Shadows of Our Forgotten Ancestors* (1964).

Another unique stylist to emerge unexpectedly during the 1960s was the Georgian director Sergei Paradjanov (1924–90), but whereas Jancsó's work earned him the title 'Hungary's film poet', Paradjanov's resulted in his imprisonment in 1974. At a time when Soviet audiences were accustomed to such reverential adaptations as Grigori Kozintsev's *Don Quixote* (1956), *Hamlet* (1964) and *King Lear* (1970), and Sergei Bondarchuk's *War and Peace* (1965–7), Paradjanov's *Shadows of Our Forgotten Ancestors* (1964), an audacious assault on the conventions of narrative and visual representation, was a revelation. In seeking to redefine the relationship between causal logic and screen space, and thus challenge accepted theories of audience perception, Paradjanov paradoxically juxtaposed subjective and objective viewpoints and used angular distortions, intricate (and seemingly impossible) camera movements, 'rack focus', telephoto-zoom and fish-eye lenses, and what he termed a 'dramaturgy of colour' to recount his tale of doomed love. Rich in Freudian and Jungian imagery, the film's

120

vision of a disorderly world was considered formalist and subversive by the authorities and, despite the completion of numerous scripts, Paradjanov was permitted to make only three more films, *The Colour of Pomegranates* (1969), *The Legend of the Suram Fortress* (1985) and *Ashik Kerib* (1988), before his death.

Although considered dangerous by the state, Paradjanov's stylized films were intrinsically personal statements, unlike the articulations of national aspiration that incited the Czech New Wave. Released around the time of the liberal Alexander Dubček's rise to prominence in the Communist Party, *Sunshine in a Net* (Stefan Uher, 1962) is usually considered the first feature of the 'Czech Film Miracle'. However, the pictues of Vera Chytilová (b. 1929) provided the movement with much of its formal inspiration.

A graduate of the Prague Film Faculty of the Academy of Dramatic Arts (FAMU), Chytilová adopted a blend of 'direct cinema' and *cinéma-vérité* for her graduation project, *Ceiling* (1962), and her first commercial ventures, *A Bag of Fleas* (1962) and *Something Else* (1963). In the case of *Daisies* (1966), she employed collage, superimposition, stylized colour and décor, and prismatic distortion to concoct a Surrealist reverie on the banality and conformity of Czech society. Chytilová was denied funds for further projects, a fate which also befell Jaromil Jireš after *The First Cry* (1963). Rehabilitated during the Prague Spring, he completed *The Joke* (1968), a more formally restrained but nevertheless mordant impugnment of authoritarianism, based on Milan Kundera's novel.

The movement's best-known director was another FAMU graduate, Miloš Forman (b. 1932), whose films in this period exhibited the influence of silent slapstick, Neo-Realism, *cinéma-vérité*, Free Cinema and the *nouvelle vague*. Episodic comedies shot on location with non-professional performers and improvised scripts, each of Forman's New Wave features was an allegorical homage: *Peter and Pavla* (1964) to Olmi's *Il Posto*; *A Blonde in Love* (1965) to screwball comedy; and *The Firemen's Ball* (1967), a parody of Soviet Socialist Realism. Choosing exile after the Soviet invasion of Czechoslovakia in 1968, Forman went to Hollywood, where he enhanced his reputation with distinguished adaptations of *One Flew over the Cuckoo's Nest* (1975), *Ragtime* (1981) and *Amadeus* (1984).

Indeed, the majority of the directors associated with the Film Miracle were FAMU-trained. Among the first to come to prominence was Vojtěchy Jasný (*The Cassandra Cat*, 1963, and *All My Countrymen*, 1968), and he was soon followed by Ivan Passer (*Intimate Lighting*,

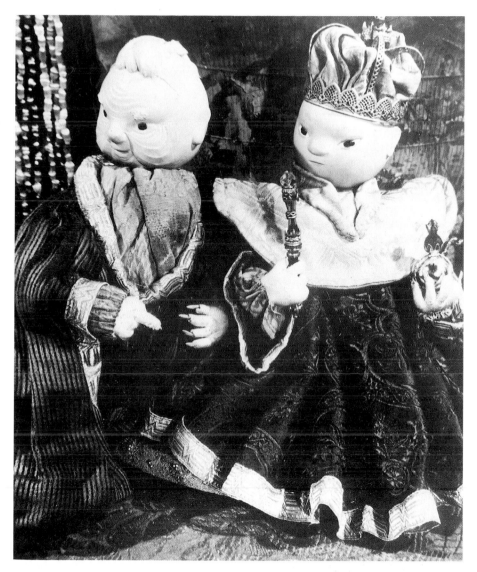

121 Jiří Trnka, *The Emperor's Nightingale* (1948). Head of the 'Trick Brothers' animation unit at Barrandov Studios, Trnka became internationally famous for such puppet features as *The Czech Year* (1947), *Old Czech Legends* (1953) and *A Midsummer Night's Dream* (1958).

1965) and Evald Schorm, a more formally traditional film-maker, who was considered the 'conscience of the New Wave' for his 'social criticism' trilogy *Everyday Courage* (1964), *The Return of the Prodigal Son* (1966) and *Saddled with Five Girls* (1967). More outspoken and experimental was Jan Němec, whose Kafkaesque allegory of Czech repression, *The Party and the Guests* (1966), starred Schorm as 'The Guest who refused to be Happy'. A former assistant to Schorm and Chytilová, Jiří Menzel demonstrated a bold approach to literary adaptation, with both *Closely Watched Trains* (1966) and *Capricious Summer* (1968) notable for their equation of sexual and political freedom. The leading non-FAMU figures Jan Kadár and Elmar Klos employed a similarly inventive yet anti-heroic style for their most important collaborations, *Three Wishes* (1958), *Death is Called Engelschen* (1963), *The Shop on the High Street* (1965) and *Adrift* (1968).

As Czechoslovakia underwent a 'normalization' process following the crushing of the Prague Spring, all these film-makers, with the exception of Uher and Jireš, were accused of 'antisocial activity' and blacklisted. Four films – *The Firemen's Ball, All My Countrymen, The Party and the Guests* and Schorm's *Pastor's End* (1968) – were 'banned for ever'. Although some New Wave directors were permitted to resume their careers in the 1980s, the Czech cinema has never recovered its enterprise and status.

Influential throughout Europe, the impact of the Czech New Wave was perhaps most keenly felt in Yugoslavia, which was itself experiencing a period of popular agitation known as the 'Second Revolution' in the mid-1960s. Since the war, the majority of features produced in Yugoslavia had conformed to such generic types as action adventures, adaptations, historical re-creations, Partisan films (which focused on the socialist role in the National War of Liberation), and documentaries, newsreels and compilation films on the theme of reconstruction under Tito known as *kinokronika*.

While these were produced mainly for domestic consumption, the animation of Vatroslav Mimica, Dušan Vukotić and the other members of the Zagreb School succeeded in gaining international recognition. Indeed, many Eastern European countries possessed animators of wide renown: Karel Zeman, Jan Svankmajer and the puppeteer Jiří Trnka (Czechoslovakia); Alexander Ptushko (USSR); Attila Dargay (Hungary); Ion Popescu-Gopo (Romania); Todor Dinov (Bulgaria) and the Poles Jan Lenica and Walerian Borowczyk.

In 1961 the features *Two* (Aleksander Petrović) and *A Dance in the Rain* (Boštjan Hladnik) heralded the arrival of a new direction in

121

Yugoslav cinema. '*Novi*' or 'new film' was as much a reaction to cinematic cliché as it was a means of making political capital. Nevertheless, the earliest films still aroused governmental ire and it was not until 1965 that the movement finally began to gain momentum. Many of the most important pictures were produced at Film City outside Belgrade, although the Zagreb Studio also made a significant contribution with Vatroslav Mimica's *Kaja, I'll Kill You* (1967), Zelimir Zilnik's *Early Works* (1969) and the documentarist Krsto Papić's *Handcuffs* (1970).

Among Serbia's leading film-makers were Aleksander Petrović (*Days*, 1963, *Three*, 1965, and *I Even Met Happy Gypsies*, 1967), the prolific Zivojin Pavlović (*Awakening of the Rats*, 1966; *When I Am Pale and Dead*, 1967, and *Ambush*, 1969) and Puriša Djordjević, whose acclaimed 'war quartet' comprised *Girl* (1965), *Dream* (1966), *Morning* (1967) and *Noon* (1968). The director whose work enjoyed the greatest international circulation was the avant-garde satirist Dušan Makavejev (b. 1932). *Man Is Not a Bird* (1966), *The Tragedy of the Switchboard Operator* (1967) and *Innocence Unprotected* (1968) were remarkable for their blend of Brechtian and Godardian methodology, and social comment. However, it is *W.R. – Mysteries of the Organism* (1971), his Surrealist interpretation of the writings of the psychoanalyst Wilhelm Reich, on which rests his reputation for dauntless formal and thematic experiment.

Novi film was one of the first casualties of the centrist reaction to the political crises of 1968–72. A number of its leading artists were presented with the options of silence or exile and many key works were withdrawn. Anxious to redress the negative image given by the 'open film', the Yugoslav authorities resorted to Socialist Realism. The first 'black films' (so called after an anti-*novi* essay entitled 'The Black Wave in Our Film') were released in 1973, by which time the foundations had been firmly laid for the last major European new wave to date, *Das neue Kino*.

CHAPTER EIGHT

World Cinema since 1970

'The old cinema is dead. We believe in the new', declared the signatories of the Oberhausen Manifesto in the spring of 1962. To those critics who considered the German film industry to have been moribund since the early 1930s, the call for a fresh approach was long overdue. Unlike the other Axis powers, Germany had not experienced a post-war film revival, despite hopes that *Trümmerfilme* ('rubble films') like *The Murderers Are Among Us* (Wolfgang Staudte, 1946) and *Ballad of Berlin* (Robert Stemmle, 1948), exploring the process of reconstruction, would instigate Neo-Realist movements on both sides of the East–West partition. However, there was a dearth of talent that was capable of exploiting the conditions, particularly after deNazification, and few German artists were prepared to abandon their Hollywood exiles for the prospect of strict censorship and primitive facilities.

Throughout the 1950s, the two German film industries developed along diametrically opposed lines. What little production there was in the East was limited to Socialist Realism, while the emphasis in the West was placed on mainstream entertainment. West Germany was soon the world's fifth largest producer – mostly of *Heimatfilme* ('homeland films') like *I Often Think of Piroshka* (Kurt Hoffman, 1956) – but Hollywood escapism ruled supreme at a box office already under threat from television. By the time of the 1962 Oberhausen Film Festival, West German cinema was on the verge of collapse.

According to the twenty-six writers and directors who signed the Oberhausen Manifesto, the sole future lay with a *junger deutscher film* ('Young German Cinema'), which, in order to be fluent in 'the international language of the cinema', needed complete freedom 'from the conventions and habits of the established industry, from intervention by commercial partners, and . . . from the tutelage of other vested interests'. Following a three-year campaign, Alexander Kluge (b. 1932), the leading figure, persuaded the federal government to institute the Young German Film Board in order to implement the Oberhausen proposals, and between 1965 and 1968 this *Kuratorium* not only sponsored nineteen features, but also founded film schools in Munich and Berlin and a national film archive.

However, much of the *Kuratorium*'s achievement was vitiated by the formation in 1967 of the Film Subsidies Board, which engendered a boom in tawdry, block-booked movies of little critical or commercial value that merely compounded the crisis facing the German film industry. Four years later, in an attempt to regain the impetus provided by the Young German Cinema, a number of directors, again led by Kluge and including Rainer Werner Fassbinder, Wim Wenders and Edgar Reitz (later renowned for his epic TV films *Heimat*, 1984, and *The Second Heimat*, 1992), established their own distribution collective, Der Filmverlag Autoren Group ('The Authors' Film-Publishing Group'), thus instigating *das neue Kino*. United primarily in an enterprise to ensure the exhibition of their work rather than to pursue common political or aesthetic goals, the members of the New German Cinema produced films of great diversity. Common to much of their output, however, was a marked formal beauty and an intellectual indeterminacy that manifested their upbringing in the 'cultural limbo' of post-Nazi Germany.

Volker Schlöndorff's independently produced *Young Törless* (1966) is traditionally considered to be the prototype film of *das neue Kino*. A former assistant to Louis Malle, Alain Resnais and Jean-Pierre Melville, Schlöndorff (b. 1939) was perhaps the least innovative of the *Autoren*, although he enjoyed more domestic success than many of his contemporaries, particularly with subsequent literary adaptations like *Baal* (1969), *Coup de Grace* (1976) and *The Tin Drum* (1979). In the course of shooting his *Heimatfilm* parody, *The Sudden Wealth of the Poor People of Kombach* (1970), Schlöndorff met (and later married) Margarethe von Trotta, with whom he collaborated on three subsequent films, most notably *The Lost Honour of Katharina Blum* (1975). A former actress, von Trotta (b. 1942) emerged as an important New German director in her own right with *The Second Awakening of Christa Klages* (1977) and became its leading exponent of the *Frauenfilm* ('feminist film') with *Sisters, or The Balance of Happiness* (1979), *The German Sisters* (1981), *Rosa Luxemburg* (1985) and *The African Woman* (1990).

Alexander Kluge began his career as an assistant to Fritz Lang in the late 1950s. Having made his debut feature, *Yesterday Girl* (1966), fittingly under the auspices of the *Kuratorium*, Kluge laid one of the keystones of the New German Cinema with *Artists of the Big Top: Disorientated* (1968). This drew heavily on the techniques of the *nouvelle vague* to explore the difficulties besetting artists seeking to break with tradition. Throughout the 1970s, he enhanced his reputation as an incisive, yet objective, socio-political satirist and confirmed his position as the 'godfather' of the movement by amalgamating the talents of ten other *Autoren* and the novelist Heinrich Böll in the semi-documentary *Germany in Autumn* (1978).

If Kluge was the leader of the New German Cinema, its most influential film-maker was Rainer Werner Fassbinder (1945–82). Between *Love Is Colder than Death* (1969) and *Querelle* (1982), the prolific and versatile Fassbinder directed more than 40 features, as well as scripting and acting in many more pieces for stage, screen and television. His first 10 pictures, including *Katzelmacher* (1969) and *Beware a Holy Whore* (1971), featured the ensemble of his 'anti-theatre' group and owed much to *film noir*, Godard, Jean-Marie Straub and the theories of Bertholt Brecht. Establishing his custom of completing projects within budget and ahead of schedule, these austere, minimalist films were critically acclaimed but failed to attract the mass audiences Fassbinder craved.

As a consequence, in *The Merchant of Four Seasons* (1971) Fassbinder elected to couch his Marxism in more melodramatic terms and thus embraced the style that was to characterize much of his remaining work. Fassbinder maintained that, as melodrama was the stuff of real life, it was the perfect medium for exploring such everyday themes as bourgeois hedonism, 'the political economy of human desire', the plight of the outsider and the misuse of power. In order to heighten this realism, he made expressive use of colour, lighting and décor and invoked cinema's other great melodramatists in devising his own distinctive style. Fassbinder's claustrophobic sets undoubtedly bore the influence of the theatre, the stylized symmetry of Fritz Lang, Expressionist 'studio realism' and the controlled *mise-en-scène* of Max Ophüls, but his chief inspiration was Douglas Sirk. In addition to the narrative structure, oblique angles and garish colour schemes of films like *Imitation of Life*, Fassbinder also assimilated Sirk's fondness for reflective surfaces as a means of conveying the falsity and frigidity of life, and for glass, as both a symbolic barrier to communication and an alienation device.

Working in a variety of genres, Fassbinder invariably set his films in one of five vividly evoked milieus: the everyday – *Fear Eats the Soul* (1973) and *Mother Küsters Goes to Heaven* (1975); the world of the rich and famous – *The Bitter Tears of Petra von Kant* (1972) and *Fox and His Friends* (1975); the past – *Effi Briest* (1974) and *Despair* (1978); the war

122

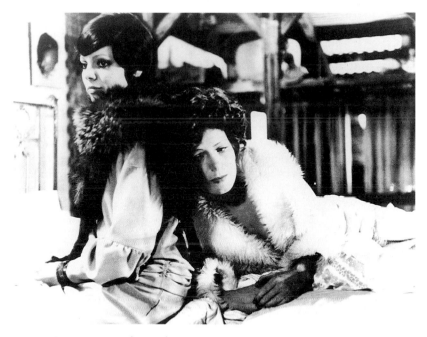

122 Irm Hermann as Marlene and Margit Carstensen as Petra, her sado-masochistic lover in Rainer Werner Fassbinder's *The Bitter Tears of Petra von Kant* (1972).

– *The Marriage of Maria Braun* (1978) and *Lili Marleen* (1980); and its aftermath – *Lola* and *Veronika Voss* (both 1981). However, his bold statements on racial and sexual intolerance, middle-class complacency, terrorism and political inertia touched too many nerves at home, and it was only abroad that he was considered 'the most original talent since Godard'.

Fassbinder's assertion that 'new realism' was the result of 'a collision between film and the subconscious' echoed the Marxist aesthetic of the avant-garde film-maker Jean-Marie Straub (b. 1933) and his French partner Danièle Huillet (b. 1936). While their minimalist features, like *The Chronicle of Anna Magdalena Bach* (1968), disavowed the physical elegance of the *Autoren*, they nevertheless shared the conviction that film was a material form with a duty to compel the viewer to engage with content rather than passively observe it. Similarly dedicated to the evolution of a new cinematic language was Hans-Jürgen Syberberg (b. 1935), whose low-budget amalgams of myth, psychology and history were hugely dependent on Brechtian theatrics, painted backdrops and rear projection. An associate rather than a member of *das neue Kino*, his trilogy of fictionalized documentaries, culminating in *Hitler: A Film from Germany* (1977), earned him a reputation as 'the chronicler of the German soul'.

Werner Herzog (b. 1942) was the 'romantic visionary' of the New German Cinema. Characterized by their measured, hypnotic pace, intricate blend of soundtrack and intense silence, expressive use of colour and almost mystical atmosphere, Herzog's films were remarkable studies of eccentricity, alienation and indomitability. Using the textures and rhythms of his images to convey emotional and physical sensation, his fictional features invariably involved characters driven by overpowering obsessions to their undoing in inhospitable environments: barren wildernesses – *Signs of Life* (1968) and *Heart of Glass* (1976); untamed jungles – *Aguirre, Wrath of God* (1972) and *Fitzcarraldo* (1982); and strange towns – *The Enigma of Kaspar Hauser* (1974) and *Nosferatu the Vampyre* (1979). Herzog's documentaries covered much the same thematic and stylistic ground, with *Fata Morgana* (1969), *Even Dwarfs Started Small* (1970) and *La Soufrière* (1977) all concerned less with objective 'truth' than with 'the subjective and symbolic aspects of undergoing a particular event, process or condition'.

Traditionally acknowledged as the least political and most existentialist of the group, Wim Wenders (b. 1945) was the last of the *Autoren* to come to prominence with *The Goalkeeper's Fear of the Penalty Kick* in 1972. Although the themes of loneliness, anxiety and dislocation recur in his work, the underlying current of all his films is the 'Americanization of Germany'. Cinematic references, particularly to *film noir*, abound in Wenders' pictures, the majority of which are hybrids of the 'road movie': *Alice in the Cities* (1974); *The Wrong Move* (1975); *Kings of the Road* (1976); *The American Friend* (1977); *Paris, Texas* (1984) and *Until the End of the World* (1991). Such is his affection for Hollywood genres that *Wings of Desire* (1987), in spite of its dedication to Ozu, Truffaut and Tarkovsky, irresistibly recalled the 'angel' cycle best typified by Frank Capra's *It's a Wonderful Life*.

The impact of *das neue Kino* on post-war international cinema has been surpassed only by that of Neo-Realism and the *nouvelle vague*, yet it was coolly received in West Germany, where Hollywood products retained a 65 per cent share of box-office receipts. The generation of directors that emerged in the wake of the New German Cinema, among them Percy Adlon, Dorris Dorrie, Reinhard Hauff, Rosa von Praunheim, Niklaus Schilling, Helma Sanders-Brahms, Werner

123

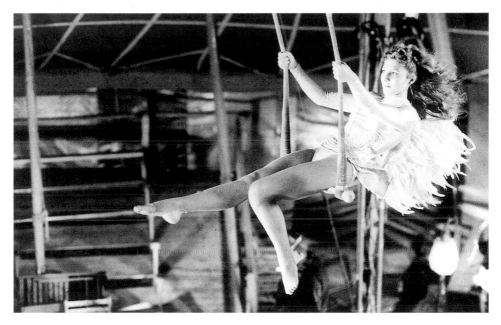

123 Solveig Dommartin as Marion, the trapeze artist for whom the angel Bruno Ganz risks mortality in Wim Wenders' *Wings of Desire* (1987).

Shroeter and Jutta Bruckner, has enjoyed marginally more domestic success than its predecessors, although it has yet to gain comparable international recognition.

After *das neue Kino*, the most significant new waves of the 1970s occurred within the British Commonwealth and in the African states that had recently gained their independence from France.

Despite having produced the world's first feature film, *The Story of the Kelly Gang* (Charles Tait, 1906), and a few popular silents like Raymond Longford's *The Sentimental Bloke* (1919), Australia had been something of a cinematic backwater in the sound era. With Hollywood and British films dominant at the box office and just one production company operational between 1932 and 1956, Australia was considered little more than an exotic location when in 1970 the federal government formed the Australian Film Development Corporation (later the Australian Film Commission) to sponsor the evolution of an authentic national cinema. Three years later, the foundation of the Australian Film and Television School was followed by the implementation of a system of tax incentives to encourage foreign investment, although all films were obliged to employ Australian casts and crews and explore indigenous themes. As a result of these measures, more than 400 features were produced over the next fifteen years, an increasing number of which enjoyed critical and commercial success worldwide.

Bruce Beresford's *The Adventures of Barry Mackenzie* (1972) is generally regarded to have been the first film of the Australian New Wave. Further assaults on the macho mentality of the Australian male followed in *Don's Party* (1976) and *The Club* (1980). But, as Beresford (b. 1940) demonstrated in *The Getting of Wisdom* (1977) and the powerful Boer War courtroom drama *Breaker Morant* (1980), his real talent was for precise characterization and re-creation of period, and the best of his subsequent films have been the costume pieces *Driving Miss Daisy* (1989) and *Black Robe* (1991).

Beresford was invited to Hollywood to direct *Tender Mercies* in 1982 and his compatriots Fred Schepisi (*The Chant of Jimmie Blacksmith*, 1978), Gillian Armstrong (*My Brilliant Career*, 1978) and George Miller (*Mad Max*, 1979) followed in the wake of the unprecedented success in America of *Crocodile Dundee* (Peter Raiman, 1986). However, apart from films actually set in Australia – *Mad Max 2* (Miller, 1981), *Cry in the Dark* (Schepisi, 1988) and *The Last Days of Chez Nous* (Armstrong, 1991) – they have largely failed to reproduce the quality of their earlier work.

An exception to this rule is Peter Weir (b. 1944). He established his reputation in Australia with *Picnic at Hanging Rock* (1975), *The Last Wave* (1977), *Gallipoli* (1981) and *The Year of Living Dangerously* (1982). Each picture explored the impact on its central characters of an alien culture or environment, and Weir has singlemindedly continued to pursue this theme in such Hollywood films as *Witness* (1985), *The Mosquito Coast* (1986), *Dead Poets Society* (1989), *Green Card* (1990) and *Fearless* (1993).

Not every New Wave director was lured to Hollywood at once; Tim Burstall (*Alvin Purple*, 1973), Simon Wincer (*Phar Lap*, 1983), John Duigan (*The Year My Voice Broke*, 1987) and Philip Noyce (*Dead Calm*, 1989) are among the more significant film-makers who remained in Australia. However, by far the most important member of this group was the Dutch-born Paul Cox (b. 1940), whose poignant and naturalistic studies of people gripped by obsession – *Man of Flowers* (1983) and *Golden Braid* (1990) – or racked with pain – *Lonely Hearts* (1981), *My First Wife* (1984) and *Cactus* (1986) – were notable for their precise pace, literate scripts and restrained performances.

124

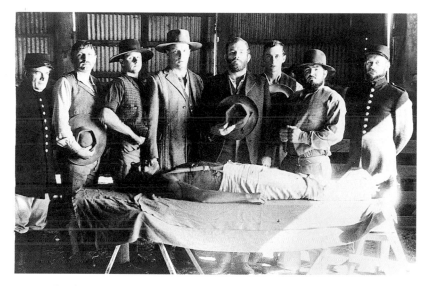

124 Fred Schepisi, *The Chant of Jimmie Blacksmith* (1978). The posse poses with the Aborigine Jimmie Blacksmith (Tommy Lewis) at the end of his killing spree in 1900 New South Wales.

Although Australian cinema has lost much of its momentum since the passing of the New Wave, it is still capable of producing remarkable films that exploit the continent's unique landscape and characteristic iconoclasm – for example, *The Man from Snowy River* (George Miller, 1982), *Bliss* (Ray Lawrence, 1985), *Proof* (Jocelyn Morehouse, 1991) and *Strictly Ballroom* (Baz Luhrmann, 1992).

Before the success of Roger Donaldson's *Sleeping Dogs* (1977), New Zealand had produced fewer than 60 features since its first in 1916. Since then, with the films of Vincent Ward (*Vigil*, 1983; *The Navigator*, 1988, and *The Map of the Human Heart*, 1993) and Jane Campion (*Sweetie*, 1989; *An Angel at My Table*, 1990, and *The Piano*, 1993), New Zealand's reputation for provocative and visually arresting cinema has recently been considerably enhanced.

Canada's feature output had been negligible, although it had been producing internationally acclaimed documentaries and animated shorts since the establishment of the National Film Board in 1939. With Hollywood commanding 80 per cent of the Canadian box office, leading talent inexorably drawn south and hits like *The Apprenticeship of Duddy Kravitz* (Ted Kotcheff, 1974) rare in the

225

extreme, few were willing to finance domestic production before the introduction of a new tax shelter system in 1978. Many of the features in the boom that followed – including the science fiction and horror movies of Canada's best-known director David Cronenberg (*Scanners*, 1980; *Videodrome*, 1983, and *Dead Ringers*, 1988) – were usually indistinguishable from a typical Hollywood product. Notable exceptions were the dark, self-reflexive satires of Atom Egoyan (*Family Viewing*, 1987; *Speaking Parts*, 1989, and *Exotica*, 1994) and social comedies like *I've Heard the Mermaids Singing* (Patricia Rozema, 1987).

125

A more genuine new wave has occurred in *le cinéma québécois* since the 1960s. Owing more than a little to the *nouvelle vague*, film-makers like Jean-Pierre Lefebvre, Gilles Carle, Michel Brault and Claude Jutra were responsible for some of the most controversial films ever produced in Canada. More recently, French Canadian cinema has begun to acquire an international following thanks to the socially and politically committed satires of Denys Arcand (*The Decline of the American Empire*, 1986, and *Jesus of Montreal*, 1989) and the abrasive films of a new generation that includes Yves Simoneau, Francis Mankiewicz and Jean-Claude Lauzon.

In stark contrast to its Commonwealth partners, India boasted the biggest and fastest growing film industry in the world, although most of its movies were still *masala* melodramas. In the late 1960s, however, prompted by the films of Satyajit Ray and the *nouvelle vague*, the Marxist Bengali directors Mrinal Sen and Ritwak Ghatak inaugurated a 'Parallel Cinema' in order to produce features of greater social realism and intellectual depth. Sen, the more prolific and formally innovative of the two, is traditionally credited with launching the New Indian Cinema with *Mr Shome* (1969), an allegorical love story that recalled *Jules et Jim*, and the Godardian essays *Interview* (1971) and *Calcutta '71* (1972). Increasingly symbolic in style, he remained a fierce critic of the exploitation of the poor (*The Royal Hunt*, 1976) and the hypocrisy of the urban middle classes (*The Case Is Closed*, 1982).

Although Ghatak completed just eight features, including a trilogy on the plight of East Pakistani refugees and the autobiographical *Reason, Argument, Story* (1974), he was also a tutor at the Calcutta Film and Television Institute, where such uncompromising 'parallel' film-makers as Mani Kaul and Kumar Shahani were among his students. Basu Chatterji and M. S. Sathyu similarly hailed from Bengal, but the movement also had adherents in the south, most notably Girish Karnad, B. B. Karanth, Girish Kasaravalli, Aravindan and Andoor Gopalkrishna.

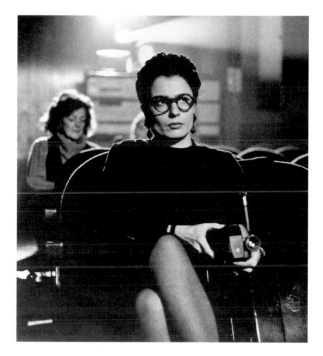

125 The film censor Arsinée Khanjian secretly films pornographic movies for her sister in Atom Egoyan's typically self-reflexive *The Adjuster* (1991).

The most commercially successful director of the New Indian Cinema was Shyam Benegal, who produced in pictures like *The Seedling* (1974) and *The Obsession* (1978) a polished blend of politics and melodrama that inspired the emergence of 'middle cinema' in the 1980s. However, films like *The Occupation* (Gautam Ghosh, 1982), *36 Chowringhee Lane* (Aparna Sen, 1982) and *Salaam Bombay!* (Mira Nair, 1987) testified to the continuing vitality of Parallel Cinema itself.

Masala musicals, along with martial arts adventures from Hong Kong and escapist entertainments from France and Hollywood, have long been the staple of the African cinema-goer. Despite the continent's size, Africa's market for films is comparatively small, with cultural, political and socio-economic diversity precluding widespread box-office appeal. In spite of the fact that more than ninety nations have gained their independence since the Second World War, cultural colonialism is still a powerful force in Africa and much of the continent's distribution system remains in foreign hands. As a consequence, indigenous film-makers are often denied access to local audiences and are thus unable to generate the revenues they require to undertake personal projects. In view of these obstacles, the achievements of Africa's national cinemas are all the more remarkable.

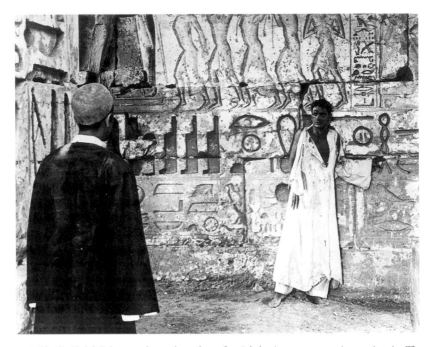

126 Shadi Abdel-Salam explores the value of a rich heritage to a starving nation in *The Night of Counting the Years* (1969).

The Egyptian film industry has become increasingly committed to social realism since the 1940s, producing several acute studies of rural and urban poverty, including Youssef Chahine's *Cairo Station* (1958) and *The Night of Counting the Years* (Shadi Abdel-Salam, 1969). Although the emphasis has shifted back to popular entertainment since the 1970s, Chahine has continued to explore serious themes in films like *The Land* (1968) and *Alexandria . . . Why?* (1978).

Cinema mudjahad ('freedom fighter cinema') dominated Algerian production in the first years after the war of liberation with France. Since the 1970s, however, *cinema djidid* ('new cinema') has prevailed, with Mohamed Lakhdar-Hamina (*Chronicle of the Years of Embers*, 1975) and Mohamed Bouamari (*The Charcoal-Burner*, 1973) among its best-known directors. Tunisia has the smallest industry in francophone North Africa, but a number of its films have performed well at international festivals, including Nouri Bouzid's *Man of Ashes* (1986) and the compilation documentaries of Ferid Boughedir. Moroccan cinema has only recently come to prominence, but through the features of Southel Ben Barka (*The Thousand and One Hands*, 1972) it has gained a reputation for formal innovation.

It is sub-Saharan cinema that has proved popular with both critics and audiences around the world. Following Paulin Soumanou Vieyra's *Africa on the Seine* (1955), more than a hundred features were completed by Black African film-makers under the auspices of a production programme sponsored by the French Ministry of Co-operation (1963–81). But funding was dependent on the forfeit of distribution rights and few films were widely exhibited.

Trained in Moscow by Mark Donskoy, the Senegalese novelist and *cinéphile*, Ousmane Sembene (b. 1923) was determined to circumvent the Ministry system in order to consider authentically national themes. *Borom Sarret*, his 1962 short, is recognized as the first indigenous black African film. His debut feature, *The Black Girl* (1965), established his reputation for acutely satirical studies of French neo-colonialism, although for *The Money Order* (1968) and *Xala* (1974), he abandoned its monochrome *cinéma-vérité* style for a colour realism that owed much to Bazin's aesthetic of *mise-en-scène*. Since then Sembene has

127

127 A traditional dance to mark the removal of the French from a Senegalese Chamber of Commerce in Ousmane Sembene's neo-colonialist satire *Xala* (1974).

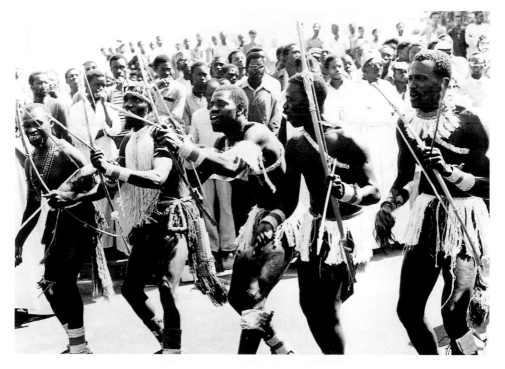

adopted a docudrama approach to explore the maltreatment of Senegalese conscripts in the French army during the Second World War (*Emitai*, 1971, and *Camp Thiaroye*, co-directed by Thierno Faty Sow, 1988) and the cultural impact of Christianity and Islam (*Ceddo*, 1977, and *Guelwar*, 1992).

Senegal remains the cradle of sub-Saharan cinema, with Djibril Diop Mambety (*Touki-Bouki*, 1973, and *Hyenas*, 1992) and the first black African woman feature-director Safi Faye (*The Grandfather*, 1979, and *Mossane*, 1992) among its leading film-makers. But important films have also been made elsewhere, including *Harvest: 3000 Years* (Haile Gerima, Ethiopia, 1975); *Aiye* (Ola Balogun, Nigeria, 1980) and *Mapantsula* (Oliver Schmitz, South Africa, 1988). More sustained levels of production have been achieved in countries such as Burkino Faso, where the clash of tradition and progress has informed the work of Gaston Kaboré (*The Gift of God*, 1982, and *Zan Boko*, 1988) and Idrissa Ouedraogo (*The Choice*, 1987, and *Yaaba*, 1989). In Mali another VGIK graduate, Souleymane Cissé, has produced such thoughtful studies of village society as *Finyé* (1982) and *Yeelen* (1987), which contrast sharply with the pessimistic view of town life presented in *Baara* (1978). The Mauritanian Med Hondo is one of Africa's most experimental film-makers, variously employing the techniques of the *nouvelle vague* (*Soleil O*, 1970), modern dance (*West Indies*, 1979) and classical Japanese cinema (*Sarraounia*, 1986) to condemn racist and neo-colonialist attitudes.

The films of sub-Saharan Africa and those of the Filipino director Lino Brocka (*Manila: In the Claws of Neon*, 1975, and *Bayan Ko: My Own Country*, 1984) were probably closer to the precepts of 'third cinema' than any produced in Latin America in the same period. Although directors like Mauricio Wallerstein (Venezuela), Carlos Mayolo (Colombia) and Francisco José Lombardi (Peru) began to establish feature traditions in their own countries, the rest of the continent was hamstrung by political and economic instability.

The Brazilian film industry has concentrated on the production of soft-core comedies called *pornochanchadas* since the 1970s, but a number of films have enjoyed international success: *Dona Flor and Her Two Husbands* (Bruno Barreto, 1976); *Bye Bye Brazil* (Carlos Diegues, 1979); *Kiss of the Spider Woman* (Hector Babenco, 1985); and *The Hour of the Star* (Suzana Amaral, 1985). A similar fate has befallen Mexican cinema, which had produced few indigenous films of any quality since the 'golden age' of Emilio Fernandez, whose partnership with the cinematographer Gabriel Figueroa yielded such poetic epics as *Maria*

128

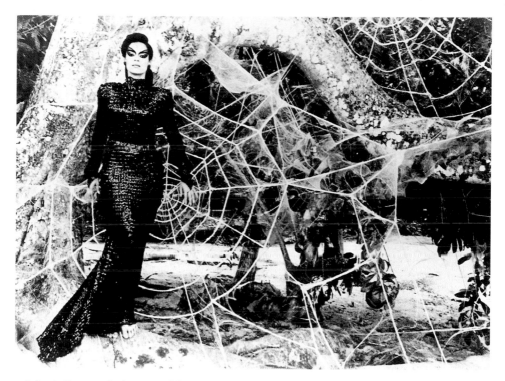

128 Sonia Braga as the heroine of the B-picture William Hurt describes to his cellmate Raúl Julia in Hector Babenco's intricately structured *Kiss of the Spider Woman* (1985).

Candelaria (1943) and *The Pearl* (1946). In the 1980s, however, directors of the calibre of Jaime Humberto Hermisillo, Arturo Ripstein and Ariel Zuniga began to emerge, but even they have difficulty securing funds within a film industry almost totally dependent on low-budget genre movies called *churros*.

In spite of the emergence of talents like Sara Goméz, Santiago Alvarez and Pastor Vega, even Cuban cinema lost its momentum in the 1970s. The situation continued to deteriorate until 1992, when the ICAIC was merged with the film division of the armed forces and production was concentrated on pornographic comedies, escapist adventures and political propaganda. Many Chilean film-makers fled to Cuba after the Pinochet *coup* of 1973, among them Patricio Guzmàn, although he completed the editing of his epic documentary *The Battle of Chile* (1975–9) in France. Helvio Soto and Raúl Ruiz also relocated to Paris, where the prolific Ruiz has since produced over 50 films of dazzling technical virtuosity inspired by diverse literary and cinematic sources, like *The Golden Boat* (1990).

Only Argentina experienced a spell of sustained creativity during this period, dating from the collapse of the military dictatorship in 1982. In the absence of censorship, film-makers began to explore the events of the recent past in four distinct categories dealing with the *desaparecidos* – *The Official Version* (Luis Puenzo, 1985); the exiled – *South* (Fernando Solanas, 1988); the exploited – *The Year of the Rabbit* (Fernando Ayala, 1987); and the repressed – *Camila* (María Luisa Bemberg, 1984). Since the late 1980s, the region's liveliest cinema has followed the trend for populist melodrama.

In the Far East, the Japanese has been one of the few Asian cinemas to experience a comparable decline in the period since 1970. Although Japan annually averaged more than 350 features in the post-New Wave era, over two thirds were in the exploitation genres, causing a drop in attendances that was compounded by the proliferation of video-cassette recorders in the 1980s. Few pictures matched the success of *The Funeral* (1985), *Tampopo* (1986) and *A Taxing Woman* (1987), Juzo Itami's satires on the slavish devotion to ritual of the Japanese middle classes, and imaginatively animated features like *Akira* (Katsuhiro Otomo, 1987), which derived from the violent, futuristic comic books known as *manga*.

Fast-paced adventures were also the mainstay of the film industries of South-East Asia for much of the post-war period. Production in Hong Kong is still dominated by the *kung fu* and swordplay genres that made the names of Bruce Lee and King Hu respectively in the 1970s, although such recent action pictures as *The Butterfly Murders* (Tsui Hark, 1979) and *The Killer* (John Woo, 1989) have demonstrated an increased level of sophistication. Social realist 'new waves' emerged in the 1980s in both Hong Kong (*Father and Son*, Allen Fong, 1981, and *Boat People*, Ann Hui, 1982) and Taiwan (*Taipei Story*, Edward Yang, 1985, and *Jade Love*, Chang Yi, 1985). The best-known director in both movements was Hou Hsaio-hsien, whose films explored the impact of urbanization and consumerism on Taiwan's past (*A Time to Live and a Time to Die*, 1986, and *City of Sadness*, 1989) and present (*The Boys from Fengkuei*, 1984, and *Summer at Grandpa's*, 1985).

129

Mainland China experienced its own 'new wave' in the mid-1980s when the Fifth Generation of film-makers rose to prominence. The First Generation had been the pioneers of the silent era, while those of the Second included the social realists of the 1930s and such artists as Zheng Junli, who worked during the late Kuomintang era, when

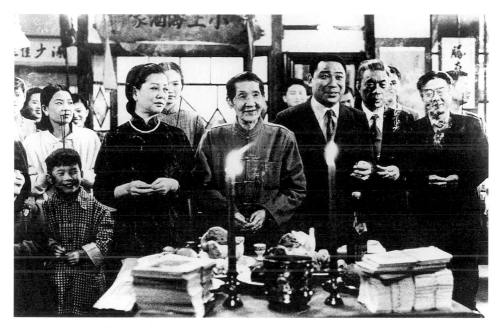

129 Hou Hsiao-hsien used medium and long shots throughout *A City of Sadness* (1989) to prevent easy audience identification in this sprawling family drama set in post-war Taiwan.

the emphasis was on such fictional accounts of the Japanese occupation as *Crows and Sparrows* (1949).

However, after Mao's victory in the civil war (1948), film-makers of the Third Generation were urged to focus on the revolution and the process of reconstruction, although they were permitted briefly to question the conduct of state affairs in such features as *Before the New Director Arrives* (Lü Ban, 1956) during the 'Hundred Flowers' era (1956–7). The first year of the Great Leap Forward saw film output double to 229 features and cartoons, the majority of which were propagandist pieces like *Loving the Factory as One's Home* (Zhao Ming, 1958).

In the early 1960s, Fourth Generation directors were given greater scope for stylistic experimentation, although, ironically, it was a member of the Third Generation, Xie Jin, who emerged as the leading exponent of such state-endorsed genres as the action adventure, social comedy and classical opera. Production then ceased altogether during the first four years of the Cultural Revolution and many directors were imprisoned or despatched to the country for 're-education'. Of the few films that were made immediately after 1970, the majority were 'revolutionary model operas' shot by non-professionals. In spite of the return of career directors after 1976, Chinese cinema remained in abeyance until the early 1980s.

The Fifth Generation graduated from the Beijing Film Academy in 1982 and entered an industry already showing signs of recovery with a cycle of features exploring the impact of the Cultural Revolution on professional and intellectual life. Under the guidance of the producer Wu Tianming, young film-makers like Huang Jianxin (*The Black Cannon Incident*, 1985) and Tian Zhuangzhuang (*Horse Thief*, 1986) began to re-evaluate Chinese social and cultural values, and even veterans like Xie Jin (*Hibiscus Town*, 1986) increased the political content of their work.

The leading figures of the Fifth Generation were Chen Kaige (b. 1953) and his former cameraman Zhang Yimou (b. 1950). Exceptional colour stylists who have emphasized the audiovisual elements of film over its traditional dramatic aspects, both directors have tended to use China's sprawling natural landscape as their *mise-en-scène*, capturing it in gliding long takes that often recall Jancsó. In *Red Sorghum* (1987), *Ju Dou* (1989), *Raise the Red Lantern* (1991) and *The Story of Qiu Ju* (1992), Zhang has demonstrated a flair for characterization and period in exploring the role of women in a patriarchal society, while Chen has concentrated on the effects of political ideology on the individual in *Yellow Earth* (1984), *The Big Parade* (1986), *King of the Children* (1988) and *Farewell, My Concubine* (1992).

The continued prosperity of Chinese cinema, despite fears of a backlash following the crushing of the Democracy Movement in 1989, is something of a repeat of the situation in Iran a decade earlier when the Islamic Revolution curtailed the activities of the New Film Group, which had been winning international prizes throughout the 1970s. Although production virtually ceased as the authorities decided how Islamic precepts were to be applied to the cinema, levels have consistently increased since the mid-1980s, and directors like Amir Naderi, Bahram Bayzai and Dariush Mehrjui have all enjoyed international festival success.

Whereas the film-makers of Iran responded to state-inspired political change, throughout the 1970s the members of the 'Third Polish School' played a vital role in shaping public consciousness about the need for reform. The movement's leading figure was Krzysztof Zanussi (b. 1939), whose films like *The Structure of Crystals* (1969) and *Illumination* (1973) made bold use of cinematic language to explore contemporary society and the conflict between personal emotion and

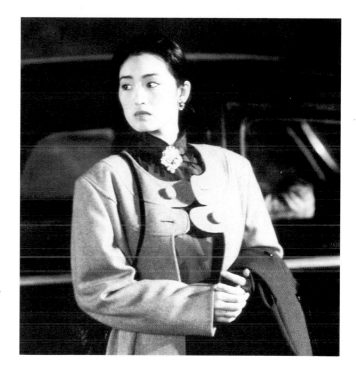

130 Zhang Yimou, *The Story of Qiu Ju* (1992). Gong Li as the peasant prepared to risk all for justice when her husband is assaulted by his employer.

professional duty. Along with Andrzej Wajda (*Man of Marble*, 1976) and Agnieszka Holland (*Provincial Actors*, 1980), Zanussi (in *The Constant Factor*, 1980) was also a pioneer of the 'cinema of moral anxiety', whose intense, low-budget features on the struggle of the individual for justice in a corrupt system echoed the demands of the burgeoning campaign for liberalization.

Following the formation of the Solidarity trade union in August 1980, Polish film-makers enjoyed 16 months of unprecedented freedom which resulted in the production of several anti-Stalinist and pro-Solidarity features, the most significant of which was Wajda's *Man of Iron* (1981). In December 1981, however, the Polish government imposed martial law and many prominent directors were driven into exile. Although Agnieszka Holland (*Europa, Europa*, 1990; *The Secret Garden*, 1994) has remained in Paris, Wajda and Zanussi returned home and the continued excellence of their work (Wajda, *Horse Hair Ring*, and Zanussi, *The Silent Touch*, both 1992), and that of Krzysztof Kiewslowski (*The Ten Commandments*, 1989; *The Double Life of Véronique*, 1991; and the trilogy *Three Colours: Blue, White, Red*, 1992) have maintained Poland's reputation for provocative cinema.

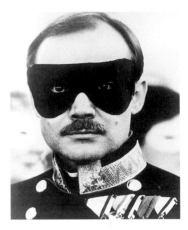

131 Klaus Maria Brandauer as the homosexual accused of spying on the Austro-Hungarian army for the Russians in István Szabó's *Colonel Redl* (1985).

Of all the film industries of the former Soviet bloc, Poland's is the only one to have emerged satisfactorily from the collapse of Communism in 1989. Deprived of state funding and protection from foreign (particularly Hollywood) imports, and forced to operate at a time of economic and political uncertainty, the remainder have experienced a dramatic fall in box-office receipts and thus productivity.

The most severely hit has been the former Yugoslavia, which had been enjoying a cinematic revival after the blight of the 'black film' before the outbreak of civil war in 1991. The resurgence had been led by the FAMU-trained Sřđan Karanović, Rajko Grlić, Goran Marković, Lordan Zafronović and Goran Paskaljević, collectively known as the 'Prague Group' because they were hailed as the heirs of the Czech New Wave on account of their absurdist humour and caustic satire. Their success paved the way for the rehabilitation of a number of *novi* film-makers and the emergence of many new ones, most notably Emir Kusturica, whose opulent tragi-comedies *When Father Was away on Business* (1985) and *Time of the Gypsies* (1988) won prizes at festivals around the world.

Despite their versatility and stylistic ingenuity, advocates of New Bulgarian Cinema like Eduard Zahariav, Rangel Vulchanov, Hristo Hristov and Liudmil Staikov and such members of Romania's 'Class of the 1970s' as Mircea Daneliuc, Dan Piţa and Mirceau Veriou have been unable to sustain the growth of their national cinemas since 1989. Even Hungary has recently experienced a marked cinematic decline, although many in the industry place the bulk of the blame on directorial self-indulgence rather than on post-communist malaise.

236

One of the most vociferous Hungarian critics is István Szabó (b. 1938), who, after Jancsó, has been the pre-eminent figure in Hungarian cinema since the 1960s. Heavily indebted to the *nouvelle vague*, Szabó's debut feature, *The Age of Illusions* (1964), revealed the influence of Truffaut, while *Father* (1966), *Love Film* (1970) and *25 Fireman's Street* (1973) all recalled the narrative strategies of Alain Resnais. Increasingly symbolic in structure and imagery, Szabó's allegories have continued to explore the impact of the past on individuals, whether under imperial control (*Colonel Redl*, 1985), Nazi tyranny (*Budapest Tales*, 1976; *Confidence*, 1979; *Mephisto*, 1981, and *Hanussen*, 1988) or democratic rule (*Sweet Emma, Dear Böbe*, 1992).

Since the emergence of Márta Mészáros, Pal Sándor, Pál Gábor, Sándor Sára, Judit Elek and Imre Gyöngyössy in the 1970s, Hungarian cinema has continued to produce talented film-makers. This consistency suggests it is only a matter of time before a profitable balance between personal vision and audience expectation is achieved.

More difficult to identify are solutions to the crises facing the film industries of the former Soviet republics as they emerge from the shadow of Socialist Realism for the first time in nearly sixty years. Strict censorship had been enforced throughout the 1970s and despite

132 Indolence on a summer's day as Alexander Kalyagin and Elena Solovei attempt to rekindle their romantic past in *Unfinished Piece for Mechanical Piano* (1987), Nikita Mikhalkov's adaptation of Chekhov's play *Platonov*.

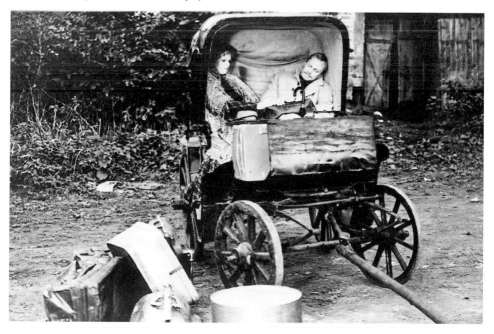

the appearance of a number of mildly satirical '*bytovye*' or 'everyday life' films like *Moscow Does not Believe in Tears* (Vladimir Menshov, 1980) in the early 1980s, Russia's leading film-maker, Andrei Tarkovsky (1932–86), could not be dissuaded from exile in 1982.

Whether tracing the exploits of a young partisan in *Ivan's Childhood* (1962) or the career of a medieval iconographer in *Andrei Rublev* (1966), Tarkovsky's films were notable for their austerity, poetry and depth of personal vision. His primary concern, 'the absence from our culture of room for spiritual existence', pervaded his entire *oeuvre* of stately, multi-layered and visually arresting features, which also shared an ethereality, whether in outer space (*Solaris*, 1972), the war-torn Russia of the director's youth (*Mirror*, 1975), the wasteland 'zones' of *Stalker* (1979), the Rome of *Nostalgia* (1983) or the Baltic island of *The Sacrifice* (1986).

Tarkovsky did not live to see the effect on Soviet cinema of Mikhail Gorbachev's liberal policies of *glasnost* and *perestroika*. With the abolition of post-production censorship in 1987, a number of long-banned films like *I'm Twenty* (Marlen Khutsiev, 1963), *Asya's Happiness* (Andrei Konchalovsky, 1967), *The Theme* (Gleb Panfilov, 1979), *Farewell* (Elem Klimov, 1981) and *Repentance* (Tengiz Abuladze, 1984) finally secured release prior to the appearance of such formally and dramatically innovative features as *Letters from a Dead Man* (Konstantin Lopushansky, 1986), *Plumbum, or A Dangerous Game* (Vadim Abdrashitov, 1986) and *Little Vera* (Vasili Pichul, 1988). However, since the disintegration of the Soviet Union not even the Russian industry has been able to resist Hollywood saturation, and a descent into the production of exploitation quickies threatens the future existence of 'art' cinema in an area that yielded so many of its most influential practitioners.

In contrast to the disruptions in the East, the situation in Western Europe has been one of continuity, with film-makers consolidating the formal and dramaturgical developments of the previous quarter-century. The proliferation of international festivals and specialist 'art' cinemas and video distributors, as well as network and pay television stations, has meant that the films of even the smallest European industries are now reaching considerable audiences. Yet few of Europe's national cinemas can claim to be self-sufficient, in consequence of which there is an increasing dependence on television sponsorship and co-production, with casts and crews drawn from all participating nations to enhance box-office appeal. The move towards internationalism had coincided with an absence of discernible national move-

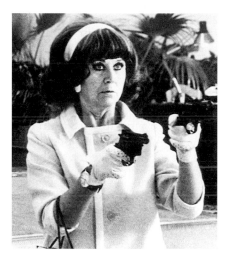

133 Julieta Serrano as one of the
*Women on the Verge of a Nervous
Breakdown* (1988), Pedro Almodóvar's
fraught comedy of, amongst much
else, infidelity, terrorism and drugged
gazpacho.

ments like Neo-Realism or the *nouvelle vague*, and the period since the
early 1970s has been characterized by the emergence of the journey-
working film-maker capable of completing projects within a variety
of cultural contexts.

Notwithstanding the sources of funding or the location of princi-
pal photography, national cinemas remain highly possessive of their
leading directors. Many talented artists have emanated from all parts
of Western Europe – Belgium: Chantal Ackerman and André
Delvaux; Holland: Paul Verhoeven and Fons Rademakers; Ireland:
Neil Jordan and Jim Sheridan; Portugal: Manuel Oliveira; Denmark:
Bille August and Gabriel Axel; Sweden: Bo Widerberg, Jan Troell and
Lasse Hallström; Norway: Ola Solum; and Iceland: Hrafn
Gunnlaugsson and Agust Gudmundsson – but a concise history pre-
cludes considering more than a few in any detail.

Spanish cinema, for so long hidebound by the dictates of the Franco
regime, began in the 1970s to build on the legacy of Luis Buñuel, Luís
Garcia Berlanga and Juan Antonio Bardem. Carlos Saura (b. 1932)
established himself as Spain's leading film-maker with such political
allegories as *Peppermint Frappé* (1967), which were influenced by the
national artistic tradition of *esperpento*, a dark, absurdist blend of fact
and fantasy, and flamenco dramas like *Carmen* (1983). The 1980s were
marked by the emergence of the cult director Pedro Almodóvar
(b. 1951), whose films include *Women on the Verge of a Nervous*   133
Breakdown (1988) and *Tie Me Up, Tie Me Down* (1990). In addition to

recalling the textures of Sirk and Fassbinder, these irrational comedies reflect the concerns of the gay community and the subculture of the *pasota* ('couldn't care less') generation.

Another independent director with a highly individual style who has come to prominence is Finland's Aki Kaurismäki (b. 1957). Profoundly influenced by American B movies and the French New Wave, Kaurismäki specializes in revisionist adaptations (*Hamlet Goes Business*, 1987, and *La Vie de bohème*, 1992), working-class portraits (*Ariel*, 1988, and *The Match Factory Girl*, 1989) and absurdist comedies like *Leningrad Cowboys Go America* (1989).

Switzerland has been hampered in establishing a single domestic market by its linguistic tripartition. However, while there is little Italian-language production, an appreciable German-speaking film industry has developed in Zurich, with Rolf Lyssy and Daniel Schmid among its principal figures. The Geneva-based francophone cinema has merited even wider recognition, largely as a result of the achievements of the Group 5 film-makers, the best-known of whom is Alain Tanner (b. 1929). A champion of the individual, an acute analyst of modern European values and a firm believer in co-production, Tanner demonstrated in films like *The Salamandar* (1971) and *Jonah*

134

134 The road movie Finnish style: Aki Kaurismäki's laconic, Jarmuschesque comedy *Leningrad Cowboys Go America* (1989).

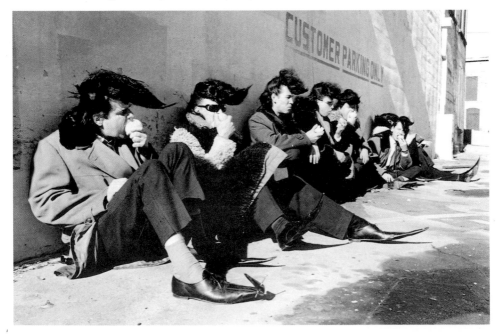

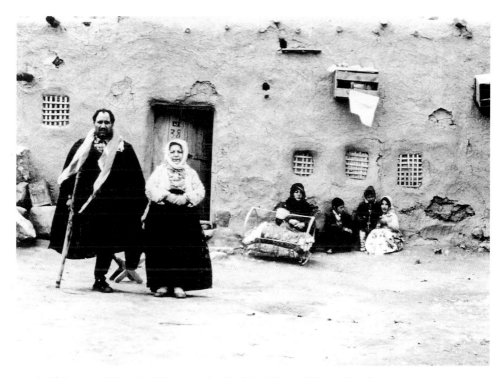

135 Serif Goren, *Yol* (1982). Written and edited by Yilmaz Güney, this allegory on Turkish underdevelopment traces the experiences of 5 prisoners on a week's parole.

Who Will Be 25 in the Year 2000 (1975) the influence of the British Free Cinema and the *nouvelle vague*.

Reminiscent of the films of Miklos Jancsó, Theo Angelopoulos's meditative amalgams of history and myth, *The Travelling Players* (1975) and *The Beekeeper* (1986), are among the best features produced in Greece since *Zorba the Greek* (Michael Cacoyannis, 1965). Neighbouring Turkey also produced an exceptional film-maker in Yilmaz Güney (1937–84). A passionate advocate of national cinema, his stark studies of poverty and repression, with provocative titles like *Pain* and *The Hopeless Ones* (both 1971), resulted in his imprisonment in 1972 on a charge of harbouring subversives. Released briefly, he was jailed again in 1974 for the alleged murder of a judge. He continued to write, and his former assistants Zeki Otken (*The Herd*, 1978, and *The Enemy*, 1979) and Serif Goren (*Anxiety*, 1975, and *Yol*, 1982) directed on his behalf. Güney escaped in 1981 to edit *Yol* himself in

135

Paris, but he was able to complete only one more feature, *The Wall* (1983), before his death.

It is Italy that remains the cardinal force in Mediterranean cinema. Many of the key films produced there since the 1970s have been the work of *auteurs* like Francesco Rosi, Marco Bellochio, Lina Wertmuller, Marco Ferreri and Ettore Scola, who made their feature debuts during the New Wave. The most widely acclaimed member of this group is Bernardo Bertolucci (b. 1940).

Inspired by Godard, Visconti and Pasolini (who scripted his first feature, *The Grim Reaper*, 1962), Bertolucci made his name with three studies of the impact on individuals of political ideology – Marxism in *Before the Revolution* (1964) and Fascism in *The Conformist* and *The Spider's Stratagem* (both 1970). The influential 1970 features marked the start of his association with the cinematographer Vittorio Storaro and the maturation of his distinctive style, which combined literary and philosophical allusion with an expressive use of *mise-en-scène*, complex narration, fluid camera movement and rhythmic editing. The problem of reconciliation to emotional or political turmoil has, to some degree, informed all of Bertolucci's work, and provides a link between such explorations of contemporary Italy as *Partner* (1968) and *The Tragedy of a Ridiculous Man* (1981) and lavish co-productions like *Last Tango in Paris* (1972), *1900* (1976), *The Last Emperor* (1987), *The Sheltering Sky* (1990) and *Little Buddha* (1994).

While perhaps no longer at the forefront of cinematic innovation, the Italian film industry is still more than capable of discovering exciting talent, as Paolo and Vittorio Taviani, Giuseppe Tornatore, Gianni Amelio, Nanni Moretti and Maurizio Nichetti testify.

French cinema in this period has benefitted from a similar blend of experience and exuberance, with veterans of the 1960s like Claude Sautet, Constantin Costa-Gavras, Jean-Pierre Mocky, Philippe de Broca and Claude Lelouch, and such newcomers as Maurice Pialat, Bertrand Blier, Diane Kurys and the documentarists Marcel Ophüls and Claude Lanzmann, all making notable contributions to post-New Wave film. The most significant director to emerge in this period was the eclectic Bertrand Tavernier (b. 1941). A former *Cahiers* critic, he has proved himself adept at period reconstruction, character study, police procedural and documentary, but it is his ability to combine 'Tradition of Quality' scripts with New Wave technique in such adaptations as *The Watchmaker of St Paul* (1973), *Clean Slate* (1981) and *A Sunday in the Country* (1984) that has won him pre-eminence. In addition, as both producer and president of the French guild of direc-

136

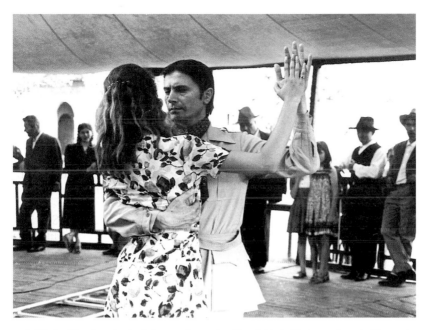

136 Giulio Brogi as both father and son in *The Spider's Stratagem* (1970), Bernardo Bertolucci's Borges inspired investigation of the obfuscatory nature of Italy's Fascist past.

tors, he has encouraged the talents of many of the younger generation of film-makers that includes Luc Besson, Jean-Jacques Beineix and Patrice Leconte.

In keeping with its past, the British cinema since 1970 has persisted with its obsessional fashioning of indigenous subject matter into facsimiles of the Hollywood product in the hope of finding a formula that will revive its fortunes on both sides of the Atlantic. Only the epic biographies of Richard Attenborough (*Gandhi*, 1982, and *Cry Freedom*, 1987) and the adroit adaptations of the British-based Indian-American partnership of Ishmail Merchant and James Ivory (*A Room with a View*, 1985; *Howards End*, 1991; and *The Remains of the Day*, 1993) have come close to repeating the success of Hugh Hudson's *Chariots of Fire* (1981). Thus, it has been a period of recurrent false dawns for the industry as a whole, with many leading performers and talented directors like John Boorman, Alan Parker, Nicholas Roeg, Ridley and Tony Scott, Adrian Lyne, Bill Forsyth and Stephen Frears ultimately forced to pursue their careers in Hollywood.

Few of the film-makers who chose to work almost exclusively within the British industry have enjoyed consistent commercial success, although the mordant social commentaries of Ken Loach (*Riff-Raff*, 1990) and the ironic observations of Mike Leigh (*Naked*, 1993) have usually been well received by the critics. Ken Russell's brash explorations of eroticism have rarely met with approval of any kind, although there is undeniable originality and flair in both his adaptations (*Women in Love*, 1969) and unconventional biopics (*Gothic*, 1986).

Russell's former set designer Derek Jarman (1942–94) cited him, along with Jean Cocteau and Kenneth Anger, as one of the major influences on his uncompromisingly experimental features, the first seven of which, including *Sebastiane* (1976) and *Jubilee* (1978), cost less than £3 million to complete. A principal figure in the flourishing gay and lesbian cinema movement, Jarman invariably focused on homosexual issues in films like *Caravaggio* (1986), *War Requiem* (1988), *Edward II* (1991) and *Wittgenstein* (1993), although they were also piquant impugnments of contemporary society and the conventions of narrative cinema.

Jarman shared a painterly eye with another avant-garde artist, Peter Greenaway (b. 1942), whose earliest works were structuralist pieces like *A Walk through H* (1978). His first feature, *The Draughtsman's Contract* (1982), introduced such recurrent themes as creativity, death and decay, and indicated a fondness for precise composition, visual symbolism, intellectual allusion and droll witticism. Since *Belly of an Architect* (1987) and *Drowning by Numbers* (1988), he has erred towards pictorialism, even in the technically and dramaturgically ambitious *Prospero's Books* (1991).

Several short-lived independent production companies attempted to resuscitate British cinema in the 1980s. The ex-Beatle George Harrison's Handmade Films, formed to ensure the completion of *Monty Python's Life of Brian* (Terry Jones, 1979), also sponsored such features as Terry Gilliam's Orwellian view of the future, *Brazil* (1985), and Neil Jordan's compassionate portrait of London low life, *Mona Lisa* (1986). The latter was co-produced by Palace Pictures, which entered into similar arrangements with the film company Goldcrest and Channel Four television. Films like *Chariots of Fire*, *Local Hero* (Bill Forsyth, 1983) and *The Killing Fields* (Roland Joffe, 1984) briefly cast Goldcrest and its chief executive David Puttnam in the roles of industry saviours. But the future seems to lie with descendants of 1960s social realism, that are wholly or partially funded by television – the

BBC: *Truly, Madly, Deeply* (Anthony Minghella, 1990); and Channel Four: *My Beautiful Laundrette* (Stephen Frears, 1985), *A Letter to Brezhnev* (Chris Bernard, 1985), *Distant Voices, Still Lives* (Terence Davies, 1988), *Hear My Song* (Peter Chelsom, 1991) and *Four Weddings and a Funeral* (Mike Newell, 1994).

The American film industry has also spent much of this period in pursuit of commercial success, to the point that its main preoccupation seems to be making money rather than movies. The primary reason for this was the impact of spiralling costs and audience caprice on the fortunes of the major studios, whose preparedness to sacrifice creative autonomy for financial security led to their absorption by various multinational conglomerates. Universal was purchased by MCA Inc. in 1962, which was itself taken over by the Japanese Matsushita company in 1990; Paramount was acquired by Gulf+Western Industries in 1966 and then Viacom in 1994; Warner Brothers was incorporated into Kinney Services in 1969 before merging with Time Inc. in 1990 to form Time Warner Inc.; Twentieth Century-Fox changed hands twice in 1981 and is now part of the Australian Rupert Murdoch's multimedia empire; while Columbia was consumed by Coca-Cola in 1982 and merged with Tri-Star before passing to the Japanese Sony Corporation in 1990. Even more tortuous was the round of dealing that saw United Artists become part of the Transamerica group in 1967, amalgamate with MGM (owned since 1970 by Kerk Kerkorian) in 1981, pass into Turner Broadcasting Systems in 1985, return to Kerkorian a year later and ultimately become part of the Australian Qintex Entertainment operation in 1990, leaving MGM free to merge with Pathé Communications to form MGM-Pathé the same year.

Despite the efforts of Robert Altman, Paul Mazursky, Hal Ashby, Paul Schrader, William Friedkin, Peter Bogdanovich and others to debunk many of Hollywood's most cherished myths with their revisionist approach to genre film-making in the post-Vietnam and post-Watergate era, the enthusiastic reception accorded disaster movies like *The Towering Inferno* (John Guillermin, 1974) convinced corporate executives of the need to reduce output and concentrate on the production of big-budget spectacles. The 'blockbuster' mentality came to dominate Hollywood thinking after the phenomenal success of Steven Spielberg's *Jaws* (1975) and George Lucas's *Star Wars* (1976) and its 137 sequels, which also established a new, younger audience, whose taste for all-action adventures, packed with star names and special effects, prompted a proliferation of escapist entertainment.

Following the calamitous failure of Michael Cimino's $35 million Western *Heaven's Gate* (1980), the studios became increasingly dependent on 'kidpix' that, released nationwide on the back of extensive pre-publicity, were expected to return unprecedented profits. Aimed specifically at the teenage market and frequently supported by lucrative merchandising campaigns, these were produced across a range of traditional and hybrid genres – action adventure: Spielberg's Indiana Jones trilogy and the films of Arnold Schwarzenegger; comic-book adaptation: *Superman* (Richard Donner, 1978) and *Batman* (Tim Burton, 1989); science fiction: *Star Trek* (Robert Wise, 1979) and *Back to the Future* (Robert Zemeckis, 1985); 'sword and sorcercy': *The Dark Crystal* (Jim Henson, 1982); horror: *Gremlins* (Joe Dante, 1984) and *Ghostbusters* (Ivan Reitman, 1984); pop musical: *Saturday Night Fever*

137 George Lucas, *Star Wars* (1977). 'A long time ago in a galaxy far far away', Darth Vader (Dave Prowse) and Ben (Obi-Wan) Kenobi (Alec Guinness) cross light sabres in episode 4 of a projected 9-part series.

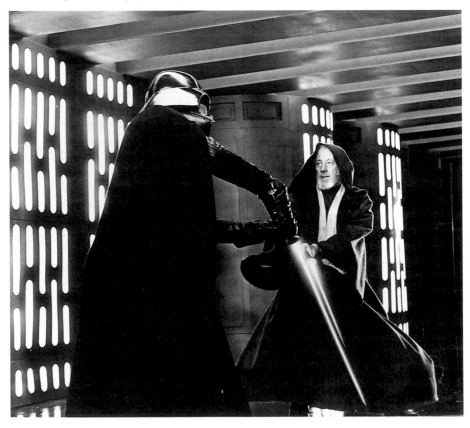

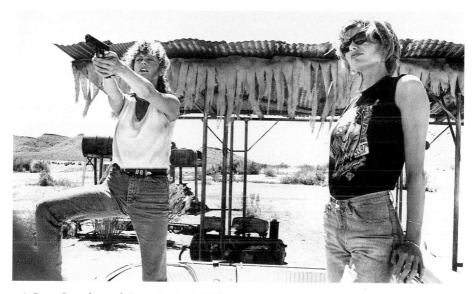

138 Susan Sarandon and Geena Davies in Ridley Scott's *Thelma and Louise* (1991) which prompted a fierce debate about whether it was a genuinely feminist road movie or an exploitative example of genre revision.

(John Badham, 1977) and *Fame* (Alan Parker, 1980); and high-school comedy: *Fast Times at Ridgemont High* (Amy Heckerling, 1982) and *Ferris Bueller's Day Off* (John Hughes, 1986).

Doses of explicit sex and graphic violence were injected into other genres to encourage the new audience to keep coming in adulthood – 'slash and splatter' horror: *The Texas Chainsaw Massacre* (Tobe Hooper, 1974) and *A Nightmare on Elm Street* (Wes Craven, 1984); *film noir*: *Body Heat* (Lawrence Kasdan, 1981) and *Fatal Attraction* (Adrian Lyne, 1987); the cop thriller: *Beverly Hills Cop* (Martin Brest, 1984) and *Lethal Weapon* (Richard Donner, 1987); the gangster picture: *The Godfather* trilogy (Francis Ford Coppola, 1972, 1974, 1990) and *The Untouchables* (Brian De Palma, 1987); 'body count' crime: *Reservoir Dogs* and *Pulp Fiction* (both Quentin Tarantino, 1992 and 1994); the Western: *Dances with Wolves* (Kevin Costner, 1990) and *Unforgiven* (Clint Eastwood, 1992); the road movie: *My Own Private Idaho* (Gus Van Sant, 1991) and *Thelma and Louise* (Ridley Scott, 1991); and the Vietnam war film: *Apocalypse Now* (Francis Ford Coppola, 1979) and *Platoon* (Oliver Stone, 1986).

The leading mainstream directors throughout this period have been

138

the college-trained *cinéastes* Francis Ford Coppola (b. 1939), Martin Scorsese (b. 1942) and Steven Spielberg (b. 1947). The erratic Coppola has rarely managed to repeat his success of the 1970s with subsequent blockbusters like *The Cotton Club* (1984) and *Bram Stoker's Dracula* (1992). An inspired technician, he has too often allowed visual flamboyance to overwhelm his smaller-scale studies of individuals fighting the system, like *The Conversation* (1974) and *Tucker: The Man and His Dream* (1988). Scorsese, like Coppola a former assistant to Roger Corman, has relentlessly explored the dangers of obsession in a series of robust features, many of which have starred Robert De Niro – *Taxi Driver* (1976), *Raging Bull* (1980), *The King of Comedy* (1983) and *Casino* (1995). His exceptional ability to develop character can be seen in many stylish adaptations, including *The Last Temptation of Christ* (1988), *GoodFellas* (1990) and *The Age of Innocence* (1993). Spielberg's control of tension and pace and his capacity for evoking wonder have guaranteed the box-office triumphs of kidpix like *Close Encounters of the Third Kind* (1977) and *E.T. The Extra-Terrestrial* (1982). However, a lack of emotional restraint has marred his adult ventures like *The Color Purple* (1985), although *Schindler's List* (1993) managed to avoid melodramatic excess in its exploration of the Holocaust.

Pre-eminent among independent *auteurs* were Robert Altman (b. 1925) and Woody Allen (b. 1935). Altman's savagely satirical observations on contemporary American society have invariably taken the form of either intimate profiles of eccentric individuals (*McCabe and Mrs Miller*, 1971, and *The Long Goodbye*, 1973) and coteries (*Thieves Like Us*, 1974, and *Three Women*, 1977) or congested, complex dissections of revered institutions (*M*A*S*H*, 1970; *Nashville*, 1975; *The Player*, 1992 and *Short Cuts*, 1993). Religion, the impermanence of romance and the foibles of the New York intelligentsia are the recurrent themes of Woody Allen's intensely personal films. Cinematic *hommages* abound in his work, from the parodies he dismissed as 'the early funny ones' in the Felliniesque *Stardust Memories* (1980) through his Bergman-inspired dramas to such mature social comedies as *Annie Hall* (1977), *Manhattan* (1979), *Hannah and Her Sisters* (1986), *Crimes and Misdemeanours* (1989) and *Husbands and Wives* (1992).

Indeed, much of the most innovative cinema released in America in recent years has been produced independently by directors such as the late John Cassavetes, David Lynch, Ethan and Joel Coen, Hal Hartley, Jim Jarmusch, Alan Rudolph, John Sayles and Whit Stillman. Independence has also afforded women film-makers the opportunity denied them by Hollywood to explore gynocentric themes. However,

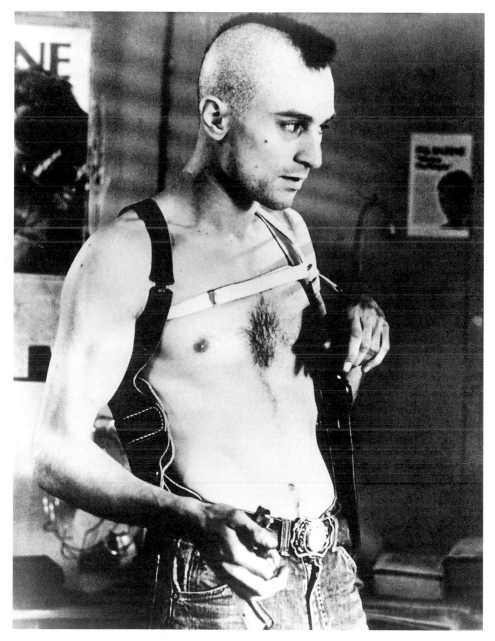

139 Robert De Niro as Travis Bickle, the personification of mid-1970s American angst in *Taxi Driver* (1976), Martin Scorsese's amalgam of horror, Western and *film noir*.

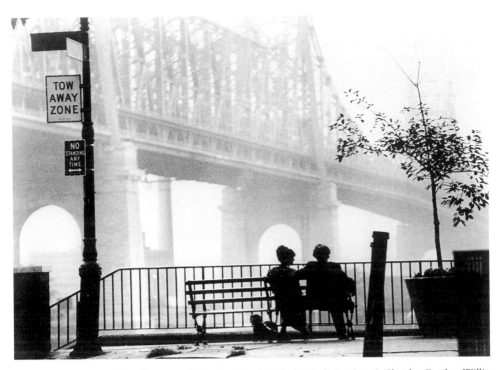

140 Diane Keaton and Woody Allen in Allen's *Manhattan* (1979). Shot by Gordon Willis in Panavision on Technicolor stock, the film was printed in monochrome.

the need to demonstrate commercial potential to secure funds for further independent projects, let alone break into the mainstream, has meant that Kathryn Bigelow, Lizzie Borden, Martha Coolidge, Yvonne Rainer, Barbara Kopple, Susan Seidelman, Joan Micklin Silver and others have usually been forced to sublimate their feminist concerns.

While the Hollywood emphasis on traditional genres and sexual stereotypes persists, challenging roles for women in non-voyeuristic films will remain scarce. The clichéd representation of black character and experience has created a similar situation for African-American artists. Following a decade of liberal-conscience features starring Sidney Poitier, black cinema began to emerge as a mainstream phenomenon in the wake of the Civil Rights campaign with films like *Putney Swope* (Robert Downey, 1969) and *Sweet Sweetback's Baadasssss Song* (Melvin Van Peebles, 1971). Anxious to capitalize on this, Hollywood released a handful of 'blaxploitation' films like *Shaft* (Gordon Parks, 1971); but as Robert Townsend's *Hollywood Shuffle*

(1987) astutely demonstrated, black performers were still invariably consigned stereotypical or tokenist roles. Matters were radically altered with the emergence of the confrontational Spike Lee (b. 1956). His authentic examinations of intra-racial (*She's Gotta Have It*, 1986, and *Malcolm X*, 1992) and inter-racial (*Do the Right Thing*, 1989, and *Jungle Fever*, 1991) tension prompted an outpouring of films by young African-American directors, notably *Boyz N the Hood* (John Singleton, 1991), *New Jack City* (Mario Van Peebles, 1991), *Juice* (Ernest R. Dickerson, 1992) and *Just Another Girl on the IRT* (Leslie Harris, 1993).

141

By 1991, 76 per cent of American households possessed a video cassette recorder or laser disc player and the combined revenue generated by the rental or direct sale of films to satisfy this home entertainment market, in an era of record receipts, was twice that taken at the theatre box office. Even at a time of multiscreen complexes, an increasing number of films go 'straight to video'. Indeed, so important is small-screen income that films that are not 'letterboxed' to retain their widescreen format are 'panned and scanned', or cropped, so that the essential action occurs within a 'TV-safe' area. Such procedures deprive the viewer of seeing the feature the filmmaker envisaged and, moreover, television's electronic images are incapable of adequately reproducing the lustre of chemically created celluloid colour or the subtlety and definition of monochrome.

The average cost of a motion picture had risen to over $20 million by the early 1990s and studio executives were increasingly reluctant to

141 Ossie Davis, who directed such early examples of Black Cinema as *Cotton Comes to Harlem* (1970) and *Black Girl* (1972), with Spike Lee on the set of *Do the Right Thing* (1989).

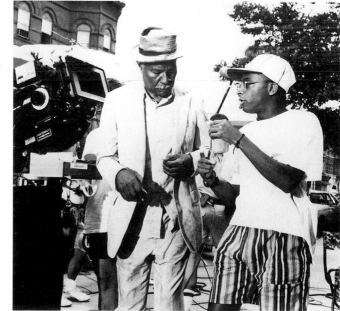

gamble on untried formulae. As a consequence, the decade has thus far followed the trends set in the late-1980s for sequels, remakes, restorations, director's cuts and adaptations of 'presolds', like blockbuster novels or successful foreign-language films. The majors themselves no longer produce features but distribute (and, in the case of MGM-Pathé, exhibit) them on the basis of 'negative pick-up' deals, by which producers sell completed pictures in return for 'front end' funding or 'back end' percentages of box-office receipts. This revenue is then used to meet production costs and pay for the original 'package' of concept and creative personnel that has been assembled by a talent agency from its own client list.

Hollywood has changed beyond all recognition in the last twenty-five years. Yet in spite of the collapse of the studio system, the introduction of new business practices, the proliferation of independent production and the interpolation of new audiovisual and dramaturgical strategies from a variety of national cinemas, the Hollywood film retains both its classical look and its unrivalled commercial appeal throughout the world. This remarkable propensity for adaptability should stand it in good stead as the cinema prepares to enter another age of technological transformation.

Epilogue: For Future Presentation . . .

Cinema has always approached new technology with extreme caution. Sound, colour, 3-D and wide-screen processes were all originally resisted for fear of disturbing the commercial status quo, until financial crises made the risk of their introduction seem worthwhile. Thus, the increasing sophistication of home entertainment systems like laser disc, video CD and CDi suggests that exhibitors might be about to resort to scale once more as a means of inducing customers into their theatres.

Although Cinerama had proved too cumbersome and costly to be commercially viable, the unique illusion of depth and involvement it created undeniably thrilled audiences. First demonstrated at Expo 70 in Osaka, the Canadian Imax system attempted to surpass the Cinerama experience. Shot on 65mm stock passed horizontally through the camera and projected in a similar way from a 70mm print, Imax cast an image three times the size of Panavision-70 onto a gigantic curvilinear screen without perceptible loss of definition. A modified version, called Omnimax, heightened the sense of participation by projecting images through a fish-eye lens onto a dome. However, costs are as prohibitive as they were for Cinerama, particularly as the necessary equipment is exclusive to the Imax Corporation. Fewer than ninety theatres worldwide can accommodate the system, but the number is set to increase in the light of the success enjoyed by Julien Temple's record of the Rolling Stones At the Max (1992).

Patented by the special effects expert Douglas Trumbull, the Showscan system also employs 70mm film and specially tailored screens, but it achieves image clarity by projecting at a phenomenal speed of 60 frames per second. In contrast, Dynavision, requiring only an adapted 70mm projector and a portable screen, can produce sizeable, well-defined images even from standard 35mm prints. However, over a decade after its launch, the system has yet to establish itself.

The potential of videotape (VT) was similarly overlooked for nearly thirty years. The idea of recording visual images on magnetic tape had occurred to the Soviet scientist Boris Rtcheouloff in 1922, but it was not until the early 1950s that the first machines appeared. Another quarter of a century elapsed before Sony introduced the Betamax video-cassette recorder (VCR) for home use, only to see it supplanted as the industry standard by JVC's Video Home System (VHS) format in 1977.

Individuals like the Korean Nam June Paik began to explore the possibilities of 'video art' in the early 1960s, but it was not until Scott Bartlett and Tom DeWitt demonstrated with otton (1967) the effects that could be achieved by manipulating images on videotape and returning them to celluloid for exhibition that feature film-makers began to take the form seriously. Godard was the first director of any renown to experiment publicly with VT (Numéro deux, 1975) and he has since taped a number of films and television programmes, but full-length presentations shot on high definition video (HDV) and converted for standard theatrical release have been rare since Julia & Julia (Peter Del Monte, 1987). In the early 1990s the movement towards 'electronic cinema' gained momentum and it is only a matter of time before HDV theatres, equipped with video projectors and serviced by satellite links or fibre optic cables, make their appearance.

In the meantime, videotape will continue to play a prominent role in the production of traditional motion pictures. Re-usable and capable of instant playback, it enables film-makers and performers to evaluate both rehearsals and takes on the set itself. It is also becoming common to edit features on video by copying images onto tape, computer-cataloguing them and then resequencing them until a satisfactory workprint is obtained. This then acts as a guide for the editor, who assembles the final negative in the conventional manner. During the production of One from the Heart *(1982)*, Francis Ford Coppola developed the interactive storyboard, which enabled him to conduct compositional experiments with scenes computer-generated from drawings, photographs, rushes and mattes.

One of the least laudable applications of video technology is colorization, by which computer-allocated hues are electronically added to video copies of monochrome films purely to enhance their commercial appeal. Among the first colorized pictures released in *1984* were the Laurel and Hardy feature Way Out West *(James Horne, 1937)* and two Laurel and Hardy shorts, Topper *(Norman Z. McLeod, 1937)*, and Yankee Doodle Dandy *(Michael Curtiz, 1942)*. In *1985*, these were joined by Miracle on 34th Street *(George Seaton, 1947)*. While reasonably popular with audiences, they were castigated by critics and artists alike, who argued that rather than ameliorating a film, the process simultaneously destroyed its original compositional values, misrepresented the artistic vision and technical accomplishment of the director and cinematographer, and perverted the course of cinema history. In spite of the protests, it seems likely that the vogue for colorization will endure.

As Steven Spielberg's Jurassic Park *(1993)* testified, 3-D computer animation has come a long way since it was first used to generate special effects for science fiction films like Futureworld *(Richard T. Heffron, 1976)*. Sony opened a 3-D theatre in New York in *1994*, which used special headsets to give the pictures added depth. However, more authentic stereoscopic images are provided by holograms, which enable the viewer to discover different aspects of the objects represented, according to their vantage point. Holography was pioneered by the British physicist Dennis Gabor in *1947*, but since Alex Jacobson and Victor Evtukov succeeded in producing real-time holographic moving images of an aquarium in *1969*, little progress has been made towards holographic cinema.

In the novelty-hungry era of the *1950s*, a couple of experiments were conducted in olfactory cinema: Behind the Great Wall, *produced in Aromarama in 1959 and* Scent of Mystery, *a Smell-o-vision (or Scentovision) experience that was released the following year. The cult director John Waters is the only film-maker to have revived the concept to date for* Polyester *(1981)*, which provided on-screen cues for the audience to scratch-and-sniff their 'Odorama' cards. The 'king of the gimmicks' in the *1950s* was William Castle. In addition to patenting spoof processes like 'Emergo' (a plastic skeleton that passed over the audience during The House on Haunted Hill, *1959*) and 'Percepto' (an electic buzzer fitted to the seat and activated during The Tingler, *1959*), Castle also devised such forms of audience participation as the 'Fright Break' towards the climax of Homicidal *(1961)*, during which patrons would be guaranteed a refund if they stood in 'Coward's Corner' and the 'Punishment Poll' conducted at the close of Mr Sardonicus *(1961)* to decide the villain's fate.

The first genuinely interactive process was the Czech 'Lanterna Magika', which was demonstrated at Expo 67 in Montreal. This provided viewers with the opportunity to select from a variety of plot options. A similar capability will soon be available to owners of CDi players, but the most exciting interactive process devised so far is 'Virtual Reality'. Two techniques have been investigated to date – digital holograms and viewing helmets containing camera or computer-linked liquid crystal displays. In time, viewers will be able to enter and interact with stereoscopic simulations of historical or fantasy environments, but even though multiple participation will be possible, it is difficult to envisage how it can be satisfactorily accommodated in the theatrical presentation of a motion picture.

Film-makers have been finding aesthetic solutions to the problems posed by technology throughout the history of cinema. It remains to be seen whether the processes already in development (or those that will follow) will have any lasting impact on the audiovisual language of film, as opposed simply to its exhibition. Past experience suggests that technological advance is irresistible, but no matter what the future course of the motion picture is, it is essential that the personal vision of the film-maker is retained if cinema is to continue to merit its place in the world of art.

Select Bibliography

General

For the numerous monographs available on the stars, readers are advised to consult the bibliographies of the books listed under *General*. Halliwell, Leslie, with John Walker, *Halliwell's Filmgoer's Companion*, 10th edition (London, 1993). *The International Dictionary of Films and Filmmakers* 4 vols (London): *Films* (1990); *Directors* (1991); *Actors and Actresses* (1992); *Writers and Production Artists* (1984) Karney, Robyn, *Who's Who in Hollywood* (London, 1993). Katz, Ephraim, *The International Film Encyclopaedia* (London, 1980). Kuhn, Annette, with Suzannah Radstone, eds, *The Women's Companion to International Film* (London, 1990). Magill, Frank N., ed., *Magill's Survey of Cinema: English Language Films: First Series* (London, 1982). —, *Magill's Survey of Cinema: Foreign Language Films* (Englewood Cliffs, NJ, 1985). Mast, Gerald, *A Short History of the Movies*, 4th edition (New York, 1992). Monaco, James, and the editors of Baseline, *The Encyclopedia of Film* (London, 1991). Quinlan, David, *Quinlan's Illustrated Dictionary of the Film Comedy Stars* (London, 1992). —, *Quinlan's Illustrated Dictionary of Film Stars* (London, 1986). —, *Quinlan's Illustrated Directory of Film Character Actors* (London, 1985). —, *Quinlan's Illustrated Guide to Film Directors* (London, 1983). Rhode, Eric, *A History of the Cinema: From its Origins to 1970* (London, 1976). Robinson, David, *World Cinema: A Short History* (London, 1973). Roud, Richard, ed., *Cinema: A Critical Dictionary* (London, 1980). Slide, Anthony, ed., *The American Film Industry: A Historical Dictionary* (London, 1986). —, *The International Film Industry: A Historical Dictionary* (New York, 1989). Thomas, Nicholas, ed., *The International Dictionary of Films and Filmmakers*, 2nd edition (Chicago, 1990).

Film Theory

Arnheim, Rudolf, *Film as Art* (London, 1969). Bazin, André, *What is Cinema?*, Vols I and II, transl. H. Gray (Berkeley, CA, 1971). Mast, Gerald, Marshall Cohen and Leo Braudy, eds, *Film Theory and Criticism: Introductory Readings*, 4th edition (New York, 1992). Metz, Christian, *Psychoanalysis and the Cinema*, transl. Celia Britton, Annwyl Williams, Ben Brewster and Alfred Guzzetti (London, 1982). Mulvey, Laura, *Visual and Other Pleasures* (London, 1989). Penley, Constance, ed., *Feminism and Film Theory* (London, 1988).

Chapter One

Barnouw, Erik, *The Magician and the Cinema* (New York, 1981). Burch, Noël, *Life to Those Shadows*, transl. and ed. Ben Brewster (London, 1990). Coe, Brian, *The History of Movie Photography* (New York, 1981). Fell, John L., ed., *Film Before Griffith* (Berkeley, CA, 1983). Hammond, Paul, *Marvellous Méliès* (London, 1974). Hendricks, Gordon, *Eadweard Muybridge: The Father of the Motion Picture* (London, 1975). —, *The Edison Motion Picture Myth* (Berkeley, CA, 1961).

Chapter Two

Brownlow, Kevin, *The Parade's Gone By . . .* (London, 1968). Everson, William K., *American Silent Film* (New York, 1978). Koszarski, Richard, *The Man You Loved to Hate: Erich von Stroheim and Hollywood* (New York, 1983). Petrie, Graham, *Hollywood Destinies: European Directors in Hollywood, 1922–1931* (London, 1985). Robinson, David, *Chaplin: His Life and Art* (London, 1985). Schickel, Richard, *D. W. Griffith: An American Life* (London, 1984).

Chapter Three

Abel, Richard, *French Cinema: The First Wave, 1915–1929* (Princeton, NJ, 1984). Eisenstein, Sergei M., *Film Form: Essays in Film Theory* and *The Film Sense*, transl. and ed. Jay Leyda (London, 1951). Eisner, Lotte H., *The Haunted Screen: Expressionism in the German Cinema and the Influence of Max Reinhardt* (London, 1969). Knight, Arthur, *The Liveliest Art* (New York, 1957). Kracauer, Siegfried, *From Caligari to Hitler: A Psychological History of the German Film* (Princeton, NJ, 1947). Leprohon, Pierre, *The Italian Cinema*, transl. Roger Greaves and Oliver Stallybrass (New York, 1972). Leyda, Jay, *Kino: A History of the Russian and Soviet Film* (London, 1983). Monaco, Paul, *Cinema and Society: France and Germany during the Twenties* (New York, 1976). Youngblood, Denise J., *Soviet Cinema in the Silent Era, 1918–1935* (Austin, TX, 1991).

Chapter Four

Altman, Rick, *The American Film Musical* (London, 1989). —, ed., *Sound Theory, Sound Practice* (New York, 1992). Dyer, Richard, *Heavenly Bodies: Film Stars and Society* (London, 1986). Gallagher, Tag, *John Ford: The Man and His Films* (Berkeley, CA, 1986). Geduld, Harry M., *The Birth of the Talkies: From Edison to Jolson* (Bloomington, IN, 1975). McBride, Joseph, *Frank Capra: The Catastrophe of Success* (London, 1992). Schatz, Thomas, *The Genius of the System: Hollywood Filmmaking in the Studio Era* (London, 1988). —, *Hollywood Genres: Formulas, Filmmaking and the Studio System* (New York, 1981). Shadoian, Jack, *Dreams and Dead Ends: The American Gangster/Crime Film* (Cambridge, MA, 1979). Walker, Alexander, *The Shattered Silents: How the Talkies Came to Stay* (London, 1986).

Chapter Five

Aitken, Ian, *Film and Reform: John Grierson and the Documentary Film Movement* (London, 1990). Aldgate, Anthony, and Jeffrey Richards, *Britain Can Take It: The British Cinema in the Second World War* (Oxford, 1986). Anderson, Joseph L., and Donald Richie, *The Japanese Film: Art and Industry* (Princeton, NJ, 1982). Barnouw, Erik, *Documentary: A History of the Non-Fiction Film*, 2nd edition (New York, 1992). Bergan, Ronald, *Jean Renoir: Projections in Paradise* (London, 1992). Landy, Marcia, *Fascism in Film: The Italian Commercial Cinema, 1931–1943* (Princeton, NJ, 1986). Renoir, Jean, *My Life and My Films*, transl. Norman Denny (New York, 1974). Richards, Jeffrey, *The Age of the Dream Palace: Cinema and Society in Britain, 1930–1939* (London, 1984). Schindler, Colin, *Hollywood Goes to War: Films and American Society, 1939–1952* (London, 1979). Truffaut, François, *Hitchcock*, rev. edition (London, 1983). Welch, David, *Propaganda and the German Cinema, 1933–1945* (Oxford, 1983).

Chapter Six

Bock, Audie, *Japanese Film Directors* (London, 1978). Bondanella, Peter, *Italian Cinema: From Neorealism to the Present* (New York, 1983). Buñuel, Luis, *My Last Breath* (London, 1984). Cowie, Peer, *Ingmar Bergman: A Critical Biography* (London, 1982). Navasky, Victor S., *Naming Names* (New York, 1980). Nyce, Ben, *Satyajit Ray: A Study of His Films* (New York, 1988). Ray, Robert, *A Certain Tendency of the Hollywood Cinema, 1930–1980* (Princeton, NJ, 1985). Richie, Donald, *The Films of Akira Kurosawa*, rev. edition (Berkeley, CA, 1984). Silver, Alain, and Elizabeth Ward, eds, *Film Noir: An Encyclopedic Reference to the American Style* (London, 1979).

Chapter Seven

American Federation of Arts, *A History of the American Avant-Garde Cinema* (New York, 1976). Bondanella, Peter, *The Cinema of Federico Fellini* (Princeton, NJ, 1992). Chanan, Michael, *Twenty-five Years of the New Latin American Cinema* (London, 1983). Chatman, Seymour, *Antonioni: Or, The Surface of the World* (Berkeley, CA, 1985). Hill, John, *Sex, Class and Realism: British Cinema 1956–1963* (London, 1986). Hillier, Jim, ed., *Cahiers du Cinéma, the 1950s: Neo-Realism, Hollywood, New Wave* (London, 1985). —, *Cahiers du Cinéma, 1960–1968: New Wave, New Cinema, Re-evaluating Hollywood* (Cambridge, MA, 1986). Monaco, James, *The New Wave: Truffaut, Godard, Chabrol, Rohmer, Rivette* (New York, 1976). Mordden, Ethan, *Medium Cool: The Movies of the 1960s* (New York, 1990)

Chapter Eight

Clark, Paul, *Chinese Cinema: Culture and Politics since 1949* (Cambridge, 1987). Dyer, Richard, *Now You See It: Studies on Lesbian and Gay Film* (London, 1990). Elsaesser, Thomas, *New German Cinema: A History* (London, 1989). Guerrero, Edward, *Framing Blackness: The Politics and Culture of the Black Image in American Cinema* (Philadelphia, PA, 1993). Kolker, Robert Philip, *A Cinema of Loneliness: Penn, Kubrick, Scorsese, Spielberg, Altman*, 2nd edition (New York, 1988). Liehm, Mira, and Antonin J. Liehm, *The Most Important Art: East European Film after 1945* (Berkeley, CA, 1977). McFarlane, Brian, *Australian Cinema* (New York, 1988). Malkmus, Lizbeth, and Roy Armes, *Arab and African Film Making* (London, 1991). Wood, Robin *Hollywood from Vietnam to Reagan* (New York, 1986).

Illustration Credits

Numbers refer to plates, roman numerals refer to colour plates

Courtesy of ABC Cable and International Broadcast, Inc: X. Artificial Eye: 73, 83, 135. BFI Stills, Posters & Designs: VIII, IX, XI, XII, 8, 9, 11–19, 21, 23–27, 30, 31, 36–75, 77–84, 86–88, 91–116, 119–124, 126–129, 131–140. Courtesy of BetaFilm (KirchGroup) & RHI Entertainment, Inc: XIII. Photo The Bettmann Archive: 89. Photo courtesy Robert & Mylene

Bresson/Argos Films, Paris: 103. Printed with permission of Gearóid de Brún, Cultural Centre of Aran, Eire: 27. Still courtesy of CTE & The Samuel Goldwyn Company. © 1933 United Artists Corporation. All Rights Reserved: 70. Raymond Cauchetier: 105. Central Office of Information, Footage File: 71, 82. Photo courtesy of Brian Coe: VII. Courtesy of Columbia Pictures. All Rights Reserved. Columbia Pictures Corporation, © 1946 Renewed 1973: 64; © 1939 Renewed 1967: 65; © 1963 Renewed 1990 Horizon Pictures (GB) Ltd: 111; © 1964: 113; © 1976: 139. Contemporary Films, London: 98, 118, 126, 127. Photo Macusa Cores/El Deseo S.A.: 133. © 1950 Daiei Co., Ltd: 97. ERA International HK Ltd: 129. International Center for Photography at George Eastmam House: 28. © Roy Export Company Establishment: 20, 21. Filmverlag der Autoren GmbH: 122. Les Grands Films Classiques, Paris: 44, 77. Photo The Huntley Film Archive: 20, 33, 34, 101. Archives Joris IVENS – CAPI FILMS: 72. Photo The Kobal Collection: 29. François Lehr/Sipa Press: 123. Photo The Arts Council, London: 22. Courtesy of Lucasfilm. TM & © Lucasfilm Ltd (LFL) 1977. All Rights Reserved: 137. Lumiere Pictures Limited: XIV, 102, 109. M.P.C.-CMF: 75. © 1959 MGM/UA Communications Co. All Rights Reserved: 94. © 1991 MGM-Pathe Communications Co. All Rights Reserved: 138. Mafilm Plc: 119. © Mme M. Malthête-Méliès: 12. Mosfilm: 47–49, 80, 120, 132. F. W. Murnau-Stiftung/Transit-Film: XI, 38, 39, 40. Photo The Museum of Modern Art/Film Stills Archive, New York: 16. Copyright ORF/Mafilm Plc: 131. Photo Cinémathèque Française, Paris: 10, 32. Pegaso: XV. Panoramic Films: 104. Photofest: 117, 118. Radiotelevisione Italiana: 136. By courtesy of the Rank Organisation Plc: 68, 69, 101. Courtesy of Republic Entertainment Inc: 92, 115. Photo Agenzia Giornalistica Italia, Rome: 85. Courtesy of the Romulus Collection, CTE (Carlton) Ltd: XII, 108. NMPFT/Science & Society Picture Library: I–VI, X, XIV. Seawell Films: 124. Still reproduced with the kind of permission of Services Sound and Vision Corporation: 79. Shochiku Co., Ltd: 96. Photo Edwin Smith: 2, 4, 6. © AB Svensk Filmindustri: 37, 99. Turner Entertainment Co. All Rights Reserved, © 1939: IX; © 1926: 28; © 1927: 29; © 1921: 30; © 1926, 31; © 1927: 50; © 1933: 52; © 1931: 54; © 1937: 55; © 1930: 58; © 1939: 59; © 1943: 61; © 1941: 91; © 1952: 95; © 1968: 112. RKO Radio Pictures, Inc. Used by Permission Turner Entertainment Co. All Rights Reserved, © 1935: 53; © 1938: 56; © 1933: 66; © 1941: 67. Courtesy the Estate of Jiří Trnka: 121. Twentieth Century Fox Film Corporation. All Rights Reserved, © 1928: 32; © 1926: 42; © 1953: 90. Uninci: 87, 100. Copyright © by Universal City Studios. Inc. Courtesy of MCA Publishing Rights, A Division of MCA Inc: 26, 51, 60, 63, 88, 93, 141. Motion Picture, Sound and Video Branch, U.S. National Archives and Records Administration: 84. © 1979 United Artists Corporation. All Rights Reserved: 140. © 1962 United Artists Company & Danjaq S.A. All Rights Reserved: 110. Villealfa Filmproductions Oy: 134. Photo Wisconsin Center for Film and Theater Research: 35.

Glossary

Animatic A rough test version of a sequence. **animation** Any technique that allows inanimate objects to move on screen. **aspect ratio** the relationship of a frame's height to its width. **asynchronous sound** Sound that does not emanate from within the frame. **back lot** Open land behind a studio on which imitation locations were built. **Belasco staging** A style of *mise-en-scène* in which the whole set is fully decorated in authentic detail, originally developed for the stage by the theatrical impresario David Balasco (1854–1931). **chorine** A member of a chorus line. **continuity editing** An editing method that matches screen direction, position and temporal relations from shot to shot to ensure clarity of narrative. **creative geography** The juxtaposition of footage shot in diverse locations to create spatial and temporal unity. **cross-cutting** Editing technique that alternates shots of two or more simultaneous actions (also called parallel editing). **day-for-night** The use of filters and/or underexposure to give footage shot in daylight a night-time look. **deep focus** The exploitation of depth of field to keep near and distant planes in sharp focus, thus allowing compositional depth. **diegesis** the world in which a narrative film's action takes place. **direct sound** Speech, noises and music recorded at the moment of filming. **dissolve** A transition between scenes in which a second image is gradually superimposed over the first, which recedes at a similar pace. **dolly** A wheeled support permitting the smooth movement of the camera. **dubbing** The post-production recording of speech or sound effects, often to post-synchronize or translate dialogue, or correct errors. **eyeline match** The consistency of a performer's line of vision between the shots of a scene. **fades** Fade-in: the gradual appearance of an image from a darkened screen; fade-out: the gradual disappearance of an image to a darkened screen. **feature film** Any film over three reels in length. **fish-eye lens** A wide-angle lens with an angle view of approximately 180°. **frame** A single photographic image on a filmstrip. **front office** A synonym for studio head or mogul used in Hollywood at the height of the studio system. **gauge** The width of a filmstrip in millimetres. **iris** A circular masking device that reveals or conceals an area of the screen to isolate key details, or to open or close a scene. **jump cut** A break within a continuous shot or a mismatch between shots to create discontinuity and thus emphasize a motion picture's filmicness as opposed to its content. **long shot** A framing device in which full-length figures are shown in their physical context. **long take** A single unbroken shot, sometimes the duration of an entire scene. **mask** An opaque sheet placed before a camera or optical printer to block off part of a photographic image. **matte shot** A composite shot in which part of an image is masked so that it can be printed together with elements from another frame. **medium shot** A framing device presenting objects midway between close-up and long shot. **microcinematography** The use of a camera and a micro-

scope to film minute objects. **mise-en-scène** 'Putting in the scene' all the elements necessary for a shot. **montage** An alternative term for editing. Also the juxtaposition of images to create ideas not contained in the images themselves. **non-diegetic sound** Sound emanating from a source outside the narrative space, such as a voice-over or the musical soundtrack. **pan** A shot in which a turning camera body surveys horizontal space while fixed to a stationary tripod. **panchromatic stock** Monochrome film stock sensitive to colours across the spectrum. **plan-séquence** A long shot pioneered by Jean Renoir that conveys meaning through intra-frame action rather than montage. **process photography** Either rear projection photography or the photography of shots produced by matte processes or optical printing. **rack focus** An intra-shot lens adjustment to focus on a new subject within the frame. **rear projection** A studio technique in which a location is projected onto a translucent screen before which the performers act out a scene. Also called back projection. **reel** A spool bearing the filmstrip. A 35mm reel holds about 1000 feet of film lasting approximately 10 minutes when played at sound speed (24 frames per second) and some 15 minutes running at silent speed (16 frames per second). **reverse angle** A shot taken from an angle that opposes the one used in the preceding shot. **rushes** Prints of a day's shooting processed in a rush overnight to allow a film-maker to evaluate the quality of completed scenes. Also called dailies. **sequence** A segment of action made up of one or more shots or scenes. **sequence shot** A synonym for a long take. Also called sequence take. **shallow focus** A depth of field in which sharp focus is restricted to planes close to the camera. **shot** The length of film exposed during a single take. A completed film is made up from the juxtaposition of shots. **shot-reverse-shot** The alternation of camera angles during a conversation sequence. **sound stage** A vast, soundproof building in which sets are constructed. **superimposition** The exposure of multiple images on the same filmstrip. **swish pan** A rapid panning movement that causes the screen image to blur. Often used as a transition device to suggest parallel action. **synchronous sound** Sound with an identifiable source within the frame. **take** The single continuous recording of a shot. **tilt** A shot in which a tilting camera body surveys vertical space while fixed to a stationary tripod. **tracking shot** A shot in which a camera moves towards, away from or parallel to the action by means of a mobile support. Also called a travelling shot. **track-zoom** A zoom lens shot taken with a travelling camera. **undercranking** Shooting film at less than the standard speed so that accelerated action is achieved on projection. **wide-angle lens** A lens with a focal length of 30mm or less that increases the illusion of depth by distorting straight lines at the edge of the frame. **wipe** A transition between scenes in which a line crosses the screen leaving the next scene in its wake. **zoom lens** A variable-focus lens that can achieve wide-angle and telephoto effects. Often used to create optical motion without moving the camera.

Film Index

Roman numerals refer to colour plates; page numbers in *italics* refer to illustrations

General Index